Urban Policing in Canada:
Anatomy of an Aging Craft

In *Urban Policing in Canada* Maurice Martin identifies a variety of factors that exert enormous influence on contemporary police practice, including traditional organization and personnel practices, government management, public attitudes, and the changing urban landscape. In doing so he makes a compelling case for the professionalization of Canada's urban police.

Martin examines the environment of policing, a profoundly urban enterprise that has been greatly influenced by the pace and nature of urbanization. While police continue to serve the criminal justice system well, he finds that they have become less effective in carrying out the larger function of maintaining order, which must be tailored to changing urban circumstances.

Policing still functions as a craft, with its hallmark in-at-the-bottom entry requirements and emphasis on skills attained through experience. In *Urban Policing in Canada* Martin makes a convincing case for transforming policing into a knowledge-based profession.

MAURICE A. MARTIN is a retired Canadian Forces officer and a retired executive of the Canadian Police College. He now lives in Toronto.

Urban Policing in Canada

Anatomy of an Aging Craft

MAURICE A. MARTIN

McGill-Queen's University Press
Montreal & Kingston • London • Buffalo

© McGill-Queen's University Press 1995
ISBN 0-7735-1284-5 (cloth)
ISBN 0-7735-1294-2 (paper)

Legal deposit second quarter 1995
Bibliothèque nationale du Québec

Printed in Canada on acid-free paper

This book has been published with the help of a grant
from the Social Science Federation of Canada, using
funds provided by the Social Sciences and Humanities
Research Council of Canada.

McGill-Queen's University Press is grateful to the
Canada Council for support of its publishing program.

Canadian Cataloguing in Publication Data

Martin, Maurice A., 1925–
    Urban policing in Canada: anatomy of an aging craft
    Includes bibliographical references and index.
    ISBN 0-7735-1284-5 (bound)
    ISBN 0-7735-1294-2 (pbk.)
    1. Police – Canada.   2. Law enforcement –
    Canada.   3. Urban policy – Canada.   I. Title.
    HV8157.M37   1995   363.2'0971   C95-900204-9

This book was typeset by Typo Litho Composition Inc.
in 10/12 Baskerville

To the memory of Norma Martin

Contents

Acknowledgments   ix

Preface   xi

1   Introducing Themes and Topics   3

2   The Conventional View of Law, Order, and
Community   25

3   The Roots of Policing – The Urban
Community   39

4   Maintaining Order – The Neighbourhood
Policing Function   69

5   The Structure and Resources of Urban
Policing   98

6   Accountability and the Supervision of
Policing by Governments   141

7   Competent, Accountable, and Autonomous:
Professionals in Urban Society   170

Epilogue: Order, the City, and the
Occupation   201

Notes   209

Bibliography   223

Index   233

Acknowledgments

My daughter, Diane Martin, provided much encouragement and support as well as her considerable experience and editing skills and for this I am much in her debt. I am equally grateful to Valerie Frith for her enthusiasm and her experience as an incisive editor. Her skill contributed much to this book, as did the conscientious editing of Claire Gigantes.

Preface

The time has arrived when police leaders in Canada must
do some serious soul searching. They must take a hard
look at their traditional priorities. Should the police
service continue to consider itself a creature of statute,
insular and inward looking, answerable to no one except
for budgetary reasons, or should we serve the social
needs of the community that pays our bills? It seems that
policing has drifted significantly from its original
mandate, that traditionally we have decided unilaterally
what our priorities will be; that we have become
essentially one dimensional crime-fighters; and that we
are not very successful at what we have chosen to do.[1]

Canadian policing has been as effective and responsive to community
voices as that of any other country in the western world. By prevailing
standards, our urban police would be judged as incorrupt, committed
to bias-free law enforcement, adept at technical innovation, and as dismayed by violent crime as their fellow citizens are. Whereas in many
countries officers are inured to public hostility, ours are concerned
about the status of police in society and their dependence on a public
support that is easily damaged by arrogance or abuse of authority.

Many administrators, however, have failed to grasp the need for new
urban policing programs that acknowledge certain ongoing transforma-
tions in Canadian life. More than three-quarters of Canadians now live
in urban centres, and more than eighty percent of Canada's police serve
in cities. Patterns of urbanization determine the nature of policing. The
perennial question is – as it has been since the first urban police force
hit the streets in nineteenth-century London – will the police respond to
urban change as a challenge, or will they react to it as a curse?

To control crime by apprehending offenders and thereby protecting
citizens from victimization may once have been axiomatic as the mandate of urban police, but today the notion is little more than a shibbo-
leth. The effectiveness of police-car patrols has been challenged by
recent research. The urban contexts for which such programs were designed are being transformed. Crime rates continue to rise. The tough
problems of order and security in city neighbourhoods are proving resistant to familiar police approaches.

It is time to rethink the functions of urban policing in terms of the
quality of day-to-day life in our cities rather than those of the rigours of
law enforcement. Further, an examination of the current status and

capacities of urban police reveals that basic changes in the police occupation itself, in its spheres of competence, management, and organization, are needed if renewed sets of priorities and programs are to be devised.

We in Canadian society have tended to view police as predominantly law enforcers, the protectors of society at large whose functions are enduringly writ in law and whose programs, legal in purpose, are subject to the impartial oversight of the courts. I will argue that ongoing urbanization inevitably subjects police functions to pressures that require a response geared to changing social conditions. But the public continues to view law enforcement as the *raison d'être* of its police forces. In order for any public policy debate on urban policing to produce genuine reform, citizens need to be more informed. If prevailing attitudes to police functions are to change, a radical reappraisal of the role of police in our collective mythology of urban life is required.

In cities specialized occupations emerge, and if their social worth is recognized, they are professionalized. The police force provides services that are vital to the well-being of the citizenry – one characteristic of a profession – and it also exercises the professional prerogative of defining its own roles. So police usually consider themselves to be professionals, in the broad sense of the term. But professions in the narrower sense of the word – for example, medicine – insist on clear standards of performance, on competence flowing from high qualifications, and on accountability to those served. Among the cornerstone professions, overarching values and ethics supplant lesser loyalties such as those to a department or a union.

Thanks to the impressive results of social-science research since the 1960s, we now have a body of knowledge that indicates the direction that the police occupation might now take. We are entering the "research reform" era of policing as we are leaving the reform period, whose hallmark was modernization through managerial competence and the rationalization of resource deployment through the preventive-patrol function. Concentrating on means rather than ends, this latter approach assumed that "progressive management" practices and techniques of organization, staffing, and equipping would improve efficiency. And so they did, in many ways. The current "research reform" more and more equips police with the capacities to formulate goals that meet the complex needs of a diverse urban society. My objective in this book is to go further: to examine the status of the police occupation itself, to analyze its competence to achieve those capacities, and to assess its professional attributes.

In more than ten years at the Canadian Police College, I heard or read innumerable recommendations that the police should change this or that management practice or engage in this or that operations practice. Many reflect so shallow a grasp of policing as a demanding public endeavour that the tendency of the police to turn a deaf ear is understandable. Not only prescriptions from the management sciences but those from the social sciences must be met with caution, burdened as they often are with an insensitivity to the complexities of policing. Many police activities attract public attention, discussion, and even agitation, so the police executive listens warily. Police functions and police accountability are uneasy matters and the subject of heated debate. Exhortations that they be more "professional" in some vague way or engage in "community policing" by placing more officers on foot patrol contribute more to the temperature of the debate than to its substance.

Although science must be value-neutral in its methods, one enters a field – often a minefield – of values, special interests, and political considerations with every attempt to apply the results of scientific enquiry to policing practices. The police enforce laws that are formal expressions of values. Order-maintenance activities are sociopolitical and often reflect not so much universal values as those of a specific time and place.

We are constrained in discussion of fundamental aspects of police functions and accountability. Police are "impartial servants of the law" and "sheltered from political influence": such linguistic conventions hobble our capacity to speak of this public institution as part of the social and political processes of public policy. Our tradition has it that the terms police and politics are inimical. Meanwhile, the terms we might use to open a fresh perspective – terms describing citizens' duties, collective responsibilities, and mutual obligations at the heart of communal well-being – have been allowed to atrophy. Individualism and individual rights have monopolized sociopolitical language and thought.

Security is as much or more the collective achievement of social and political endeavours as the maintenance of order by police. Today, the proliferation of local associations and groups representing particular interests in a city – whether long term or *ad hoc* in their aims – can be read as an encouraging sign that tasks requiring communal attention are still recognized and that a sense of collective obligation survives. But community participation in public security, however desirable it may be in principle, raises complex and even intractable questions when we begin to think about putting it into practice. I think I can promise, though, that readers of this book will emerge as informed participants in this debate.

Despite the many fine studies of policing that have been produced during the past thirty years, we still need work that contributes organizing themes through which policing in urban society may be better understood. Given the urgency of crime-related issues, it is hardly surprising that researchers tend to focus on doing better what is already being done (fighting crime) and on other police-management issues. Few authors recognize that the issues of policing and urban society are inextricably linked and do not, therefore, examine them together; most take one or the other for granted. Conventional attitudes to law and order hold that the law is an expression of an objective reality, that is is defined without regard to particulars of circumstance or person. In the case of criminal law especially, the law is blind. The quality of universality ascribed to morals and laws suggests that when one sins or breaks a law, the site, be it city or farm, is irrelevant and it is treated as such before the law. There is a range of behaviours, usually of a minor nature, which, in threatening the orderliness of a neighbourhood, is defined by the particulars of place and people in relation to that neighbourhood and not necessarily by law. The failure to account for varying community standards inside the law persists throughout the literature, though with notable exceptions.

If we are to improve the job police forces do for us, we must attempt to understand the complex and often amorphous urban environment in which police conduct their business. I echo Robert Reiner from *The Politics of the Police*: "[The] 'softly, softly' approach to police reform and accountability ... far from being a sop, may be the most feasible chance for improving the standards of policing. To rebuild an ancient edifice brick by brick requires time and patience. But it is more likely to succeed than either calling it names or charging at it head-first."[2]

While I argue for change, particularly for the professionalization of urban police, I am not here to warn of dire consequences should change not occur in the near future. I cannot predict that the security of our cities will soon collapse under the pressures of criminality and social disorder. The crooks still need to be caught, and the legal establishment fed. Crime rates will continue to fluctuate in their own difficult-to-understand way. Instead, I invite you to witness a maturity of major social trends that coupled with some illuminating recent research, permits a fuller understanding of security and order than one would have thought possible even a decade ago. Through such reflection a renewed sense of purpose might emerge.

Urban Policing in Late-Century Canada

CHAPTER ONE

Introducing Themes and Topics

THE URBAN AND INDUSTRIAL ROOTS OF POLICING

The first modern police department was established in London in 1829 against widespread, ardent, and reasoned public opposition. The nature of that opposition across much of English society was exemplified by the fear that police would be a means of government control and of intervention in private lives. The policies that the Home Secretary, Sir Robert Peel, used to overcome this fear, gave the police enduring attributes that have limited their capacities, even in Canada, to this day.

Industrialization and urbanization are the terms used to characterize the baffling changes that British society witnessed from the late eighteenth century on through the nineteenth. Habituated though they were to the contrast between the metropolis of London and the provincial life of the rest of Britain, neither the British people nor their government were prepared for the rapid growth of industrial centres like Manchester and Birmingham. In London, the influx of unemployed veterans of the Napoleonic and Crimean Wars demonstrated once again that no solution had been found to the domestic upheaval, experienced mainly as crime waves, that inevitably followed the termination of foreign hostilities. Anti-union legislation, shifts in land use, and migrations promoted not only social turmoil and riots – a common form of political activity – but the emergence of movements that threatened the established or orthodox view of society. The consequences of social and economic dislocations were widely interpreted in terms of lower-class immorality.[1] To be fair, social decay was then largely understood as moral decay (and social reform as moral reform). The same emphasis now placed on economic factors when we analyze social instability was then placed on the collective moral fibre. However, primitive central and local governments were challenged by new and difficult urban conditions. It was felt that the alienated members of the working class had to be persuaded to acquiesce in, if not accept, new political and public processes in which they could reasonably expect to take part. Such acceptance was essential if working-class opposition to being policed, as it were, was to be overcome. The origins of the acceptability of policing, then, should be viewed in the context of the emerging activist role of a modernizing government. And this, in turn, must be understood in terms of the expanding apparatus of government, electoral reform, and the pressures for a wider franchise that culminated in the Reform Act of 1832. The characteristics of and divisions in society that evolved across the period of industrialization and dramatic urbanization are thus directly relevant to an analysis of urban policing today. Histories of the medieval origins of policing, shire reeves and all that, reflect an approach as tangential as it is quaint.

The 1830s and 1840s, saw considerable growth in government (a "revolution," according to one observer[2]). Legislation addressed, for example, the poor, children, municipal-government systems, education, factory reform, sanitation, railways, and social services. Functional departments with political heads and career administrators were established to improve efficiency. Much of this was, of course, spurred by urbanization and the gross inadequacies of local governments.

Similarly, in the United States of the mid-nineteenth century, urbanization forced local governments to face the need for administrative efficiency, which in turn spurred the establishment of various specialized municipal departments, including, on the English model, those of police. So the incentive for government to set up police departments sprang, largely from the modernization of government, not rising rates of crime.[3] Nevertheless, the public remained sceptical. In the United States, which was less class-bound than Britain, political authority – indeed, any official or "expert" authority – aroused suspicion in the democratically minded frontier society.[4] The United States strategy, unlike Britain's, clearly placed policing under local political control. Ever since, police have successfully resisted amalgamation or regionalization and now number about forty thousand agencies. But the American faith in local democracy has been rewarded with the corruption of city departments by politicians from whom the police have not fully escaped.

In England, opposition to Peel's Metropolitan Police Act, which re-placed local watchmen and parish constables with the prototype de-partment that became known as the "Met," focused on the fear, common to most classes and especially the recalcitrant working class, of a system of control reminiscent of the surveillance and "dossier" practices of French police. All things French, with the exception of wine and fashion, were, as ever, anathema to the freeborn Englishman. Prussia, with its paramilitary force, was also regarded as a cautionary example.

The course leading to the tolerance of urban police was long and uneven, and it would be difficult to attribute public acceptance to po-lice performance. Rather, the improvement in social conditions wrought by prosperity and the steady habituation to a government presence in everyday life probably did more to pacify the opposition than any perception of declining crime. Britain was being policed in a recognizably modern fashion by the early 1870s, but the number of drunkenness offences grew from 75,000 to over 200,000 in the two de-cades before 1876, or from a quarter to over forty percent of the total of minor offences (stabilizing at about thirty percent at the turn of the century). This category included, among others, common assaults, petty thefts, game law, vagrancy, highway law, as well as by-law offences. The second more numerous category of offences concerned the street life of the working class: obstruction (of movement), nuisance, solicit-ing, loitering with intent to commit a mischief, suspicion of causing a breach of the peace, as well as offences against by-laws regulating trad-ing, street performers, street games, street betting, and others, to a to-tal percentage of fifteen to twenty percent or more of all offences. Thus, well over half of police work in the latter part of the century was concerned with regulating not merely drunks but street life thought of as unruly, apparently immoral, or, at the very least, unattractive. The interest and intervention of the influential upper middle classes in the morality of working people and their families was repressive and sanc-timonious, but it did eventually serve to enhance the social status of re-spectability and provide an incentive to educate children. (Early schools were private- and religion-centred.) Maintaining "respectabil-ity" became an effective influence in community life.[5]

Much homely conduct was swept away – assembling to gossip, loiter-ing, playing games – largely by police activity but also by the availability of other facilities in growing cities: about five hundred music halls opened in London between 1860 and 1880, and as housing improved, homes became more suitable for social activity. Much police action simply displaced undesirables to some less visible district. The people who experienced the sharpest end of this policing were those at the

poorest level of the community. The image of the helping neighbourhood "bobby" was a myth to most.[6]

Although it is essential to recognize the broad social forces that contributed to the eventual acceptance of police in Britain, one must also
acknowledge a set of policies Reiner identified aimed at facilitating the
process.[7] First, police organization was bureaucratic and hierarchical
in its chain of command; rule-bound and impersonal. The public was
to be assured that constables acted under strict control. Entry requirements were minimal. Promotion was reserved for those who never
breached discipline. (Training was not taken seriously until the 1920s
at the earliest.) Second, adherence to the rule of law was the prime
characteristic of police operations; the police were to be legalistic in
procedure, constrained by statute, and overseen by the courts. Their
obvious subjection to the specifications of law rather than the political
order was their best defence against opposition in a nation that considered the rule of law as the cornerstone of liberty and liberty as a
uniquely British inheritance. Discretionary powers were derived from
applying the minor-order statutes such as vagrancy so that the police op-
erated within the confines of explicit law in routine order maintenance.

Third, the police came to be seen as nonpartisan and insulated from
direct political control. The Home Secretary tended not to intervene
in operational policy. (This should not be confused, however, with
wholesale constabulary independence from policy direction, which
was a 1920s innovation of dubious constitutional legitimacy.) Fourth,
the strategy of minimal force – win by appearing to lose; no weapons
but the truncheon – was particularly important in handling industrial
disputes and political demonstrations. Heavy police violence did occur
but the evidence suggests a decline during the twentieth century to
1970.

Fifth, the image of policing as a service was emphasized, though to a
large extent this came about through the twenty-four-hour availability
of the police and their authority to act. But the image did much to promote legitimacy and acceptance.

Finally, the notion of preventive policing proved attractive. Peel
used the term prevention, much overblown in recent decades. He gave
police a preventive – in Reiner's terms, largely scarecrow – function,
meaning being on the street and being visible. Originally, law enforcement was downplayed. Detectives were a later development: in 1880,
in a department of eight thousand, there were but fifteen.

The English experience suggests that policing may successfully attend
to disorder, provided consensus and stability exist. Both permit mini-

mal use of authority and force; acceptance of policing activities and their legitimacy follows. One can say that policing works if it is part of the successes of society, in which case police incapacities are a part of society's failures. The British institution of policing is founded on this balance, and Reiner's comment is pertinent: "policing is embedded in a social order riven by structured bases of conflict, not fundamental integration. The manner of policing such a divided social order may be more or less harmonious and based on some consensus, or overtly oppressive, with important consequences."[8] It is in the nature of policing to be viewed as representative of both society and government with comparable virtues and blemishes. During the latter half of the nineteenth century, for example, as overall figures indicate, the greater part of police resources were devoted to promoting the conformity of citizen behaviour to "official" standards that deemed as disorderly much activity of no apparent threat to anyone. That the police officer was representative of the established class and its version of morality was understood; stamping out popular pleasures gave an unavoidable impression that government had no sympathetic intentions in policing the lower orders. Thompson has suggested that laws and the growing numbers of police did not so much produce changes in social habits as growing numbers of offenders.[9] Laws facilitating the regulation of behaviour such as loitering and gambling left the initiative with the police themselves. The counterexample, then, would read: Where dissension is relatively widespread, a consensus is improbable, social stability is eroded and a general distrust of official agencies probable. At the more extreme point of major unrest, it may be said that when government occasions or tolerates persistent social problems or social disrepair, as Chief Constable John Alderson learned,[10] policing may well become part of the problem; its mandate, which favours the *status quo*, will fail to achieve consensus with the policed and hence may incite the disorder so deplored. Even the big-city riots of the 1980s were not uniformly amenable to police action as some situations were aggravated by official determination to continue vigorous policing or, ultimately, to "regain control of the streets."

There is, then, an ambiguity or uncertainty about the place of police in the social and political order. Some weight of this observation falls on the difficult nature of consensus as to what is to be regulated or enforced. Many people tend not to conform to established norms but nonconformist activity is tolerated, if not accommodated, under conditions of otherwise wide political consensus and social stability, the two going together. (In situations of violent and predatory crime, policing is needed and accepted even at the price of basic freedoms being suspended.) The notion of consensus contrasts with, among other aspects of the current situation, the policing establishment's successful claim to the prerogative of defining its own roles, leaving citizens and civilian police authorities in Canada and in Britain squeezed into lesser roles. These major issues, of police accountability and management by government, are addressed in a later chapter.

In the nineteenth century, the campaign to overcome social instability was won by the state, and the police fitted into that wider political achievement, as the late Victorian scene attested. Police came to symbolize "the existence of a functioning legal order" with "routine public order policing" enthusiastically supported by the increasingly dominant middle class.[11] Whatever their demonstrable effect on crime rates may have been, the police served as the physical embodiment of order and stability, the most treasured values of the middle class and the preconditions of commerce.

The modern police agency bears the structural characteristics of its prototype in Peel's England. It is bureaucratic and rule-bound, with chain-of-command control; discipline-centred, with compliance tending to be a qualification for rank while training is not taken seriously. Police are seen to act according to the law, bound by procedure, with legalistic constraints and accountability and oversight that is judicial rather than local or political. They are to operate within the confines of explicit law even during routine order-maintenance tasks. Police are to act with minimal use of force. They are to be relentlessly nonpartisan and insulated from direct political influence.

Modern policing appears to be diverging from some of its original characteristics. The essential strategy of minimal force, for example, has been battered during social and political unrest or during the acting out of violent illusions by seemingly increasing numbers of psychotics. Police personnel in tactical units or special-weapons teams are often seen on television behaving with commando-like zeal. The display of paramilitary tactics and weapons in the control of potentially disruptive demonstrations and protests, perhaps beset by threats of terrorist acts, is now fairly common in presumably stable Western countries. The parade of riot shields, the appearance of blackened faces, camouflage, and armoured vehicles and automatic weapons on newscasts are common, here and elsewhere; the notorious if exceptional case of police bombing a residence in a United States city underlines the point. So even in dramatic circumstances, the role of the police is perplexing; once the principle of minimal coercion is challenged by the threats of disorder and crime in a flawed social and political setting, the goals, competence, and strategies of policing soon become issues.

Of all the sacred cows in the legacy of policing, perhaps none is more in need of reappraisal than its putative insulation from "political influence." Any policy respecting the deployment of public resources for some social or community purpose is political, though not necessarily partisan in origin or intent. Political acts are inherently discriminatory, favouring one or another segment of the public in the distribution of public benefits – such is the stuff of politics, especially partisan politics, and of democracy. So a distinction must be made between police activities that invoke the ideally bias-free processes of criminal justice, i.e., law enforcement, and those that serve some social good, i.e., the maintenance of order. Applying this distinction to the activities of a police officer on the street is difficult at best – the distinction between law enforcement and order-maintenance functions is important but blurred. When an officer is dispatched to an incident, for example, it cannot be known until the officer arrives and, using discretion, categorizes the incident whether it constitutes a crime under the Criminal Code or an event that disturbed the orderliness of a place and requires only the restoration of orderliness. In all such cases, the officer's authority under the Code is essential regardless of outcome.

The criminal-justice and social purposes involved in police activities are usually so intertwined as to be inseparable. Law-enforcement tasks were removed from the role of patrol officers in the pioneering Flint foot-patrol experiment, for example, but were soon returned because of this interweaving of functions and officers' consciousness of being hobbled. Still, the maintenance of order is political, raising, as Reiner noted, questions of definition, equity, and accountability.[12]

Within a society divided along economic, ethnic, gender, and other dimensions of inequality, the discriminating impact of law is virtually unavoidable. The impartial intent of criminal law and criminal justice and, by extension, of law enforcement is something police are quick to point out. The law is universal and its enforcement marches to a legal beat. Order maintenance hinges on discretion and may well be discriminatory in intent; it may favour one group in a community over others. Order-maintenance practices may not be uniformly acceptable among different groups in a community – laws regulating behaviour fall into this category.[13] Disorders, for example, tend to have local peculiarities; to categorize and treat them as singularly criminal misses the mark if their roots in neighbourhood troubles are untouched.

Gaining freedom from corrupting political control and so regaining legitimacy, the United States police became neutral agents of the law, and the weakness of apolitical police departments became evident in the mid-1960s. Police showed a lack of orientation towards, and experience in, managing local troubles with or without local support.[14]

Recent racial problems faced by many police departments further illustrate the need for a clearer grasp of what is meant by politics. Clinging to the neutrality of the uniform and insisting that law enforcement has no racially biased intent is senseless. A politically sophisticated occupation would be fully aware of the various dimensions of the issue, the discriminating quality of law in its impact being one and the political nature of the maintenance of order another.

THE FUNCTIONS OF LAW ENFORCEMENT AND THE MAINTENANCE OF ORDER

The two functions of urban policing – law enforcement and the maintenance of order – are central to much of the discussion that follows in this book while specialized tasks, such as investigations, are beyond its scope. The greater part of police resources are mobilized around preventive patrols, whether on foot or in cars; it is the premier program, but patrol officers engage in both functions. Given a common response to incidents – the dispatch of patrol officers – it is often difficult to determine at any one point whether an officer's reaction is enforcement or order maintenance. So a brief commentary on the patrol task may be useful.

The challenge to patrol officers is to respond to an incident, whether they come upon or are sent to resolve it. The incident may be a relatively minor matter or one of serious crime. Heightened anticipation, even apprehension, attends these moments and may be transmitted to the citizens involved. The patrol officer may seem aloof or hostile and suspicious and, if so, may meet with resentment. Spiralling antagonisms may follow.

In the case of a more serious crime, the officer's discretion is limited. Wider resources and more senior personnel are called in, procedure becomes the rule and the patrol officer's role subsidiary. Nevertheless, on arrival, the imperative is to take control of the incident. A uniform does little to encourage cooperation and the task tends to become one of asserting personal authority in an often hostile situation. Officers soon become habituated to these hothouse conditions, dealing with people when they are aggressive, emotionally upset, savage, rowdy, lying, deceptive, injured, drugged, or depraved. Incidents often involve some interest of desperate importance to a person – matters of livelihood, of physical well-being, of family relationships, or of reputation – but to the officers, such incidents become matters of familiarity and routine. As James Q. Wilson has observed, "the police have seen it all before and they have come to distrust victim accounts."[15] Officers seem to be – and are – sceptical and detached from the complaining citizen's interests. The truthfulness or integrity of the victim may be doubted. Such doubts are learned through repeated experiences. Police perceptions of a hostile public derive, in part, from their contacts with those victims, suspects, and onlookers and from the deceit, even of so-called respectable citizens, aimed at protecting friends and relatives.[16]

The job is complex; officers work alone or in pairs without close supervision and cannot let a complaining citizen, victim, or onlooker be the sole judge of the quality of their services. An officer's response to an incident will be viewed as incomplete, for the dominant goals of the law may prevail; outcomes may be delayed or obscured from public view. If a charge is likely, then the constraints and procedures imposed by law will dominate and discretion will be largely removed. Wilson[17] has noted that in low-income areas, violence is more frequent and the unfavourable impressions people and officers have of each other are heightened. In the United States of the mid-1960s, about seventy percent of the victims of crimes against the person had incomes of under $6,000 per year while fifty-five percent of victims of crimes against property had incomes of over $6,000. In most crimes against the person the victims know the offender; hence the officer is likely to be suspicious of the victim's story. There are levels of legitimacy, something akin to stereotypes: a middle-class person who has been mugged has legitimacy as a victim in the officer's eyes, less so if a victim of stolen but insured property; lower-class persons have far less legitimacy, having "brought it on themselves," and are likely to be less truthful in cases of, for example, assault.

Although administrators and patrol supervisors recognize, in principle, the need for standards of conduct, officers exercise considerable discretion in most situations, so the issue for the police executive is how to determine, evaluate, and influence a street officer's performance and ensure that such officers act in accordance with the policies of the department. Wilson emphasized the point that the matter depends more on the "organizational and legal definition" of the police task in the department than on the personal qualities of the officer. For example, a department with a vice squad will produce more prostitution arrests and one with a traffic unit, or a quota system, will issue higher numbers of tickets.[18] The influence of the police subculture and how it defines the police task is also a potent influence. Because incidents are contentious and potential sources of police-public conflict, the operative policy in "legalistic" departments emphasizes the seemingly noncontentious function of enforcing laws. I recall discussing this aspect of police-public conflict with the chief of a large, highly regarded department who indicated that he would prefer to reform his departmental policies and strategies into a legalistic style and drop purely order-maintenance functions ("not true policing in any event") where possible, knowing that the issue of conflict might thereby be managed if not fully avoided. But a patrol officer knows that acting against only those who break or are likely to break a law is unworkable in practice.

Disorder disturbs the tranquillity or the predictability of events in a neighbourhood. It is local, tied to the particulars of people and place. It either disturbs or threatens to disturb the public peace and involves face-to-face conflict among two or more persons. It is a dispute over what is "right" or "seemly" conduct or over who is to blame for conduct deemed to be wrong or unseemly. But a noisy drunk, a panhandler, a rowdy or noisy teenager will not agree to be classed as disorderly, and intervention by a street officer will be disputed. In the case of a fight in a tavern or in a home, intervention may be seen as proper but who receives blame may be disputed for in many cases of disorder an infraction of at least minor law is involved.

It is necessary to establish a rudimentary understanding of law enforcement. Urban police are well versed in the function of law enforcement and their considerable competence is not in question here; little will be said of it. Law enforcement comprises those practices and programs aimed at violations of the Criminal Code: the detection of crime and the apprehension of offenders with the benefit of whatever deterrent effect police rates of success may have. It is the occasion of diminished discretion. The more serious the crime the more resources devoted to apprehending the offender; the more evidence available, the further an investigation will be pursued and any latitude to downgrade an originating complaint will be diminished. In this function policing becomes highly technical, in surveillance and intelligence work, in identification and scenes-of-crime examinations. On these practices some claims to professionalism are based. If policing now counts among its objectives the suppression of crime because crime corrodes a community's quality of life, then it may be said that law enforcement has crucial, if less tangible, outcomes beyond the protective (such as the removal of predators from the street). These include sustaining a respect for the law, satisfying a commonly held sense of retributive justice, and providing assurance to the law abiding that vigilantes are unwarranted. None of these purposes has a specific focus on a neighbourhood's concerns about order.

About two-thirds of all the arrests made in the United States are for misdemeanours: drunkenness, disorderly conduct, larceny, driving under the influence, simple assault, vagrancy, gambling, and violations of liquor laws.[19] Many of these, though not all, contravene laws of regulation rather than of serious prohibition, so that law enforcement with this component of behaviour management is not sharply distinguishable from the maintenance of order.

Although we must distinguish between order maintenance and law enforcement for purposes of conceptual clarity, the distinction collapses more often than not on the ground – or, more precisely, on patrol. If we pursue this a little further and ask why this should be so, we come to one of the themes that recurs in the chapters ahead. The city is not a backdrop for policing but the challenge itself. Either urban stability and orderliness are sustained or they fall among the victims of economic deterioration and social transience. The maintenance of order is tied to the vicissitudes of daily life in the full diversity of the urban environment. Though it commands the greater portion of police resources, it does not command their zest and zeal as does law enforcement. To many police, there is a satisfying symmetry in law enforcement: flight and pursuit, stealth and detection, crime and punishment, an offence and an accounting, the exalted place of law and the inexorable retribution for deviance. The messy social environment in which all of this is played out cannot be ignored. Still, the maintenance of order remains the quintessential function of the urban police.

The salience of order maintenance is increasingly recognized by police and elected officials alike. John Alderson, a former chief constable of the Devon and Cornwall Constabulary, noted that the "police role in the social order is primarily that of keepers of the peace, and prevention of crime. This function can only be activated where the primary level of activity is rooted in neighbourhoods. It is here that police officers have to toil in the foothills of the social order. The enforcement of laws is adjunct to this primary function and should not be its usurper."[20] A one-time mayor of Toronto, John Sewell, said that the maintenance of order seems paramount.[21] Sir Kenneth Newman, once commissioner of the London police, quoted Lord Scarman approvingly to the effect that, of the police functions – the prevention of crime, the protection of life and property, and the maintenance of public tranquillity – the last ought to have priority. Newman gained attention for programs reorienting his immense department to the concerns of community and to the problems of race, the disadvantaged, and the pluralities of public interest.

Order maintenance is the central problem for patrol officers, who give to it as much as two-thirds of their activity. With it comes danger, often when least expected, so that the preoccupation with danger is a central element in patrol officers' "working personality" and in their subculture.

The maintenance of order is the use of authority to impose solutions to immensely varied problems or conflicts. It defies any but the vaguest definition and, within departments, defies rules and procedural niceties; hence it is the stuff of discretion. Discretion includes, for example, deciding that it is not "worth" pursuing some unlawful act to an official stage of action. An officer's sense of what a particular incident requires includes what citizens seem to prefer, the demeanour of suspects, and, at times, the possibility of a public complaint.[22] The contrast with enforcement is extensive and is widely discussed in the literature. In maintaining order, police officers seem to fulfil a complex multidisciplinary role. Constables in their discretion make social policy. For example, police tend not to charge for offences that yield light sentences in the courts. Police duties have elements of social work, of confessional or priestly functions, and of the magisterial role of judging.

To officers, not all people are equal under the law; policing differs from a procedural emphasis on equality and innocence. People are assessed according to how they act and appear and, often, who they are. Through this filter the potential for disorder on the street is perceived. Order is seen to rest on civility, ordinary clothes or appearance, sobriety, and any outward evidence of employment or innocent intent. It is often a matter of status, not objective equality. Being cooperative and showing courtesy and deference to the officer is part of the equation of inequality when discretion is applied on the street in meting out "informal" justice.

Maintaining order is potentially disputatious; the salient question is whose order is being maintained and to what purpose. Clive Emsley has drawn attention to local conflicts in Britain arising from order-related laws that lack unanimous or properly achieved support.[23] Moore and Kelling have described "Victorian" laws in the United States as difficult to enforce and therefore unevenly applied.[24] Even today, such "regulations" as prostitution and liquor laws have quaintly Victorian tinges and police are highly discretionary in their enforcement.

Whatever the officer does to restore order is outcome rather than process. Judgments are not made on the basis of guilt alone. Officers are inclined to believe that a person who shows disregard for them is likely to disregard laws. Thus, to be stopped and challenged by the police is discriminatory and is felt as such. "In sum, the order maintenance function of the patrolman defines his role and that role, which is unlike that of any other occupation, can be described as one in which *sub-professionals, working alone, exercise wide discretion in matters of utmost importance (life and death, honor and dishonor) in an environment that is apprehensive and perhaps hostile"* (emphasis in the original).[25] The skills needed are neither recognized nor rewarded in the department and are not widely understood. Order maintenance – with its acts of judgment and informal and varied means of handling conflict and meting out informal justice, as well as its wide potential for attracting error and complaints – is the primary source of police secrecy and solidarity and of their entrenched belief that they alone comprehend the job.

MATCHING THE POLICE OCCUPATION TO THE PROFESSIONAL OCCUPATIONS OF MODERN URBAN SOCIETY

Policing is often spoken of as a profession, but the occupation has no professional characteristics except the vital service it is charged to provide and, significantly, its unilateral claim to self-regulation. "Crime-fighting" technology and laboratories, centralized fingerprint and data banks, and rapid communication facilities may create an aura of professionalism, but such technical devices may be found in a wide variety of employment settings.

The possession of advanced, research-based knowledge and its application by qualified practitioners might entitle some skilled workers to claim professional status. But how apt is this description to policing? Patrick V. Murphy, a former commissioner of the New York Police Department and later head of the Police Foundation, said that police must be held accountable politically to ensure that values at the core of police work are cultivated in a department. These values will, in turn, yield the perspectives needed to make ethically sound decisions, leading to true professionalism: all this in contrast to practices directed by tradition or the comfort of familiar ruts, "which, even today, govern many of our police departments."[26] He went on to say: "In my opinion *professionalism* means questioning through research old and new policies and tactics and establishing continuity in a growing body of knowledge about what works and what does not work in controlling crime and maintaining order. For too long, police practices have been based on untested hunches. Only over the last two decades have we begun to learn through research that many of our hunches and assumptions were wrong. At the Police Foundation, we have been able to shatter many of our policing myths about response time, about deadly force, and about patrol. Research and evaluation efforts like these must continue if our professionalization attempts are to succeed."[27]

Being professional, he noted, also meant the continuing effort to enhance abilities to perform as police officers through training and education, so that "we can understand the full depths and dimensions of policing." [28]

In the United States, August Vollmer and O.W. Wilson launched a reform movement that culminated in a particular brand of professionalization, the hallmarks of which include technical modernization, managerial competence, the development of the modern version of a preventive patrol strategy, and the near-universal organization of departments around it.[29] Under way before the Second World War and completed only in recent decades, Vollmer and Wilson's efforts centred on achieving freedom from political interference and the corruption that flowed from it. Of the several components in their thinking, two are relevant here: the grave threat posed by criminal enemies of society, and the need for experts (police generals) to defeat them. Vollmer believed that scientific policing, with centralized control and communication and record keeping, suited general concerns and the priority given to fighting crime. Vollmer advocated a role for police as "non-specialist crime fighters" combining both apprehension and prevention undertaken along with other community agencies. The criminal, a public enemy, had to be fought with the use of modern science and technology.[30]

"Professional" leadership meant managerial sophistication, which combined crime-fighting competence with the ability to ward off criticisms of police inefficiency that could open up the possibility of external supervision. This notion of professionalization was not exclusive to the United States, as developments in Canada showed. In a political/governmental emphasis on rational or objective management, the accepted view must be that police administrators are not to be subject to interference, provided they act in accordance with prevailing police doctrine, and that no segement of the public should receive special attention.

In hindsight, we can now see the tension between the O.W. Wilson approach and accountability. Emerging policing practices were elevated to "professional doctrine." The traditional attention to lesser crimes in the maintenance of order was downgraded in police thinking because of the status granted to the "war on crime." With the narrower goal of combating serious crime, the "politically neutral" police could permit themselves a certain indifference to enforcing "minor" laws such as those governing loitering, vagrancy, and excessive noise, the very by-laws by which police officers might otherwise regulate conduct in a neighbourhood so as to sustain order.[31]

O.W. Wilson's notion of police professionalism – administrative competence, political neutrality, and reliance on technology, all to combat serious crime – was largely successful in loosening the bonds of political influence. But, as Moore and Kelling have pointed out, the bonds with citizens were also eventually loosened.[32] This approach reinforced the conventional law-and-order belief that crime can actually be controlled or suppressed, a well-entrenched view, for as Klockars noted, "because the early chiefs had pushed the war on crime analogy so hard as a way of getting the traditional general's privileges, they were stuck with the crime fighting image and expectations the analogy had promised. So strong was that image in fact that virtually every purchase of equipment, every request for additional personnel, and every change in operational procedure had to be promoted or defended in terms of its role in fighting crime."[33]

Much has been made of the fatherly, supportive, and tolerant officer of the last century, the mythic policeman who looked after the indigent, the inebriated, and the lost children of his precinct. In the United States, the need to maintain order, combined with a pioneering spirit based on a strong sense of individualism and the varying, culturally related needs of diverse immigrant groups in larger cities, generated a kind of social tension that the fatherly officer was seemingly well suited to deal with. There is a political attractiveness in the notion. Pondering the virtues of that fatherly person, however, amounts to a nostalgic simplification and brings a misleading bias to the tougher notion of community policing. It is what Samuel Walker calls part of "fractured" history.[34] Still, the reform movement that so profoundly shaped the development of the police between 1870 and 1970 tended to deflect policing from maintenance functions. As a result, police made a near-exclusive commitment to a crime-fighting doctrine that tended to starve them of options and of a wider repertoire of knowledge and skills by which to accept a public-policy role.

Compare this trajectory in the "professionalization" of policing to the standard characteristics of other fields recognized as professions, including the grant of provincially legislated authority to manage themselves. To the same extent that a service to the public is vital it is also potentially dangerous, so the protection of the interests of clients and the public needs to be assured. The process of providing such assurance is the process of professionalization – that is, the attainment within an occupation of certain capacities such as, for example, an association concerned with occupation-wide standards including self-regulation; public recognition; and a substantial body of knowledge and skills that are unique to the profession and underpin its competence. On such capacities the grant of self-government rests. It is the client to whom the professional is primarily accountable, while the profession, collectively, is accountable for the conduct of its members and the quality of service they provide. Implicit in the grant of autonomy is the realization that the better judges of occupational standards and conduct are members of the profession itself, for their knowledge is unique to them.

Both the police claim to immunity from external scrutiny and the issue of police accountability beg the question whether or not policing is a profession. Professional practice is a democratic process in that accountability to clients in particular and the community in general requires consent and support so that the regulation or intervention by central administrative bureaucracies becomes largely redundant, or is avoided.

This definition of professionalism, demanding as it is, must be kept in mind when probing the development of policing as an occupation, since it compels examination of the contentious issues of management of police by government, their accountability and responsiveness to the community, and the nature and quality of the services they provide.

Professionalization offers the opportunity of autonomy based on the triple notions of independence from external influence, the integrity of the practitioner/client relationship, and competence. Police officers, for several reasons, continue to be concerned about political influence over their work and about the competence of any external authority to judge the quality of their actions. The history of policing over the course of this century reflects a sensitivity to political influence. The occupation, as it now exists, was profoundly shaped by the quest for autonomy, an autonomy achieved by a narrow focus on managerial practices at the price of occupational development.

The professional imperative that assigns primacy to the interests of clients in a practitioner/client relationship seems anomalous to the mandate of a police force devoted to the rule of law and to the public at large rather than to particular clients. Yet the notion of community policing implies this sort of orientation to clients; sets of distinct clientele may well become those to whom police are accountable in working out matters of local order. The contrast between the forms of accountability that may be expected of police and those that may be assumed from, for example, a medical practitioner, will be explored in the chapters ahead.

At this point, however, another aspect of professionalism must be introduced. Over the centuries, cities provided the setting for new occupations to emerge, from medieval guilds and crafts and the trades of the Industrial Revolution, to the specializations and professions that now dominate contemporary society. That this remains a characteristic of urban society is evident in the explosion of new occupations supporting the swift application of high technologies even to routine daily activities. Equally, many older occupations are being transformed by the growth of subspecializations in, for example, medicine, law, and engineering. Obviously, no individual has the capacity or the time to absorb the full body of knowledge attending these fields. Whether or not they are deemed to be professions, extensive education, training, and practice are required before one can be accepted into such occupations. In short, the professionalization of vital occupations is thriving in public and private workplaces alike. Canada is entering the post-industrial age wherein the fundamental resource is not the machinery of factories but the stuff of professionalism, knowledge itself.

In this context, the practices of minor or on-the-job training – of apprenticeship – can be seen as archaic for a major multitasked public occupation. A full secondary-school certificate is not, generally, a prerequisite for entry into the police because its training programs are relatively recent and may not be classed as particularly advanced or demanding. The postwar growth in demand for extensive education or training institutions to meet the needs of other occupations and the parallel expansion of knowledge and skills unique to various occupations point to the inefficiencies of more traditional modes of qualification, apprenticeship among them. At the root of parallel trends in professionalization is the ability of occupations to generate new knowledge and skills as a basis for increased competence beyond the knowledge resources of the past.

All this points to the feasibility of the professional modernization of urban police. The question is whether they will face the issue themselves and whether there will be the political will to provide them with the supporting educational, personnel, and policy structures – as well as the incentive – to do so. To point to the labour-intensive nature of policing (ninety percent of a department's budget is given over to salaries and other personnel costs) is a commonplace. But like the traditional professions of medicine and architecture – and certainly like the emerging high-technology-based occupations – the growing fund of policing knowledge suggests that policing must become knowledge intensive. The costs of output in professional fields, it is said, are mainly the costs of knowledge, not labour, and so it should be for policing.

"Post-industrial society," as Daniel Bell said, cannot be precisely defined but rather loosely describes some trends in much of the Western world and Japan. Canada is slowly being transformed into such a society, the dominant characteristics of which include the centrality of theoretical knowledge and its codification so as to provide for advances in its application, as the relevant technologies become pervasive.[35] The notion of postindustrial society points to the direction of change in the nature or characteristics of society including certain developments in the structure and character of occupations, developments that remain alien to the police.

Science has supplanted the man/machine/capital economic arrangements of the industrial era as the primary shaper of society. According to Bell, science has become intertwined not only with traditional technologies, but with newer social technologies and social needs and so the new scientific institutions will be crucial to the processes of government.[36] Horizontal class structures will be replaced by vertical orders as the more important factors in political attitudes and attachments. The broad functions around which society might organize itself include the scientific, the technological, the administrative, and the cultural; the five institutional areas might encompass economic enterprises, government bureaus, universities and research complexes, social complexes (e.g., hospitals, social-service centres), and the military. The economy is now geared less to the production of goods than to the provision of services (in the United States, over two-thirds of the workforce are engaged in services) and the crucial commodity, knowledge, is a collective good calling for a cooperative strategy in order to increase its spread and use in society.[37]

The growth of a knowledge class comprising professional and technical workers is also characteristic of this emergent society. Influence and merit, or status, derive from education and skill rather than property, facilitating the increased participation of women in the workforce and the concomitant two-salary family. With this shift residential areas themselves will change as high-density areas spread into and beyond urban fringes. Technology has taken care of the need for unimpeded flows of information that at one time promoted urban concentrations. The diminishing need for such concentrations in central areas is creating a distinctive new policing milieu.

THE POSTWAR DECADES

The three decades after the Second World War were a period of unprecedented urban growth during which equally unprecedented demands were made on municipal government services. Migration from rural and semirural Canada contributed the greater part to expanding city populations, and the postwar boom in births further accelerated the demand for houses, schools, and so on. Net immigration between 1951 and 1981 reached 2,660,000, which, assuming a ratio of two police officers per thousand citizens, called for an increase of 5,320 officers, a large increment indeed. Overall, during much of this time, a quarter of a million immigrants settled in cities each year. Schools and teachers (education expenditures increased 334 percent, unadjusted for inflation, during the 1960s), hospitals and doctors, prisons, courts, and lawyers – all grew in rough proportion, as did the police. Large stretches of suburbia, novel to residents, had at first no familiar patterns of neighbourhood life, no network of supportive groups. But among these residents, traditional values persisted, and governments responded by providing the reliability and stability of familiar agencies and services. The suburbs became sought-after havens of respectability and security.

Telephones, which were not all that common before the war, gave the people in these larger cities access to the service agencies of government. Anyone my age can remember the disappearance of the police and fire-department call boxes on city corners. The triple technology of telephones, cars, and radios kept police in contact with citizens in the sprawl of suburban growth. Contrary to the view that police became isolated from the community once they were encased in a "cocoon of steel and glass," the postwar suburban officer was more in touch with his constituency than were his pre-war counterparts.[38] These new technologies gave rise to new patrol programs and the strategy of rapid response by which the distant stretches of suburban communities could be policed. The decades of fast-paced urbanization were the heady times of growth in police departments, leaving few moments for a calmer deliberation of mission, roles, and ends. It was a complex, largely successful growth, but, sooner or later the results would have to be assessed.

The postwar era came to an end with the economic recessions of the early and late 1980s. The buoyant incomes of municipal governments were crushed, leaving a static and even diminished tax base, while citizens switched abruptly to vigorous antitax attitudes. Not only has restraint become a near-permanent part of civic politics: it has also become clear from Proposition 13-type politics (Proposition 13 refers to the Californian case in which citizens imposed spending limits through a form of referendum) that people will support spending only if it can be demonstrated that the expenditure is vital to the community, that its authors are accountable, and that the program will be effective. Emerging research results suggested that police programs would not meet these criteria.

I doubt whether many police programs faced such an appraisal. In any event, the results of program-effectiveness studies were not widely disseminated at the time, in or out of policing. Furthermore, policing is buffered from local political scrutiny and intervention is highly limited, for example, by statute in Ontario. Nevertheless, astute managers have noted that restraint has heightened emphasis on projects that directly address public concerns for neighbourhood well-being. The place of law enforcement as the pre-eminent justification of police programs is diminished through examinations of its effectiveness and through a growing emphasis on the now better-specified activities of sustaining order.

At the same time, however, there is a countervailing pressure to maintain the *status quo.* Apolitical policing – the continued sheltering of police from wider political concerns and therefore from the public-policy debates centring on community well-being – has left the police unversed in local political processes and issues of which they are a significant part but to which they cannot effectively contribute. It is an arena they cannot enter with confidence.

A GENERAL ANGLE OF VISION –
A VIEW OF REALITY

London of 160 years ago, though socially and economically complex for the time, was a different world from the city of today. The late twentieth century presents its own particular watershed in the diversity of challenges police face: in attitudes, values, behaviour, social characteristics and demographics, in transportation and technology, even geography.

It can be said that the issue over the past two to three decades has been that of the proper function of urban police. The simple identification and categorization of the various tasks they attend to, summed up, do not constitute a rational or satisfying notion of what the role should be. Call-driven patrols or the exaggerations of crime fighting do not adequately delineate those functions, but the problems currently faced by police are now being considered in a growing body of research that provides a basis for grappling with the issue.

Some police agencies use the label "service" in their title; others use "department" or "force" still others, like the Metropolitan Toronto Police, use no tag at all. Nepean and Edmonton now call their departments services, as Calgary has done for many years, thus suggesting a difference between their role and that of other departments in the municipal government. Others, especially in Ontario, express the law-enforcement mandate by using the label "force". These variations reflect the problem and challenge among the police community of determining the functions of urban police.

One widely held position – the aging conservative view – emphasizes the doctrine that security, or the absence of crime, is the condition of a common adherence to the law, with exceptions impartially enforced. There is a congruence in this position of public and police notions, of what the police "should" be doing. The popularity of a rapid-response capability and of removing the violent and predatory from the streets is evidence of this agreement, as is the 911 emergency-response system with its dubious rationale. Underlying this congruence is the shared view of the preponderant, even consummate, place of law in a democratic society. While this overall perspective is no longer adequate, it is so entrenched in public attitudes that it must be attended to in any reassessment of police functions. (It should be said here that the history of policing developments from the early nineteenth century to this day throws up frequent references to "declining moral values," suggesting that we have been on a two-hundred-year slide. This is not the case, and it may be more useful to think in terms of shifts from a familiar set of moral emphases in to other sets.)

The occupational structure of policing retains the traits of a craft, in which skills are largely learned in a coach/apprenticeship setting and qualifications gained through experience. Medieval and early industrial craftsmen were of high status, the aristocrats of labour, and the ideals of crafts linger in policing: esteem for hard-won skills, personal authority over one's tools and over the quality of the product. Thus, there is in policing an emphasis on competent investigation of crime and apprehension of offenders. At the constable level, quality in policing has a craft-like personal or individual orientation; the patrol program is implemented and played out at the level of the individual officer.

This book examines only the police occupation and what its future might be, a limitation that is often difficult to apply given the intricate and often vague nature of the area. The scope includes broad matters of major influence: a bit of history to indicate the origin of some of the enduring but obstructive characteristics of policing, to which the early part of this chapter is devoted; the environment of influential public attitudes and of the urban setting itself, that which determines its functions; a discussion of evolving functions, especially in community policing; the supervision of police by government and government influence on policing; a detailed examination of the police occupation; the fit between policing and professionalism as defined in modern urban society; and discussion of various approaches to the problems of police accountability and supervision. Many issues of public concern are discussed at length, others only referred to. The latter include police abuse of authority including police violence, ethnocultural insensitivity and allegations of police racism, and crime rates, especially those of violent crime and family violence. The text does provide, however, an understanding of how and where many of these issues arise. For example, abuse of authority is rooted in police social-ization processes, the often ambiguous nature of patrol work, police perceptions of their roles, and, in some ways, the historical evolution of those roles, with any abuses sheltered by the nature of police super-vision and by the cohesiveness of patrol officers. These connections will become apparent.

The future of policing seems to lie along two broad lines. First, polic-ing must become a more balanced endeavour. Police resources might be shaped by and reorganized in accordance with the urban environ-ment and tied to a matured sense of the local nature of consensus and accountability, with law enforcement as the counterpoint or compan-ion function. Policing will thus become an even more challenging oc-cupation. Calls for a leadership of professional calibre will follow, marking the second broad road into the future. What follows is an ex-ercise in mapping the routes that this process might follow and the so-cial terrain it must pass through on the way to occupational renewal.

CHAPTER TWO

The Conventional View of Law, Order, and Community

Ideas and cultural styles do not change history – at least,
not overnight. But they are the necessary preludes to
change, since a change in consciousness – in values and
moral reasoning – is what moves men to change their
social arrangements and institutions.[1]

THE COMMON IDEOLOGY

Our ideological roots can be traced both to the Enlightenment and to
urban experience since the Second World War. Rationalism and the
political philosophers of the Enlightenment, particularly Locke, influenced United States constitution building, while Locke, Hobbes, and
Rousseau, among others, influenced the social and political order in
Britain and Canada, which did not involve ground-breaking episodes
of constitution design as in the US, but rather processes of fine tuning
and adapting existing structures. This common intellectual legacy has
had divergent consequences; there are significant differences between Canada and the United States, for example, in terms of political and social behaviour and assumptions about security and
policing. Nonetheless, it underlies what has became the conventional, the traditional in our thinking and thus helps to explain the
assumptions we make.

The view that security is the *raison d'être* of organized society is characteristic of Western thinking. The means of achieving security and the
role of the state, of government and law, of law enforcement and order
maintenance in doing so, are shaped by conventional, formative ideology. The relevant conventions are widely shared among the more conservative segments of the public – the poor, lawyers, doctors and the
clergy, the military and the police – as well as among the many citizens
who are "law and order" oriented. Crime-control policies often reflect
this ideological bent rather than hard-headed experience. The issue is
far from academic: one need only recall the political potency of law-
and-order election platforms in the United States, the well-received

belligerence of the war-on-drugs campaign or the endless debates on capital punishment. These attitudes are well entrenched, and people in politically sensitive offices respond to them. For their part, the media tend to be conservative, reinforcing the "moderate middle," as Reiner puts it.[2]

The three pillars of the conventional are: law above politics, the human proneness to evil, and the necessity of punishment. The commitment to reforming the old Adam in us according to the prescriptions of law persists.[3]

That moral precepts limit behaviour is central to the conservative tradition. Western democracies cherish the belief that everyone is of intrinsic worth, an equal and universal worth consisting in the inviolable dignity and integrity of the person. Each of us possesses the "inalienable" right to express that worth in individual ways, whether by earning our bread by some other "higher" quest for personal growth and achievement. To interfere, in the pursuit of some individual good, with the similar endeavour of another is to attack that person's worth and security of place. If by focusing exclusively on our own good we elevate our worth at others' expense, we are victimizing them. Being human, we come to know the restraints on our behaviour that follow from being part of humanity. Morality is, then, a representation of humanity through which we become aware of restraints, that is, of the particulars of what we may and may not do. Morality is also a universal in keeping with our intrinsic worth and as such binds us all. The affront of a transgression against a person is, in our tradition, an affront to the morality we all depend on and thus to the worth we esteem in each other. This sense of the rightness of things permits us to characterize the acts of one against another as being not only unlawful but immoral, since law expresses the morality vital to our security.

The French Declaration of the Rights of Man and of the Citizen, published on 26 August 1789, reflects this ideology: "Liberty consists in the freedom to do everything which injures no one else; hence the exercise of the natural rights of each man has no limits except those which assure to the other members of society the enjoyment of the same rights. These limits can only be determined by law." John Lea and Jack Young, who are more radical in their approach, suggest that in the conservative mind, crime is wilful and "so to have justice, so that the honest person knows that his or her honesty is not to be sneered at, punishment *must* occur. The balance of justice must be maintained" (emphasis added).[4]

There is, in short, a logic, perhaps a fading logic, in the idea that law expresses a common morality and that adherence, including enforced adherence, should inspire moral habits in the service of individual security.

Moral rules have traditionally been conceived of in legal or quasi-legal terms. The state is expected to maintain just relations among citizens. When the state is secular, moral constraints are, in principle, distinct from religious orthodoxy. Still, the moral quality of law was reinforced in nineteenth-century England and Canada by the increased influence of religion and the resulting penetration of society by religious morality and convictions. In the range of conduct it regulates or prohibits, the law may stretch according to the morality of the day or, as in the less-religious twentieth century, it may contract.

The Victorian middle and upper classes professed a state of virtue such that the laws of the time, with their moral content, were employed to regulate behaviour deemed immoral or conducive to indolence (a cardinal vice in an industrial age dependent on a new work ethic). Religious tenets were assigned a public, moral character the better to promote social respectability in the working classes. Temperance, actually abstinence, was encouraged well into this century in order to strengthen working-class families, promote their economic well-being, and create an overall class respectability with the "credentials and the capacity to occupy an independent place in the political process."[5]

The newly minted British bobby played his part in this theatre of eternal truths and precepts that had protected the English since before the Norman Conquest as much from royal or governmental abuse of power as from predatory criminals. Much of the legacy remains.

As Berki said, "The image of society seen in terms of the conservative perspective is ... a reduced, two-dimensional one ... There is nothing else to the problem of law and order, to the problem of security; natural nastiness, viciousness on one side, the law and inculcated law-abiding habits of people on the other."[6] The net effect is the inclination to view law and its enforcement as having a practical function in the provision of security. Otherwise the state is without an executive role in this crucial area. This practical function flows from the belief that security exists when the law is universally obeyed; exceptions become a matter of enforcement and punishment. This rather simplistic reduction feeds into the "law enforcement" image of police work, that is so firmly entrenched in the public mind. In Carl B. Klockars's words, "It fostered the impression that police action was largely dictated by the provisions of the written law and was ultimately supervised and reviewed by the courts. Both of these notions proved highly compatible with what many Americans thought the police of a democratic society should be."[7]

By this ideology the state, an abstraction, does its duty if it "contains" crime by providing some institutional, thus visible and official, means of recognizing the place of its laws and promoting adherence to them – showing the flag, as it were, by way of a reasonable number of convictions and punishments. It provides "statistical protection," not deterrence. Reiner speaks of two fallacious assumptions underlying both the law-and-order and civil-liberties positions: that the central function of police is law enforcement, and that in a rational sense, deterrence follows from that.[8]

In this representation of rights and morality, the state and its laws stand above mere politics, which is the representation of temporary, sectional interests. The conventional view recognizes only the existence of individuals, not their particulars, but makes individual rights a focus of the rule of law. Police officers, in enforcing the law, implicitly show as much or more concern for the place of law as for the individual attributes of the people involved. Just as the state is impartial and deemed to be above the conflicts of society (while representing the interests of all components of that society), so must police be above the same conflicts. Law enforcement is not concerned with order and particular disputes.

The law occupies an exalted position in our society, as the cathedral-like surroundings of the courts and the robes of their officers attest. These trappings contribute to the persuasiveness of the law needed to sustain a supportive consensus. But the law is an abstraction that does not speak to the matter of its own application. It is silent about how security is to be sustained; the means, afterall, including enforcement, are those of daily politics. And if the law is universal in nature, there is clearly no requirement that the *politics* of security – the practices of organized society and its institutions, including policing – be separate in purpose from that of criminal law. Laws, however, are as imperfect as the political wisdom of the society that devised them.

The state recognizes the place of tolerance in relations among citizens representing a diversity of views and beliefs; it "embodies civility, stands above conflicting personal and group interests and is the only effective 'impartial' adjudicator in society."[9] But where tolerance fails, the resolution of resulting conflict cannot be such an aloof matter. The law-enforcement approach, from this perspective, may not be an effective instrument for restoring order. Robert Trojanowicz of the pioneering neighbourhood foot-patrol program noted that the inclination to believe that enforcement is not only necessary but sufficient is false, especially in the urban context of innumerable laws and a mirage of consensus.[10] The conventional attitude undervalues the role of politics and all its instruments, police as much as legislatures, in mediating the contradictions that arise between the abstracts, universal quality attributed to law and its formulation and administration in a context of competing interests.

Conventional ideology has other built-in tensions. Practical concerns about crime and its roots in society are unavoidable. Crime and disorder vary with time and local social and economic conditions, variations that are not included in the universalist perspective. Matters of security are so confounded by various social factors that attributions of cause are at best speculative, so relying on the public's sense of what is desirable becomes politically rational. At this level, objectives can be, and often are, clearer and more achievable than they are in the realm of morality and idealism. How security and crime are construed in the public mind is therefore salient, for if changes in relevant social arrangements and institutions are to be achieved, then changes in public attitudes and values are the prerequisite. High courts wrestle with the issue in much the same terms. In short, the application of law through enforcement, while objective in its intent, cannot be aloof from the competing interests of the day. It requires the mediation of policing in the pursuit of some less-lofty purpose and identifies successes on the basis of known outcomes. Ultimate causes of crime cannot be discerned, so that remedies tend to be immediate, short term, and partial. The problem cannot be dealt with by applying some general theory.

CRIME AND DISORDER

As Berki has said, "[what] ordinary common sense and our gut reactions ... tell us on the one hand, and what is disclosed in philosophical reflection and speculation on the other, suggest the same thing: that personal security is really the key to modern society, and that the problem of so-called law and order is the key to personal security."[11] Yet the programs and agencies of government are essentially retroactive: an offence must have occurred for the panoply of officialdom to act. The offence then becomes its property; it is taken over and placed in the hands of police and courts. Victims become bystanders. Law enforcers – the "unsleeping sentinels" of society, in Chesterton's words[12] – are unavoidably crime-reactive. For the victim, deterrence is lamentably retrospective; with its minimal effect, deterrence, though valued by society in principle, is of little evident value to any one person. This suggests that the power of government directly to control or reduce victimization and crime is slight. As studies have suggested, enforcement only marginally deters the commission of crime.[13] Nevertheless, laws and punishment retain a symbolic significance for law-abiding people who are committed to measures that foster a common obedience.

The conventional orientation to security and the problem of crime is an action-oriented philosophy. The goal – enforcement – is clear cut and invites no contemplation or calm deliberation. Berki puts it this way: "The conservative view is certainly best characterized in terms of its intentional 'myopia,' its almost exclusive concentration on the here and now, on what goes on at the visible, surface level, and what can be done about disorder and crime immediately. The conservative stance achieves a remarkable degree of clarity and purposiveness in a limited area; the focus is sharp on the trouble spots, while the surroundings tend to be ignored and left covered in darkness."[14] Police absorption in day-to-day crises, however minor,[15] tends to lead to the emphasis, often remarked upon, on action and action-based experience.

Berki described crime as the product of the "malevolent indifference ... of strangers."[16] One's place as a human being with a vital right to security is denied by the criminal's mere indifference to that right in pursuit of selfish ends. Although we are all in varying measures familiar to one another, the archetypal offender is unknown, so that the stranger assumes a particular significance in our perceptions. The fear of strangers is part of the fear of crime, and strangers signify the potential threat in a neighbourhood. My security rests only marginally on the state; it depends more, according to Berki, on the relative absence of hostility towards me, on malevolent indifference being randomly diffused in the community, and "on my being *one* single individual among many others."[17] In this sense, one's security rests on statistical improbability, something more likely in an orderly community.

Whatever else may stimulate individual action, personal security is the most fundamental, the *sine qua non* of society. Yet personal security, being a social achievement, is beyond the capacity of any one person alone.

The potential for victimization at the hands of some malevolent stranger affects the quality of community life at its core; the antidote tends to be assurances of orderliness: of the expected and the familiar. This helps us understand that fear of crime is directly related to community problems rather than to an actual level of crime. People sense, and rightly so, that the problems of freedom and security are the same; it is not so much the need to balance one with the other as to recognize that restrictions on freedom for the sake of security actually lessen both. In other words, freedom and security depend on the same thing: the provisions of society. As I said above, people cannot alone provide for their security; freedom and security both require a well-functioning community of people.

This characterization of crime highlights important if familiar reactions to the potential of victimization. First, we find security in the midst of those we know – relatives, friends, colleagues, and other acquaintances, along with police officers and those generally acting with public trust. At a slight distance are people otherwise unknown but similar to us in values, attitudes, and personal characteristics who bestow a sense of security, based on affinity, similar to that found within a large tribe, an affinity despite the near-infinite variety of social practices manifest at individual, family, and neighbourhood levels. Secondly, because we are a society of strangers,[18] malevolence is readily perceived in the discords and incivilities that arise in an unstable neighbourhood out of conflicting interests or suspicion of the strangeness of different groups. Mere indifference, in this context, can be read as a threat. The belated recognition of the extent of family abuse arises, in part, from this general perspective; a violent husband is not, after all, a stranger, and abuse of one's spouse, which has only recently been perceived as an intrusion into local orderliness, was more indicative of a lack of respectability and marital instability, a matter of private concern.

Criminal acts and disorderly acts are different in principle. The latter reflect an individual's relationship to a group and a deviation from its accepted norms. Order is the peaceful playing out of social relationships, or an acting out according to expectations, going by the rules.[19] Maintaining order may be called "political" policing rather than "state" policing in that identities (socioeconomic status and race, among others), social rules and relationships, and the specifics of time and place – all of which define an act as disorderly – are hardly universals. The processes of law enforcement are indifferent to those particulars in defining a criminal act. There is nothing sinister in this political reality if the distinction is recognized. However, "political" policing, by definition, involves discretion and, therefore, bias. Should the maintenance of order be classed as a form of law enforcement and placed under similar legal approaches, it will remain the lesser activity and, in being forced under some procedural control, deprived of, or seen to be without, discretionary authority.

Order does not exist in the abstract; it exists in particulars. The medieval notion of order, the condition of a common observance of (royal) law and custom, has much evolved. Order at the level of daily life is still the expectation of a tranquil unfolding in social transactions, but underlying this expectation is an ongoing, traditional arrangement of group relationships, of local custom, of an accepted and legitimized pattern in the community; not simply rules and practices, but substantive, concrete, interlocking structures with settled understandings about purposes and interests among people. In a community thus ordered, the inhabitants and their consciousness of their own identities distinguish or characterize the daily goings-on. Disorderly acts are an affront to the real nature of identity and attitudes. Within the context of group interests and purposes and the patterns of behaviour these promote, an act of disorder is political, though often illegal (more than a minor disturbance).

Order maintenance is a response to social/political conflict and thus a political enterprise, which then persistently raises questions about police supervision and accountability. Policing, involving as it does the capacity to act in settling conflict, lies at the heart of government functions. To regard the primary task of policing as crime control is inappropriate for it could not, thus defined, be effective.

Day-to-day life in any neighbourhood is a reflection of the larger context of order and thus of power relationships among politicians, police, officials of government and business, and the innumerable understandings of how responsibility is shared. Any deterioration in this broader order will be reflected in an erosion of local order: in the stability of a neighbourhood, the quality of a public service, or the attentiveness of government. Only those with greater power and wealth can rely more on their own resources than on the state for personal security, which they achieve in a form consistent with the exclusivity of their normal way of life and social position. Berki compared exclusive neighbourhoods to medieval castles: "In Sunningdale and Tonbridge, and selected suburban areas of all large modern cities, you don't need a patrolling policeman to secure the tranquillity of your siesta; the presence of your similarly privileged neighbours and the natural barriers of walls, locks, spreading lawns, alarm systems will largely suffice."[20]

Enforcement and order maintenance, then, are interdependent. But each is based on the centrality of order that crime corrodes. In the wake of a crime that task is to restore local order, the state conventionally having "taken away" the crime, and often the criminal, as its property. One is left with an image of advancing disorder merging into, or indistinguishable from, crime; an image of the run-down council estate where music blares out of windows early in the morning ... graffiti on the walls ... aggression in the shops ... bins that are never emptied ... always being careful ... it is a symbol of a world falling apart. It is lack of respect for humanity and for fundamental human decency."[21] It is the advanced social decay of neighbourhoods racked by drug-trade disturbances.

THE REALITY AND PLACE OF POLITICAL ROLES

The emergence of urban police can be attributed, though not exclusively, to the growth of municipal bureaucracies within a broader trend towards rationalized government administration with functionally defined departments led by specialists. In the case of policing, there was no apparent need for functions to be identified with explicit legal or social purposes; hence a largely unspecified set of activities emerged, varying with the political winds of the day in the United States and under the shelter of police commissioners in Canada.

Unlike various European countries or the United States, England did not develop a "high" police agency like the Federal Bureau of Investigation (FBI) – agencies that specialized in intelligence, controlling riots, and other threats to the stability of government. The then-distrust of the political establishment did not permit such a development in England. As a result, some functions did fall on "low," or municipal, police departments, devolving as tasks typical of order maintenance, regulating specific behaviour such as protests and demonstrations and even mundane picketing.

The policing institution is located in the political arena of national life although it claims allegiance to the politically neutral domain of criminal law. The hypothesis that eventual public acceptance of policing in England (perhaps acquiescence is the better word) was attributable to its depoliticization is questionable. The expansion of Victorian laws, the product of upper- and middle-class political influence, was aimed at the working classes, especially their street life, and so had an undeniably political character. Police zeal had the effect of impressing on people that the police officer was a representative of the upper middle class and its version of morality – stamping out popular pleasures – that encouraged a clear and visible impression that the authorities had no friendly or protective intentions towards the "lower" orders. At the same time, the improvement in social conditions, the ideal of respectability, and socially homogeneous housing estates produced social order more effectively than "politically neutral" policing, which did not change public behaviour so much as create new categories of offenders.[22]

The logic that regulation of some behaviours, if expressed as law, is politically neutral and therefore acceptable is faulty if the law is enacted to "cover" some bias in intent, including class bias. Nor is consensus bias free. Consensus, or an appearance of consensus, is elusive and may founder in a society of increasingly permissive values, since it has a time- and place-specific quality.

Competing interests are mediated, arranged, or satisfied by political means. Government is involved through the formulation and implementation of public policies on which it has often sought consensus through various mechanisms. The broader aspects of this process are well known. The development of policies and programs based on some measure of consensus is difficult, given the diversity of communities within late-twentieth-century cities. Differences among interest groups are sharp and consensus often capricious. When it comes to developing significant programs that affect security, the police as a public institution have not proven adept at negotiating amidst the tensions and demands of urban interests. Instead, they tend to settle for consultation with various fractious groups among which no common understanding is likely except when high rates of violent crime tap support for law-and-order reactions. Gradually, however, political pragmatism dictates the favouring of one community of interest over another, perhaps with some mollifying trade-offs for the less favoured.

At the same time, the moral quality of law reflects a humble and usually shared sense of the rightness of things, the quiet backdrop against which our views of and reactions to the day's events are thought out. We sense that tolerance, civility, tentative arrangements, compromise, and all similar democratic processes of mediation are right and proper and in them politics has its rationale. The innumerable ways people may differ one from another – in values, beliefs, social status, and property – do not isolate so much as provide the basis on which people recognize affinities of interest and form different and competing groups around them. Society as a whole, then, cannot be a political abstraction so much as a misleading fiction. While much of the mediation is left to political intervention, much is also left to society; the considerable tolerance and civility we see around us is the mark of a healthy community.

Whoever acts as one "should" to promote general security, acts politically; that is, a social good is pursued in the here and now. In the case of a police officer, performance will be partial to some interests and in large part, one expects, the partiality extends to the broader consensus, an aspect of stability in which governments have a profound investment. Acts are directed according to this consensus and for this we come to rely on individual people whom we trust such as a police officer, and not an abstraction like the police in general. Furthermore, the job of the police executive is political; the law is silent as to the ways and means of maintaining security, just as it is silent about the institutions of enforcement. The law does not decree a monolithic police establishment. The rule of law implies neither that the politics of order must be separate from the apolitical processes of criminal justice nor that the two must be the same, even if entwined in the same institution and its programs.

ORTHODOXY AND AMBIVALENCE IN POLICING

The traditional approach to crime (based on the moral nature of law and the idea that human nature is weak but amenable to correction) is a rational-deterrence notion that is largely symbolic in restraining deviance even in law-and-order politics. This sort of symbolism has a strong appeal to politicians though its rationale is questionable. It seems to elicit, Reiner observes, some common understandings that focus on law-abiding behaviour. It is an impatient approach because in the narrow view, a crime is but a single incident caused by an individual whose character or conscience is correctable; hence the problem is an individual one, clearly seen and, therefore, open to attack.

Conventional ideology is inhospitable to social nuances and to an open police dialogue on the use of discretion. William Bennett, then director of the United States Office of National Drug Policy, said at the 1990 annual convention of the International Association of Chiefs of Police that the crisis posed by drug abuse was pressing and urgent and that more police, more prisons, and more prosecutors were needed. He urged all states to build more prisons: "Let's remember that a prison is a civilizing institution. It was created by civilization for the purpose of civilized vengeance. Incarceration is a failing for the individual, but it is a victory for civilization." Bennett also urged the restoration of traditional values: "Re-establish the values of family, church and school, and in the long term eighty percent of the drug problem will be taken care of."[23]

The conventional view is reflected in policing itself. As one retired senior Canadian officer and his coauthor wrote in a widely cited book, the police priority "now, as always, is to keep the community secure and ... they try to do so through preventing crime, enforcing the law and maintaining the peace"[24] – a traditional statement with its conventional law-enforcement orientation. The authors also say, with merit, that the primary responsibility for crime prevention does not lie with "law enforcement authorities," for the more effective police means of preventing crime, the patrol program, in relation to total crime, "[has] a limited effect." [25] (The terms prevention, as in "preventive patrol," and deterrence were used interchangeably to mean that offences are discouraged through the rapid response effect.)

The authors, like others, were searching for valid statements of police functions and candidly suggested a limited police capacity for prevention/deterrence: "Most causes of crime are beyond the control of police and can be eliminated only by society in general ... Crime is obviously a chronic social disease. Without present preventive measures it would even now be beyond control, and its present rate of increase indicates that in future even broader and more sustained preventive efforts will be necessary."[26] The deterrent measures, then, are those of orthodox law enforcement and this persisting doctrinaire thinking, burdened by the admission that crime is little controlled by law enforcement, will still command increased resources needed to attend to more frequent crimes.

Police officers provide a special kind of service to the whole of society; they are "acting out the law." As the state (though not a government) in principle is impartial and deemed to be above the conflicts of society (though not above society itself), so must be the police. In this light, the police institution derives status, a special interest in and a special claim on a privileged position; their near-constant expectation of the reassurance of public respect thus becomes understandable, as does their occupational sense of the impropriety of external criticism, and the further sense that political offices do not have a superior claim to authority, including the authority of police supervision. This sense of privilege seems to fetter police thinking. Useful program options do not readily emerge; nor are wider standards of effectiveness perceived beyond the legal/moral. As others have noted,[27] one problem in this regard is not whether police act within legal bounds but whether they so act with civilized conduct, a tougher standard in order-maintenance activities. The more homely position embraces the widest range of conduct and detaches it from the protection of a privileged or suprasocial role.

Much of what is noted as conventional in this chapter is common to industrial society. Some of the past and ongoing effects of urban industrial society and its policing arrangements are among the topics of the next chapter. The industrial system joined the social structure (economy, occupational system, and technology) with a culture of character-building endeavours promoting the habits of "delayed gratification, of compulsive dedication to work, frugality and sobriety, sanctified by the morality of service to God and the proof of self-worth through the achievement of respectability."[28] But the industrial age is giving over to the postindustrial, whose attributes include: increased specialization and subspecialization within the occupational system; a multiplication of collectivities and hierarchies; formalization of rules; extension of universalism; secularization of beliefs and emphasis on the individual; syncretism, or the smoothing over of the differences among creeds and forms; and, in terms of culture, the search for novelty and sensation.[29] The orthodoxies of industrial society, the moral strength and persuasiveness of law, are battered and their grip loosened. Social relations based on property and related power structures and on an ideological ethic of restraint are being eroded. The sources of this upheaval are scientific and technological; they are also cultural and political, promoted by communications technology, huge private corporations, centralizing tendencies in governments, and continuing urbanization.

The two main characteristics of postindustrialism are the centrality of theoretical knowledge (the strategic resource) and, through it, the expansion of the service sector. The service sector has long been proliferating, of course. But it is in health, education, research, and government that service growth will prove decisive. The new élite, the intelligentsia, are increasingly grouped in universities, research organizations, professions, and government departments as well as in a restructured society: their place will be found in newly evolving professional and technical social classes.[30]

Conventional morality, oriented to the values of the past, is diminished by the rationalism of the present and its promise for the future. Knowledge-based decisions are tied to future results, as with science-based prohibitions on cigarette smoking. Morality and tradition are being supplanted by knowledge as the impetus behind the trend to seek a rational basis for social policies and objectives and for the regulation of conduct. The debate about capital punishment, for example, focuses more on the rationality of deterrence than on the moral worth of human life and a sense of retributive justice.

Absence of education – of knowledge or technical skills – is the new mark of disadvantage, and the criterion of a social and occupational status is that of professional rank. The capitalist-versus-worker conflict is being replaced by that of professional versus populace. Bell suggests that an emerging "populism" is claiming more rights and a wider participation in society; members of groups will seek power through politics since it is unattainable through the traditional avenues of property and inheritance.[31] The basis for change, and for the shape of change, once found in the man-machine technology supporting a factory system, has shifted to a cultural/political basis. This shift implies that a new work ethic is emerging that will be in conflict with the still-extant Protestant ethic, and some social tensions are inevitable.[32] For all the upheaval we may experience from these developments, they also offer some heartening prospects for hitherto intractable problems in policing. It is clear, for example, that the urban poor dislike and distrust the police and that the feeling is reciprocated and will persist until the conventional norms of the urban middle class are abandoned.

The sociocultural decisions of an industrial market society were aggregated individual decisions with hedonistic overtones, resulting in the banalities of throw-away mass culture, "the proposition that *individual* satisfaction is the unit in which costs and benefits are to be reckoned. This is an atomistic view of society and reflects the utilitarian fallacy that the sum of individual decisions is equivalent to a social decision ... The paradox is that in the nineteenth and early-twentieth centuries we had, in America, individualism in the economy and regulation in morals; today we have regulation in the economy and individualism in morals."[33]

In postindustrial society, the emphasis will be on communal rather than individual decisions. There will be movement towards further participation and consensus, and it will be a political process. Government will gain in influence over the economic sector, attracting to itself the search for advantage among segments of the community. Economic influence, that of property or commerce, will be supplanted by political influence.

Wilson's point that a change in the consciousness of values, morality, and reasoning will lead to a change in social arrangements and institutions is of consequence. What emerges will have a bearing on the capacity of urban communities to provide security and sustain order. One necessary condition is that public attitudes, the conventional and orthodox, need to change and perhaps will, given a renewed rationalism. More certain is that at the closing of the century, the reconfiguration of policing into a knowledge-based occupation is belated.

CHAPTER THREE

The Roots of Policing – The Urban Community

CITIES AND THEIR NEIGHBOURHOODS: THE PRIZED PLACE OF LIVING

The most significant trend in the more than one hundred years of police history has been massive urban, particularly suburban, growth. It is reasonable to hypothesize that urbanization will characterize the twenty-first century as it has the twentieth. Nothing has affected policing more than this. The business of maintaining order and security is conducted against a backdrop of inner-city neighbourhoods and burgeoning suburbs, two contrasting aspects of the urban whole. Much of the city has been shaped to give reality to the ideals and virtues of family life in tranquil and secure residential havens. These sought-after ideals and the physical attributes of neighbourhoods that reflect them have determined the structure, purposes, and functions of policing. As the once-pervasive suburban form of residential neighbourhood is beginning to give way to new residential forms, policing must surely keep pace.

Cities have been well studied from the spatial/geographical, historical, behavioural, cultural, and institutional/political points of view. The problems of policing, security, order, and crime, however, have only recently gained prominence among urban research topics. It may well be that as public-policy issues, they were thought to fall within the domains of criminal law or public administration, political philosophy, the psychology of deviance, or the sociology of law more than urban studies. While studies of criminality often focus on economic and social conditions, few have explicitly examined the urban context of the policing endeavour for its relationship to order and the quality of community life. Rates of crime and the heightened public concern they prompt have tended to narrow the focus on crime in the criminal-justice-system context, an effect of conventional law-and-order thinking. Widespread concern for the ills of cities, inner cities in particular, has generated a great deal of relatively recent research as well as experimental programs,[1] such as major public-housing projects in Britain and the United States and, to a lesser extent, in Canada. Slogans such as the "war on poverty" come to mind. But a review of reports centred on urban poverty does little to illuminate the role the police might have played. Not until the social turmoil and rising crime rates of the 1960s and 1970s did policing begin to attract the attention it deserves in urban studies.

Cities for most of us are fascinating and attractive, varied and endlessly expressive of human achievements and failures. They offer liberty on the one hand, and heightened constraint and regimentation on the other. Urban culture demands literacy as nonurban culture does not.[2] Donald Higgins has suggested that a city is a set of problems, of political processes that determine reactions to these problems, of public institutions set up to address them, and of people and ideas that enliven the processes set out to address them.[3] Within each city, as Wilson and Herrnstein observed, a given neighbourhood is not only an area where people live but the locus of a small if complex society whose boundaries limit what may be observed and what opportunities or constraints are set and within which particular attitudes are shaped.[4] Neighbourhood and community settings form a "complex web of interactions" that shapes attitudes, gives meaning to such abstractions as class and race, and brings people into, or keeps them apart from, the larger society. The transmission of attitudes conducive to crime throughout a particular subculture – for example, one characterized by poverty and a restriction of opportunity – deserves to be examined, however pervasive, subtle, and elusive these "neighborhood effects" may be.

Cities, then, make up the shifting, hugely variable social matrix of policing. The following pages examine the reality of policing in its urban perspective, thus avoiding an overemphasis on criminal justice and law enforcement divorced from the shifting circumstances of time, place, and people. I will argue that the present organization of police and the shape and direction police functions have taken are largely the product of urbanization, particularly in its suburban form. But while suburban needs have been catered to, attention has only belatedly been paid to older city forms. Meanwhile, the pattern of urban growth is changing again and the signs of different city forms are now being glimpsed.

Dysfunctional police services are a consequence of the police trailing behind general urban trends. Bertrand Russell said that "society cannot exist without law and order, and cannot advance except through the initiative of vigorous innovators. Yet law and order are always hostile to innovations, and innovators are almost always to some extent anarchists. Those whose minds are dominated by fear of a relapse toward barbarism will emphasize the importance of law and order, while those who are inspired by the hope of an advance toward civilization will usually be more conscious of the need of individual initiative. Both temperaments are necessary and wisdom lies in allowing each to operate freely where it is beneficent."[5] Russel said that the conventional values of law and order are reinforced by custom and a wish to preserve the *status quo*; that gregarious animals display an "instinct to conventionality"; and that feelings of insecurity are aroused by the unknowns inherent in innovation. Vested interests, too, leap to the defence of the old, the traditional, and the orthodox.

The familiar police-patrol program has long been one of the conventions of the day and is now obsolete. Once a constable patrolling a short beat, now a motorized, evenly distributed crime-oriented response service, this program works best in the suburbs. Nonetheless, it is known to be of meagre protective and deterrent value. This is highlighted, particularly in larger centres in Canada, Britain, and the United States, by the many neighbourhoods persistently threatened by disorder and crime in spite of much conventional police attention. The preventive patrols of Peel's London consisted of constables given visibility by uniforms as much so that they could be easily supervised as for any preventive purpose; as Carl Klockars said on the subject of uniformed patrol, "To anyone familiar with the origins of patrol it is nothing short of astounding to realize that what was once clearly understood as a means of controlling police could grow to acquire a front-line role in the war on crime."[6] The same concern with control is seen in O.W. Wilson's now-familiar redesign of patrol work (discussed in a later chapter), with its aim, in part, of diminishing the discretion of officers and their potentially corrupting contact with the public. The evidence that the establishment of the police and the effectiveness of the "bobby" on the streets of London reduced the incidence of crime is at best ambiguous, and in the United States of the 1850s, as Emsley noted, newspapers protested that preventive patrols did not prevent burglaries.[7] The pioneering Kansas City patrol experiment demonstrated its relative ineffectiveness in preventing or suppressing crime.[8]

At the turn of the century, fourteen percent of the world's population, and thirty-five percent of Canadians, lived in cities. The percentage in Canada remained under fifty percent until well into the 1920s. Nearly a hundred years of police experience and evolution were shaped by small-city or small-town conditions. Now the world percentage nears the halfway point and is likely to reach three in five in the coming century. Mexico City, with an estimated eighteen million people, will approach forty million during the next three decades.

The "whirlpool" effect of growing cities was noted almost a century ago: a self-sustaining pattern with more and more people drawn into the vortex. Well into this century, immigrants to Canada, especially during the great waves of western settlement, came from rural backgrounds and sought rural destinations, whereas modern migrants are city bound. Canada will continue to be an urbanizing society and no exception to the world trend as its overall population grows. Within Canada, migrants to cities tend to be the better educated, motivated by opportunity and higher pay. Cities offer opportunities for specialization and the means, especially extensive education facilities, for achieving specialized qualifications. Cities provide a release from the limiting aspects of rural social experiences. As Leonard Gertler and Ronald Crowley have pointed out, they also offer a freedom not found at all under small-town conditions where social control is prominent and effective, as it is in company towns, but also covert, imposed through gossip and social sanctions.[9]

It was not until the postwar decades of the mid-twentieth century that Canadian society began to be transformed by urban growth. In the early 1950s, Canada's urban population was about 10.7 million; in 1976, 17.5 million; in 1981, 18.4 million; and five years later, in 1986, more than 19 million; about seventy-five percent of the population lived in cities.[10] Now eighty percent of urbanites live in twenty still-spreading metropolitan areas.

The form that city growth took was suburban: neighbourhoods of lawns, trees, and curving streets in exclusively residential areas. In most Canadian cities, the surge in growth came after the suburban form was well established in Britain and the US. In general, inner-city neighbourhoods of high density were not widely built in Canada. Because the Industrial Revolution came somewhat late to this country, so did the accompanying urbanization, the specialization of labour, and the growing numbers of factory workers. Settlement in Canada occasioned some early industrialization, since factories were required to support both the building of railways and farming in the West. Only later did the war effort lead to a wider industrial base. Manufacturing tended to be based on the apprenticeship system. Early unions were craft unions, and craft practices became entrenched in the Canadian experience.

The British and North American city form, the suburb, has been pervasive in the English-speaking world and also peculiar to it: European, Latin American, and Asian cities have not used the suburban form of growth.[11] The impetus towards suburban development was complex, but some of its most obvious manifestations illuminate the evolution of urban policing.

By the dawn of the Victorian era, values had come to centre on the stability and security of a closer family unit, one that the new middle class – the pioneers of suburban living – could afford more easily than their working-class predecessors. Homes were to be separated from the workplace and wives were to become the full-time guardians of the domestic sphere, where morality, religious piety, the work ethic, temperance, and self-improvement would be fostered.

As noted earlier, social turbulence and the dislocations caused by industrialization in the early decades of the nineteenth century prompted an emphasis on moral development akin to the stress placed on physical fitness today. Young men attracted to city factories left behind the community supervision (surveillance might be a more accurate term) typical of extended kinship and the "home town." Urban institutions designed to instil or develop character – YMCAs, Sunday schools, and temperance associations among them – flourished. One leading purpose of the then newly founded public schools was character formation, primarily understood as self-restraint. The bastion of this new morality was the suburban neighbourhood.

The first suburb was designed and built 150 years ago. In *Bourgeois Utopias*, Robert Fishman describes a suburb as a place of exclusiveness:[12] it excluded places of work and anything else that was superfluous to a residential area including people from other classes, except servants. Cities were still compact, though densely occupied, and fathers were able to commute into the city by carriage. Thus separated from the inner city, suburban residents left crude urban influences behind. Gradually, the notion that other classes – as well as immigrants of differing national origins who sought out older, less-expensive city areas – were morally deficient lent substance to the sense of inner-city social decay and the need for suburban exclusiveness. Suburbs became the most effective mechanism of social segregation. With houses placed in a park-like setting, suburbs were also, as they are today, a blend of nature and city.

Meanwhile, the working class was alienated from government and its authority as much by indifference as by a suspicion of government intentions. The motives of social reformers were often suspect, and the solutions proposed for poverty and other social ills were usually repressive. In England, for example, debtors' prisons and workhouses survived despite their evident disutility. By the turn of the century, improving social and economic conditions had rendered society more orderly, though class distinctions were widely accepted as impermeable. This insulation of one class from another was reinforced by the geographical segregation that suburbanization permitted.

The suburbs boomed in successive waves with each development in transportation until, in time, workers were also able to live in suburban neighbourhoods similar to, but still separate from, those of middle-class managers.[13] The trend was most marked in the United States – less so in Canada – during the 1890s, when railway commuting was introduced. The second major wave, lasting through the 1920s into the 1930s, was spurred by the construction of streetcar lines, then of subways – the London tube dates from the 1890s – and elevated trains in many US cities. Subsequent waves of suburbanization were made possible by the automobile, first used recreationally by the better-off who had second dwellings within reach of the city, then increasingly by car-borne commuters, triggering the onset of suburban sprawl.[14] The construction of extensive freeway systems surrounding major cities furthered the dispersal of residential communities and their related institutions, as well as commercial and industrial enterprises. The suburbanization of the postwar decades has been increasingly based on the freeway system.

Urbanization in Canada both corresponded to and departed from American trends. Calgary, where I was raised, grew from a large prairie railway town into a "newer" city along suburban lines, though growth lapsed after a decade or two with the depression of the 1930s – the suburbs began about three blocks from the city centre. It resumed only in the postwar decades, with relentlessly suburban developments of single-family houses, each with a front lawn. Calgary had no true inner-city neighbourhoods of higher density, no multiple-unit housing, and few buildings of mixed use. Other Canadian cities were much the same. Even in Toronto, it is reported, ninety percent of the area devoted to residential purposes is suburban in nature,[15] though Montreal is notable for its nonsuburban, more European, flavour with streets lined by low-rise apartments in many, even recently built, areas.

Since suburban neighbourhoods are too small to provide their own services and regulation, local civic management is uncommon. Instead, there is an informal interdependence of suburban communities, even though some have sprawled across existing municipal boundaries, that seek to influence government at all levels in protecting the integrity of each. It has been estimated that in the average United States metropolitan area, there are ninety levels of government, including independently organized school districts, charged primarily with defending the integrity of the suburban neighbourhood. The same concern for neighbourhood integrity is reflected in the strength of the intransigent, not-in-my-back-yard attitude towards publicly supported housing, senior-citizens' residences, and half-way houses. In 1988, for example, in a small city suburb just north of Toronto, twenty-two rate-payer associations protested the proposed light-industry zoning of a parcel of land.

Outsiders are still not welcome, and it seems that the more exclusive the neighbourhood, the fewer the public sidewalks. Suburban residents tend to be well integrated into their local community: they know other residents; they have several group or organization memberships; they own their homes; and, in most communities, they have longer periods of residence. This exclusiveness or segregation is maintained by various means, including political influence, strong zoning regulations, and municipal land-use review and adjustment procedures developed to serve suburban interests. As Samuel Walker has said, "[The] general level of expectations about quality of life – the amount of noise, the presence of 'strange' or 'undesirable' people – has undergone an enormous change. Three generations of Americans have learned or at least have come to believe that they should not have to put up with certain problems."[16]

The London Metropolitan Police, established just as this new suburban form of development got under way, was designed to cope with disorder in presuburban cities, not with the needs of suburbs. Similarly, the establishment of the United States urban police occurred as mid-city townhouse developments gave way to suburban forms in the mid-nineteenth century. The founding structure of English and North American police, then, was oriented to high-density, multiple-use central neighbourhoods with their related matters of security and service and then quickly applied, though radically refashioned, to serve the suburbs.

In 1987, George Kelling wrote: "We're going to have to see cities and neighborhoods differently. We're going to have see cities and neighborhoods as important sources of character building in the United States, and that essentially they're a primary source of social control and the police are there to support that and to help develop it."[17] Although Kelling was prescribing a direction for the future, the suburban neighbourhood, designed for character building, has been the near-exclusive form of neighbourhood for well over a century. The suburb can be viewed as a major social "experiment" in facilitating the formation of character, even uniformity of behaviour, according to the norms of respectability and visible achievement. Suburbs may be viewed as controlled social environments marked by a homogeneity of values and attitudes; an immediate social milieu in which accepted and expected behaviours are reinforced and from which strangers and deviants are barred.

Attributing the orderliness typical of a suburb to a preponderance of stable, family-oriented people who rejected the older, inner-city districts does not bear much scrutiny. Different inner-city neighbourhoods experience different rates of disorder and crime, as have some suburban neighbourhoods in more recent years. Moreover, Europeans experience relatively lower rates of crime and disorder in spite of the high-density residential areas typical of the Netherlands, Germany, and Scandinavia. To what extent, then, does the orderliness fostered by the suburban arrangement exceed levels of orderliness achieved by people who may share certain suburban attitudes but who do not live in the suburbs?

Increases in crime rates are often associated with urbanization. James Wilson and Richard Herrnstein[18] have traced the crime waves of the 1820s and 1830s to an initial growth spurt in US cities at the onset of industrialization. But the correlation between city growth and crime rate only goes so far. Some large US cities experienced both a declining population and increased rates of violent crime during the early postwar decades, in part due to the flight of the more stable segments of the population to the suburbs. The use of older political boundaries rather than expanded demographic boundaries reflecting urban sprawl across several municipalities has resulted in an often-artificial definition of an urban entity. Crime rates declined across five decades into the 1920s although these were years of urban growth. However, crime rates then increased with increasing urbanization after the Second World War. To account for changes in crime rates in the US, Wilson and Herrnstein[19] cited one study to the effect that the combined effects of increases in the population, the relative proportion of young males (perhaps the more influential factor), and migration into metropolitan areas (for example, migration from the rural South into northern cities) accounted for forty-six percent of the increase in the absolute number of reported crimes between 1960 and 1965. The size of cities also seems to be a factor. The larger ones provide more opportunities for crime, and greater numbers of those who are prone to commit crime, notably young males.

In *Police in Urban America*, E.H. Monkonnen reported an overall steady decline in crime rates in a sample of twenty US cities from about 1860 into the 1920s, during which there were periods of urban growth, all largely suburban.[20] Police departments were established from the mid- to late nineteenth-century and personnel grew in numbers to 1.5 officers per thousand in the population. As in Canada and Britain, the post-Second World War decades saw considerable suburban growth in the US and surges in disorder and crime rates, even though police numbers grew at a proportionate or faster rate, and despite the continued grip of Victorian morality. Gross crime-rate figures do not lend themselves to detailed study of the success of suburban portions of cities in suppressing crime, though what data are available show that suburban crime rates rose but remained disproportionately lower than overall city rates.[21] So if orderliness is equated with the level of crime, then the orderliness of suburbia may flow from character building and accompanying practices of social control, though it is difficult to separate these from other factors such as a possible bias in enforcement. The heavy enforcement of regulatory laws in inner cities inflate crime rates, while changes in official systems of reporting crime, as well as varying proportions of crime-prone young males, also tend to skew the results of such comparisons.

Despite the need for caution, it should still be possible to draw some conclusions about suburban life, orderliness, and urban policing. David T. Herbert has described the "neighbourhood effect" as a contagion: sets of values and associated forms of behaviour that exist within a given "territory" may be transmitted to individuals who live there; a neighbourhood subculture develops across different categories of people,[22] reinforcing similarities in the behaviour of its constituents. Similarly Wilson and Herrnstein suggest that young males are likelier to find others with shared attitudes and motivations that predispose them to particular forms of behaviour in urban settings.[23]

With the migration within urban areas from the older, often premodern districts to modern suburban neighbourhoods, those more likely to commit crime were among the people staying behind[24] those more likely to commit crime. Numerous studies make repeated reference to exclusiveness of suburbs, their homogeneity as an essential attribute, the suburban arrangement as an effective means of social segregation, and the political influence of suburban citizens in protecting their neighbourhoods from unwanted zoning changes or similar intrusions. The value of the middle-class owner's house is tied, in large part, to resisting neighbourhood change, that is, in keeping out people of a different socioeconomic status. However unpalatable a notion, sustained social segregation may be a significant factor in the success of the suburban experiment.

During the first postwar decades, municipal services such as education, physical infrastructure, and inner-city problems dominated the political agenda, at least in the United States. With persistent annual increases in crime, however, attention shifted to law enforcement. The political clout of the suburbs attracted attention, particularly their ability to preserve their integrity against threats of spill-over disorder and their central quality of exclusiveness.

The faith millions of families placed in this great nineteenth- and twentieth-century experiment of creating a milieu that fosters morality and character building through neighbourhood-wide social attitudes and behaviour endured for generations. In this, on balance, perhaps something of a success can be seen.

Threats to the orderliness of a suburb were not and are not usually seen by residents to stem from the neighbourhood itself. Incidents of distress such as marital disputes, while internal, were not deemed to affect community order. Thus crime being the handiwork of outsiders, the police need only be on call. The traditional police-patrol strategy, with its focus on crime and even-handed, nonintrusive policing rather than on the police presence as "watchmen," protected suburban social values, including exclusiveness. The postwar surge in the growth of suburbs in Canada occurred just as the police began to rely heavily on two-way radios, telephones, and automobiles. These three technologies permitted the design of a patrol program well suited to the suburbs, characterized by centralized control, call-driven dispatch, and rapid response. Since continued police presence in suburban neighbourhoods was felt as intrusive, being neither necessary nor wanted, the patrol program was also seen as economical.

Policing suburbia dictated a shift in the meaning of prevention. Originally it referred to the "scarecrow" function of visible, uniformed patrol officers suited to high-density parts of cities; now it was coming to mean the deterrent effect of speed – a "fire-brigade" emergency service of questionable utility that is the foundation of the calls-for-service, deterrent-patrol orientation of modern city police.

James Q. Wilson has defined three styles of policing: watchman, legal, and service.[25] (These are not rigid, mutually exclusive definitions and will receive further attention in the next chapter.) The watchman style characterizes a department concerned with order maintenance. Violations of law are ignored unless they inconvenience residents or run contrary to accepted community mores. The law is viewed as a *means* of maintaining order, and order is a variable dependant on the nature of the group. Juveniles, for example, are expected to misbehave. It is a tolerant approach, suited to and acceptable in stable, long-established neighbourhoods of ethnically and culturally similar working-class people. The legal style, in contrast, is much more rigid and emphasizes full application of the law and strict adherence to the rules of procedure.

Today, it is the service style that is common in middle-class communities where there is agreement on the need for, and definition of, order. Enforcement and order-maintenance calls are taken seriously, but a resort to formal responses (such as an arrest) as a sanction is less likely. The task of protecting orderliness against outsiders is eased by wide agreement as to what illegal or immoral activities are. Suburbanites want to be left alone in their minor indiscretions; they want so-called undesirables kept away, juveniles attended to leniently, and peace maintained. Cooperation, courtesy, and deference, typical of middle-class communities, make the officer's task easier, so that when necessary, according to Wilson, police intervention tends to be more formal and more serious than in working-class or inner-city communities.[26] People in the suburbs prefer the professionalism of the legal- and service-style approaches; a tolerant watchman style is less acceptable, particularly to suburbanites of higher socioeconomic status.

The mobilization of police resources around the centrally controlled preventive patrol was well suited to the suburbs, though often decried. It fitted their traditional notions of the sources of order and the ideals of suburban living. On the other hand, this uniform, seemingly equitable service is inflexible, resistant, at best, to local adaptations and now burdened by a rigidity of habit and acceptance. It is not amenable to grave neighbourhood disorders. The escalating rates of violent crime and social turbulence of the 1960s and 1970s in the United States and Britain highlighted this deficiency. The Police response – for example, turning to the community policing approach – has been belated, fragmented, and often superficial.

In a later study, James Q. Wilson and Barbara Boland investigated the relationship of a "style" of policing to lower rates of crime (e.g., burglary, robbery, and crimes of violence) in selected cities. Higher numbers of citations for moving-traffic violations indicated a "legalistic" type of department, one in which aggressive patrol tactics were practised, especially stop-and-search/question. This tactic, a form of deterrent in that it signals an increased chance of being caught,[27] may account for the lower crime rates. Lee and Young spoke of "military policing," policing without general consent, in noting that stopping people on the street, the use of informers, and the use of stereotypes suggest a military style of policing; field interrogation becomes in itself a form of deterrence. They suggest that it is a penalty that deters because it is random.[28] It is also increasingly circumscribed by law and the focus of some police complaints about restrictions on their latitude to fight crime.

"To achieve an aggressive patrol strategy, a police executive will recruit certain kinds of officers, train them in certain ways, and devise requirements and reward systems (traffic ticket quotas, field interrogation obligations, promotion opportunities) to encourage them to follow the intended strategy. This used to be, and for many still is, the core of the concept of 'police professionalism.' "[29] This professionalism, still an improvident one in my view, forms part of the concept that police administrators should be immune to political influence so long as they act in accordance with professional doctrine, as exemplified by traditional patrol tactics, and that "public decisions be made on the basis of what is best for the community 'as a whole' and should not favour particular neighborhoods, constituencies, or interests."[30] The reform movement will be discussed in a later chapter, but one aspect should be mentioned here. The more legalistic police departments tended to be found in cities with a professional city manager, that is, in reformed city governments. Characterized by managerial competence, the professional approach, fostered by such reformist police leaders as August Vollmer and O.W. Wilson, became prevalent.

THE CHANGING FACES OF CITIES

The distinction between the terms community and neighbourhood is pertinent. A neighbourhood is usually thought of as a small district, a geographical area with certain uniform characteristics. A community, on the other hand, is more a territory of the mind, defined less by geograph than by common interests and problems and by networks of personal ties that govern how people interact and identify with each other. A sense of community is a complex notion. It will vary according to how vital its interests are to the people within its ambit. The obvious example of a community of vital interests is that of a visible minority. The two notions, neighbourhood and community, often coincide and overlap,[31] and the notion of neighbourhood is subsumed by that of community. Yet the notion of neighbourhood-as-community may be weakened as people increasingly interact across the wider urban area. The more developed the interests served by other social groupings, the less people become involved with a neighbourhood itself. Conversely, people will have no sense of being part of a neighbourhood and of its uniqueness unless they experience the differing aspects of contiguous areas. A.P. Cohen maintains that a neighbourhood is experienced on three levels: the immediate area, perhaps one city block in each direction; the area in which children are permitted to play away from home; and the more distant point at which there is a marked difference in socioeconomic class or land usage.[32] In denser or non-suburban areas, a neighbourhood may be as small as a floor of an apartment building, while a secondary "neighbourhood" may be the building as a whole. Inner-city areas often have less easily discerned neighbourhoods because of mixed use and the citizens' inability to in-fluence that use.

Thus, depending on one's the set of defining interests (a person can be a member of more than one community of interests), a neighbourhood may or may not be synonymous with community. But neighbourhoods-as-communities tend to be readily identified by civic administrators and sociologists for their easy, usually geographical, definition and have become the usual units in city land-use planning. Policing, ex-cept for such jurisdiction-wide activities as major investigations, tends to be oriented to, even organized by, fixed territory. This includes com-munity policing. However, certain communities of interest that are not geographically fixed come unavoidably to be the focus of police atten-tion and perhaps even command it. Here the interests arising out of violence against women and family abuse come to mind.

Police officers develop, through experience, internal cognitive maps of cities according to the various crimes and disorders prevalent in each district – in other words, maps that are less of topography than of the symptoms of social troubles. The diversity across this internalized map will be shared within a department and will become, through common experience, part of the pool of perceptions that influence and shape a common set of police attitudes towards particular people who tend to be categorized according to where they live.[33] This cogni-tive map suggests to police, in the first instance, which of various order-maintenance or law-enforcement activities may be appropriate. (This is where David Herbert's "contagion" effect comes in.) There remains the question of the validity of those shared attitudes, the stereotyping that ties the social problems of a district to the characteristics of indi-vidual residents, to their socioeconomic status, and other attributes.

Inner-city districts tend to be older, higher in density, and zoned to permit multiple land uses. But they also often contain high contrasts in stability and affluence. The inner city attracts both the indigent and the wealthy. In many cases, older neighbourhoods, if protected through restricted land uses, remain intact. To categorize neighbour-hoods as either inner city or suburban is crude. Some studies have at-tempted further subcategories: "gentrified" or revitalized, stable or in decline. Still, certain physical traits are adequately conveyed by the original distinction. The higher density of older neighbourhoods re-flects a greater number of multiple-dwelling-unit buildings. People tend to be tenants rather than owners. The district will usually be zoned to serve several purposes – commercial, perhaps light industry, social housing, hostels for derelicts, and entertainment, among others – so that invariably there are grave intrusions into the quality of residential use. These shifting uses, or merely the threat of them, degrades the value of a neighbourhood for residential purposes. It is comparatively inexpensive to reduce the size of rental units to increase numbers of tenants. Inhabitants tend to be single and young; family groups tend to be single parent; many people are pensioners; and overall, turnover and the number of transients are high. In many cases, these are the original and affordable home neighbourhoods of immigrants who eventually moved to the suburbs. But many high-density neighbourhoods – whether in groupings of apartment buildings, social-housing developments, or redeveloped districts – are stable and orderly.

The ills of inner cities became discernible when, for example, the provision of cheap transportation fares – working men's fares – led to a boom in the construction of working-class suburbs, enabling workers to escape the inner city and avoid the "monopoly" rent of landlords that still burdens the poor, the aged, and other disadvantaged people.[34] In older low-income areas, restricted zoning is not favoured by owners, implying as it does limitations on use, while loose zoning permits flexible use and, thus, opportunities at least for short-run increases in value, regardless of residential quality. The political influence of residents will be weak and political interest in them as residents negligible except to the extent that they are seen as burdens on municipal services.

But things change. Statistics Canada has reported that the number of people living in inner cities is rising for the first time since 1951, having increased by five percent between 1981 and 1986. The inner city is more attractive to professionals, to empty-nesters, and to young people starting their careers. Home ownership, as a result, is on the rise. In 1986, 62 percent of these inner-city adults were unmarried; 56 percent lived alone, in contrast to 22 percent outside of the city core; and immigrants still constituted a high proportion of inner-city people, about 30 percent on average. With this trend costs rise and low-cost housing units diminish in availability, so that not only low-income people, many of them young adults, but middle-class people – not the chronically poor – feel the squeeze. Increasingly, one must be very well off or very poor to live in the central cores of large cities. When high-income people remain in the core the neighbourhood will likely be mixed and not very distinct from nearby areas that harbour difficult or threatening lifestyles.[35] Turning a street corner can mean entering a different world. Such districts of sharp contrasts are reminiscent of premodern cities.

For their part, suburban neighbourhoods are better able to retain their homogeneity and stability, having the strength and political influence to resist the troubles signalled by a change in zoning, neglect of houses and other buildings, or the intrusion of unwanted commercial activity such as the establishment of a tavern. All of these signals, whether in suburb or inner city, are indicative of "broken windows" in need of repair – the community-policing thesis that attention paid to early, minor signs of disorder halts further deterioration. The political influence of suburbs increased dramatically in the 1970s and 1980s. Protecting suburban neighbourhoods from signs of decline more common in central, mixed-use areas came to the top of the political agenda.[36] Changes in a city plan, the spread of commercial enterprises, shifts in ethnic make-up, conversion of houses into multiple-unit dwellings: such dynamic features of older districts are precisely what suburbanites so vigorously resist. Wilson associated the conventional demand for tougher policing with a breakdown of neighbourhood cohesiveness occasioned by the flight to the suburbs of the middle class, those most concerned with maintaining standards, the "respectable" people.[37] As it becomes increasingly clear that social and environmental problems thrive in many mature suburban areas, the question arises whether the current flight from suburban areas is akin to the erstwhile flight from the core.[38]

The orderliness of a neighbourhood is tied to its health, its cohesiveness, how well its people interact – it is commonly said that there can be no community where there are no connections. It will be useful, then, to discuss the types of human connections that characterize the "lost city," the "saved city," and the "liberated community".

The "lost city" thesis,[39] a nostalgia for the dependable life of the past, attributes significant changes to, perhaps even a deterioration in, human connections to modern urban life. It is thought that urbanites, though members of communities, have a limited network of neighbourhood/community relationships, for example with church and charity, home and school, work and recreation. The urbanite's primary connections – to work and family – are more narrowly defined; they are less intense and have fewer points of connection within a neighbourhood. Urban ties tend to be isolated or fragmented into two-person relationships rather than rooted in a more extensive group. Even ties of kinship tend to be lax. Among the networks that do exist, connections are sparse and interests few, loose, transient, or diffuse. Clusters of groups and interests are fewer, contrasting with the clear, tightly bound clusters of primary-interest groups of the past defined by kinship, employment, or other similar close affiliations. The organizational capacity for activities based on common interests is scant and the tenuous nature of existing networks inhibits cooperative action.

Barry Wellman and Barry Leighton[40] argue that, if one accepts that these are the characteristics of modern city dwellers, policies designed to promote the development of urban roots and the regeneration of neighbourhood communities will probably fail, indeed have failed in war on poverty and many urban-regeneration programs in the United States. The required neighbourhood cohesiveness, it would seem, shows itself in a capacity to stimulate cooperation with the aim of protecting or restoring the neighbourhood, as well as a capacity to influence behaviour on its streets.

The "lost city" thesis is strained, obviously, when applied to typically stable suburban neighbourhoods. In contrast, the "saved" community thesis claims, first of all, that urbanites tend to be as committed to their neighbourhoods as they are to their other, wider networks. Members of a neighbourhood network are connected by multiple strands, many of which are strong, often embracing family and friends as well as church, parent/teacher, and neighbourhood-preservation groups, among others. Neighbourhood ties tend to be organized into extensive networks of interests and social contacts; the networks are well defined and remain local, rather than encompassing external ties. Finally, there is sufficient coherence and strength to fuel action on a range of matters.

There is merit in both the "lost" and the "saved" positions. The latter reflects a suburban neighbourhood; the former has some correspondence to the neighbourhoods of a central-city area, suggesting as it does the often-noted attitudes of aloofness from others, of noninvolvement, and the felt anonymity of people in densely populated districts, disadvantaged or affluent, who evince no vital interest in the immediate neighbourhood.

The "saved" position seems to fit healthy suburban neighbourhoods and perhaps well-organized old-city neighbourhoods best. Healthy neighbourhood communities, even with small-scale interaction among residents, have the competence to deal with large-scale organizations and government; they are tenacious in preserving their internal resources, maintaining local autonomy, and exercising social control over their members in the face of often powerful external forces.[41] This competence reinforces the practice of taking the neighbourhood as the basic unit of planning and the importance given to preserving existing neighbourhoods as mechanisms for curbing rapacious development and the perils of renewal. The healthy neighbourhood is one apparently logical client of government and of police, not just because of the proverbial middle-class suburban interest in impeccable zoning and physical attractiveness: as Wellman and Leighton suggest,[42] assistance sought through neighborhood communities is often more sensitive to local needs than that preferred by larger bureaucracies.

Many inner-city areas are stable, including those that have undergone redevelopment and the traditional neighbourhoods of working-class people, which are amenable to watchman-style policing. There is still a significant relation between poverty and delinquency in declining inner-city neighbourhoods. Density itself, however, is not inevitably related to delinquency. Persistent disorder often sets in once the inner district is depeopled by the move of the better educated and employed to the suburbs.

It was earlier noted that, according to Wilson and Herrnstein, higher densities increase the opportunity to experience certain kinds of attitudes and behaviour. Youths inclined to crime, for example, are more likely to find and associate with like-minded peers, just as they will find more cars to steal, more banks to rob, and so on.[43] Like Wilson and Herrnstein, Peter McGahan found that the higher the number of living units and the higher the density of people, the higher the rate of mobility or turnover and the higher the rates of victimization.[44] With regard to crowding and its relationship to order, Gertler and Crowley cite a Canadian study in which a sense of crowding in the survey area was not related to actual physical crowding (defined as existing where numbers of residents exceeded the number of rooms in a living unit)[45] but to perceived – but neither reported nor overt – threats to personal safety and security. Deprivation is relative and the sense of it may change over time. It has been suggested that some social disorder and turmoil reflect the dead-end realizations of young people unable to compete in the areas of housing, education, and employment. For them, the pleasures of consumption are illusory. This despair perhaps may draw a disproportionate number of young males into delinquency.

When residents of older neighbourhoods believe that their neighbourhood is in decline, they will seek out others similar to themselves to make a common cause of housing, noise, dirt, and so on. Neighbourhood boundaries come to constrain physical movement and social communication,[46] thereby intensifying social pressures depending on the mix of the neighbourhood. Wilson and Herrnstein point to a significant relation between poverty and delinquency in declining neighbourhoods of the inner city independent of density or crowding. They quoted evidence indicating that in a high-crime slum area where personal safety may not be taken for granted, people are preoccupied with each other but particularly with strangers, in terms of their age, sex, dress, race, or reputation. Threat is assessed accordingly. The relevance of boundaries in permitting one to determine another's strangeness lies in their limiting effect: daily attention to events within them is a matter of vital and habitual interest, a kind of myopic focus.[47] Perhaps what is sensed as strange or threatening is first measured against one's parallel sense of security, part of the underlying fear-of-crime dynamic.

Neighbourhoods with economically deprived people do not all have the same rates or types of delinquency. Subcultural differences, for example, seem to play a role. An analysis of two neighbourhoods, each with a high murder rate, distinguishable in that one represented at least two generations of residents while the other was populated by recent immigrants from the south, revealed that incidents of homicide tended to differ in occasion. In the case of the latter, murder was seen as instrumental in the commission of a crime such as robbery; in the other, the typical murder was "expressive," i.e. committed during a dispute.[48]

The sense of neighbourhood varies with status. In suburbia in particular, middle-class homeowners have an intimate experience of their houses that extends to a persistent and vital interest in the neighbourhood for its quality as real estate. They will defend its integrity because house values correlate with its value as a residential area. An artist, on the other hand, might value his neighbourhood not because of property ownership but because of its aesthetic qualities. Working-class awareness also centres on the house and a small part of the street; the people within this smaller area tend to socialize with a warm feeling of place. They identify with few other places except for some shops and churches within walking distance. People in stable neighbourhoods of the older city typically display the traditional domestic virtues of church attendance, local shopping, and the like – they value the quality of the neighbourhood and its orderliness. A neighbourhood, then, is as much a state of mind, a place where one feels at home, as it is an area. In contrast, the dominant characteristics of a problem neighbourhood denote economic instability: unemployment (especially among young males), poverty and the decay of buildings, civic neglect, and a loss of community strength to tackle its problems.

With city growth, successive suburban neighbourhoods become enveloped by newer suburbs and do not necessarily remain the point of contact between city and nature. Instead they become city only, and the homeowner's escape from the inner city becomes less and less complete. Further, the purely exurban city, of which the prime example is Los Angeles, also suffers from such ills as congestion, pollution, and crime, the very things suburbanites seek to avoid. In the physical design, or perhaps neglect, of suburban sprawl little or nothing was done to promote a sense of neighbourhood in successive developments. These districts seem to become "lost" in their characteristics and one senses their impersonal quality; the usual suburban defences against disorder do not emerge.

Housing preferences among two-income, usually childless families, run to clusters of housing structures with high-quality services in the immediate vicinity, a variety of amenities within safe walking distances, and high-quality retail facilities nearby. Preferred residential locales include apartment buildings, especially condominiums, which become the "neighbourhood" focus of a mutual interest in amenities and in orderliness – something frequently, if privately, achieved. In inner-city areas redevelopment or revitalization of neighbourhoods will occur to suit these two-income families, who would otherwise migrate to suburbia or, increasingly, exurbia.

Before turning to exurbia, however, I should like to consider the fear of crime in light of these reflections on neighbourhoods past and present.

People tend to believe that rates of crime are higher than they actually are. This is arguably part of, or perhaps arises from, a companion perception that the home neighbourhood is in decline or neglected. One's sense of social well-being is tied to the status of one's neighbourhood. Economic deprivation, shifting land use threatening a neighbourhood's residential character, and general deterioration and neglect of buildings signal disorder and may well promote both a sense of helplessness and social isolation through self-restricted activity. Neighbourhood conditions may either drive people apart or provide an early incentive to some positive collective activity. If police are to develop and apply the skills of social engineers (an aspect of their work discussed in the next chapter), this interneighbourhood difference is of obvious consequence, especially if communities can be nurtured to engineer their own social regeneration. Fear of crime *per se*, however, does not generally prompt an effective level or quality of community participation. Crime is clearly disruptive to a neighbourhood and changes its members into individual calculators seeking a selfish advantage, especially chances for survival amidst their fellows. Common undertakings become difficult or impossible, except for those motivated by a shared desire for protection.

Fear of crime is itself a reality, part of the social condition of a neighbourhood, impinging on its quality and on the behaviour of residents. Fear of crime has been studied to determine the security-related characteristics of neighbourhoods, of which disorder and perceived rates of crime are but two. Levels of fear have been equally prominent as measures of the effectiveness of what police do, be it in a general program (such as "preventive patrols") or an experimental one.

Fear of crime in one Canadian city, Regina, has been related to the attributes of the neighbourhood of residence and to the residents' socioeconomic status. An interneighbourhood comparison indicated that the older the neighbourhood and the more mixed its land use – the neighbourhoods in question were clustered in and around the downtown core – higher the crime rate and the higher the fear.[49] (However, a city-by-city comparison found that fear levels in Regina were among the highest in Canada without a corresponding high level of crime.) Those who felt themselves more vulnerable to crime – senior citizens, those living in the inner city rather than the suburbs, and those living, often alone, in apartments and duplexes – tended to call for a traditional emphasis on law enforcement. Other factors that affect levels of fear include socioeconomic status and, in Regina, the perceived characteristics of the various groups making up the local citizenry: Regina has a large native Canadian population living in the central areas, a factor that was not addressed in the study report and did not feature in the discussion of the results, but that may account for an exaggerated, if misplaced, level of apprehension.

At the same time, as Sally Engle Merry has observed, people tend to view their own neighbourhoods as safer at least than some others, regardless of the reality of crime rates. It is the "knowns" of a neighbourhood and a calculated practice of assessing danger and acting accordingly that supports the perception of relative safety, just as the unfamiliarity of other neighbourhoods and their people promotes fear. Fear is corrosive; as Merry noted, the language expressive of crime also expresses the fear of the strange and the unknown as well as social and ethnic hostilities. Danger is a cultural construct: perceptions of danger are embedded in belief systems shared within social groups and influenced by individual and group experiences and values. The process of forming attitudes about which kinds of people, places, and times of day and night are safe or dangerous and what signs are useful in identifying such categories is one facet of the process through which an individual becomes a member of a culture. The individual seems to assimilate and blend past experiences, information from other people, and cultural stereotypes. What constitutes a matter of insult, humiliation, or even serious injury is thereby learned and added to the individual's survival skills in the city.[50]

Thus, what is and what is not dangerous is learned; it is particular to a place and group and may bear no great relation to reality. The perception of danger may depend on stereotypes of people and of locations. In her study of one neighbourhood in a northeastern United States city, Merry found that Chinese Americans and Afro-Americans distrusted each other, each group believing the other was in one way or another dangerous, though both groups were law abiding and stable.

The definition of "fear of crime," then, has many components. The common one is assumed to be fear of victimization, and in an area marked by disorder if not crime, fear may be rooted in a sense of apprehension about unknowns, in the strangeness of and suspicions about other ethnocultural groups. That fear of crime is corrosive and ethnocultural relations particularly vulnerable to it is a plausible conclusion.

How do government agencies, including the police, collaborate in responding to fear of crime and its effects on neighbourhoods? Peter Manning [51] noted that there was no evidence that the energy and resources devoted to catching criminals increase the public's sense personal safety. The extra attention given crime through enhanced law-enforcement activity and the consequent media attention to arrests may corrode the public's sense of security and lead to dwindling community cohesiveness, thence to even tougher police action. His experience with neighbourhood foot-patrol experiments led Robert Trojanowicz to comment that the law-enforcement orientation of conventional thinking and the programs that flow from it relieve the public of responsibility for their own security; they perceive that they play a role but one that is largely subordinate or passive.[52] Intergroup tension in a high-crime-rate district promotes isolation and even antagonism, thus decreasing the potential for community action. However, one of the racially mixed neighbourhoods in Metropolitan Toronto is becoming more organized, despite intergroup tensions, in an effort to help police deter drug use.[53]

So whether or not fear and crime rates impel cohesiveness in the community is a difficult but crucial question. It seems that the preconditions for bringing people of unstable inner-city areas together include the sheer gravity and immediacy of the threat. Lesser threats will galvanize people of suburban and stable neighbourhoods perhaps because of their long-term commitment to the area, their experience in local activities, and their skill in prompting the agencies of the wider community to be attentive to their anxieties. People of lower income levels are less likely to anticipate or react to lesser threats to protect their interests, and those at the poverty level will react only to immediate, severe threats to neighbourhood well-being and security.

Social weakness is a feature, not of the physical layout and location of a neighbourhood, but of the characteristics and attitudes of the people in it. Poor central-city districts are not always unstable and socially unhealthy. The improvement of physical arrangements, for example through defensible space concepts (increased lighting, designs promoting a sense of proprietorship especially among tenants, heightened visibility, repairs and property improvements, among others), seem to have no lasting downward effect on crime rates, which tend to revive once an increased police presence is removed.[54] Two adjoining neighbourhoods in Cardiff, Wales, one with a much higher delinquency rate, differed only in parental attitudes towards delinquency, which was viewed for more seriously in one than in the other.

EXURBIA — THE SPREADING URBAN LANDSCAPE

New communication facilities and transportation systems are freeing people from territorial limitations on their personal and working lives, making them members of a "liberated" community whose interests and personal relationships span an unrestricted urban area. Narrowly based family and work networks may exist, but even when they are close or contiguous there is no one "community" in the familiar sense.[55] The importance of the neighbourhood community is minimized in this "liberated" perspective, in contrast to that of the "saved" community. In the "liberated" community, personal connections may form around some interest or issue that embraces all or much of the urban area. Given the wider implications of their concern, urbanites tend to seek the interest of politicians and government agencies. Helping networks, not necessarily tied to the neighbourhood, may become part of the formulation and implementation of public policy. Examples include groups seeking support for a symphony orchestra or for food banks, efforts to improve police/race relations, establish havens for homeless adolescents, influence land-use decisions, combat violence against women, etc. There is a tendency to seek civic attention. Significant concerns in a municipality tend to be "owned" by particular interest groups; the severity and prominence of a given concern will vary with time. So the context is dynamic and groups, each organized around their particular concerns, have to compete for attention. There are indications that they also cooperate in an elaboration of networks, including those concerned with disorder and crime. At this level of networking, the arena of action extends well beyond any neighbourhood. The need to recognize a growing category of clients, interest groups not tied to specific localities, and to respond to their variable concerns calls for much civic, including police, adaptability.

Wellman and Leighton suggest that none of the three positions – "lost," "saved," or "liberated" – is exclusively valid; as a description, one or another tends to be more accurate depending on the "social circumstances" of the territory to which it is applied. They also note that in "saved" neighbourhoods densely knit ties and tight boundaries tend to occur together, thus promoting development of ties when a common purpose arises. (There is also the element of time; a threatened neighbourhood is not in a static condition and may well become more integrated under pressure.) "Saved" neighbourhoods, moreover, are well structured for maintaining informal social control over members and intruders. The saved pattern tends to prevail in communities whose members do not have many personal resources and where conditions do not favour the formation of external ties.[56] This is common in ethnic and working-class neighbourhoods.

On the other hand, "liberated" communities are suited to conditions of affluence. Their loose networks are neither conducive to social control of members nor seen to be needed for that purpose. Home-based security is assured through affluence. Members tend to branch out and link up with external networks, "ramified liberated networks" that are for them more effective in obtaining the desired resources, which often means political influence, as noted above. Wellman and Leighton say that individuals may be members of both "liberated" and "saved" networks. Some ties, for example, of family, tend to be close. Other networks are loosely knit and diffuse but are nonetheless useful in the search for resources.

Exurbia, a now-familiar urban pattern in Canada, is a transitional stage in the advance of cities beyond the suburbs during which new urban arrangements emerge that are better suited to evolving patterns of living and working and to advanced commercial and industrial systems, and perhaps more sensitive to the environment. As London was the site of the first suburb two hundred years ago, Los Angeles, well over fifty years ago, became the first exurban city. It still has no central core, no downtown, and none of the converging roads that make a core possible.[57] This exurban residential arrangement is still novel but may be seen in other cities such as Phoenix, Arizona.

Exurbia is an urban area dispersed across rectangular grids of high-capacity roads, rather than a city centre to which thoughts and roads lead. Its constituents are neighbourhoods scattered around small cities and towns over the longer distances of a growing urban basin.

The exurban arrangement envisions not dense, mixed-use neighbourhoods but a composition of small town-like arrangements in an intermingling of districts of different uses and categories of people. There seems to be a judicious use of distance; neighbourhoods, exclusively residential, that adjoin districts devoted to other uses are common. One study, now some years old, suggested that the area of common travel, for shopping, work, school, and recreation, spreads around a small centre for about ten to twenty-five kilometres, at which point the sphere of attraction of the adjoining community is invisibly marked.[58]

The urban spread of Canadian cities is not extensively exurban, for the suburban ideal is still more than a nostalgic echo. Exurban and suburban forms, it seems, share the sense of well-being that is still found in settings that are close to nature. Flight from the urban centre means precisely the economic and social power to migrate from the bustling frontier of urban life to the security of a home in a naturally quiet area; in the US especially the "fight" against lawlessness and disorder takes place for the most part in the no man's land of depopulated city centres.

The new metropolis, growing beyond the edges of suburbia, is highly dispersed though often suburb-like in its many familiar tracts of single-family houses, though apartment and townhouse developments are also common. These new-form urban areas have been given various labels – the earlier and awkward "multinucleated" or "metropolitainism", then dispersed cities, garden cities, exurbia, slurbs, and, in Fishman's terms,[59] technocities and technoburbs. Suburbs, in their time, drew larger retail centres and many services to the intersections of major roads, but overall, they depended on a central urban core as the primary focus for commerce, retail stores, work, hospitals, cultural activities, and so on. The suburbs truly radiated from the cores and commuting was predominant. Now, satellite cities (exurbia) are being established on the farther fringes, providing places of work in close proximity to residential areas.[60] We see spreading areas of commercial and industrial "parks", medical and dental complexes as well as commercial and retail centres; major public institutions, including hospitals and advanced education centres, complete the picture.

Political jurisdiction is likely to be fragmented throughout the exurban and suburban spread across small rural or semirural municipal communities. A public good, such as education or roads, can only be provided by an authority that has the power to coerce payment through taxation. Thus, in the absence of competition in government services, the issue becomes the efficiency with which those services are provided.[61] The pull of efficiency is towards a larger, presumably more effective, central political arrangement; the seeming logic of economies of scale often prevail. While the United States experience remains one of municipal fragmentation (recall here the ninety-plus authorities in the typical urban area), the amalgamation of municipalities in Canada (or at least of many of their functions) along with close provincial supervision of many functions (including policing) has been a reality.

Political jurisdiction affects on the nature of neighbourhoods, the governmental level at which the police are organized, and the nature of their service, matters dealt with in later chapters. Higgins suggested that the one main functional jurisdiction at the municipal level was the regulation of land use and, indeed, the increase of its value.[62] Across cities, the practice of zoning by neighbourhood provides what Manuel Castells calls separate but unequal enclaves behind a barbed-wire wall of municipal regulation.[63] Similarly, jurisdictional fragmentation, according to Kevin Cox and Frank Nartowicz,[64] leads to closed jurisdictions with élitist characteristics, common in the United States, rather than to pluralist, democratic systems. It is through such political/jurisdictional currents that outlying exurban jurisdictions find their strengths and weaknesses: political influence and protective zoning without the burden of central administrative bureaucracies but with higher service costs, an absence of technical experience, and a vulnerability, due to small tax bases and inexperience, to somewhat unrestrained development. Among the service costs may be a small-sized police department, one likely to be oriented to the exclusiveness of its neighbourhoods.

Exurban and suburban neighbourhoods may share some aspects of physical layout. However, what is new to exurbia is the popularity of multiple-living-unit buildings. It is now common to see spreading townhouse developments and tall apartment buildings in densely peopled neighbourhoods incongruously nestled in rural settings with office buildings standing nearby in pastoral serenity. People who live in a widely spread area of activity "make up" their own city from among many options by working here, shopping there, and seeking entertainment somewhere else, usually over some distance on rectangular rather than radiating grids of high-capacity roads. The centre of the larger city is rarely visited. The metropolis is moving to the countryside where individuals and families can participate in the urban information flow, in economic, even cultural and social, aspects of metropolitan life without having to live in the city as we know it. Fishmanhas commented that mass-audience television programs, the uniformity of standard consumer products, and standardized services suit decentralized exurbia, with its not-so-ready access to more varied services and entertainments, and add to the ease with which a variety of such economic activities elude the higher costs of public service and congestion found in the metropolis.[65] One suspects that this homogeneous if bland mix provides a sense of sharing in a wider culture.

Exurbia is gaining in industrial and commercial attractiveness, particularly since the requirements of information-based activity can be met through high technology without recourse to close interpersonal working contacts; banking machines are one of many examples. This is not to suggest that city cores will atrophy; the matter is one of the direction and diversification, well underway, of future growth. Some regeneration of city centres may well drive poorer people into high-density areas in or near the suburbs, the highrise apartment "slums" of many cities. This newer exurban city is one of greater space, of contrasting but contiguous neighbourhoods, some of high density, creeping across more and more jurisdictional boundaries, becoming new cities without a recognizable civic centre, focus, or political direction.

Society has outgrown the attitudes and beliefs that constituted suburban morality. Women have returned to the workplace, and the belief in the moral value of a house-bound mother has evaporated. Statistics show that now, for the first time, over half of Canadian women with small children are working. The older values of a stable family have shifted, as sexual equality, divorce rates, and the debate about abortion indicate. The newer values favour individualism; moral positions once seen as crucially important to the stability of social life are now accepted as relative and even unremarkable preferences. Influential, broadly based, and strongly held morals, principles, and constraints are eroded.

At present, the costs of police services to smaller jurisdictions, the greater distance over which fewer police must operate, and the ongoing police propensity to organize on a centralized basis suggest that in exurbia expectations of the police will not develop as they did in suburbia. One exurbanite indicated to me that in his residential area, a reasonably affluent one, the police, on receiving a call would take upwards of twenty minutes, to respond, "if they came at all." Here, residents rely on local arrangements: a homogeneous neighbourhood, the heightened visibility of a stranger, no through traffic, physical security, and the greater distances across which predatory efforts have to be made.

The Toronto area is one example of the reality of exurbia: by the year 2011, Metropolitan Toronto will have grown from 2.2 million people (of whom thirty-six percent live in apartments) to 2.5 million, while the three adjacent regional municipalities will nearly double in population to 2.4 million.[66] But the range of physical spread is much greater. Adding one further regional municipality will bring the projected total to 5.3 million and still not exhaust the areas constituting the metropolitan area.[67]

In *The Coming of Post-Industrial Society*, Daniel Bell [68] spoke of widening horizons, that is, greater distances, often spanning continents, across which a person's interests and work may extend, in the wake of modern transportation and communications advances. With the breakdown of place-bound cultures, these new horizons would be accessible to all. Similarly, a break with the past renews or reshapes continuity and tradition; it fosters variety, though a contemporary inclination is the smoothing over of differences in values and ideals. Glimpses of the postexurban city suggest that few will live and work in relative social isolation; it may become commonplace for one person to communicate with hundreds, possibly thousands, of others – unthinkable, a few generations ago.

Inklings of a vaguely sci-fi urban world of highrise and high-tech living may not prove accurate. We can only speculate. Technological developments are unpredictable, as are community attitudes. A city is a social system shaped, at least in part, by social ideals and intervention; the suburban, "character-building" form exclusive to the English speaking world is a convincing case in point.[69] In some United States metropolitan areas, a "slow-growth" approach – involving tight control of development is being tested. Mixed or managed landscape proposals for metropolitan development – fostered by partnerships of governments, universities, environmental groups, and so on – are emerging. Regional planning, which is not so much an urban form as another approach altogether, has been common in Canada since regional planning was first undertaken in Alberta in the 1950s. More recently, the Toronto Centered Region Concept has endorsed the idea that extensive stretches of landscape be subject to some plan. Any plan, it seems, is better than a haphazard, piecemeal encroachment on the countryside.

Scattered neighbourhoods continue the ideal of living close to nature for the benefits it seems to yield. The terms "managed landscape," "natural landscape," and "working landscape" are the offspring of a current movement that shows signs of gathering force not only through environmentally sensitive politics but through notions of what a modern, healthy community may be.[70] Its components include landscapes, or areas left to nature, as well as working landscapes, those of farms or other productive endeavours; planned but nonintrusive transportation corridors; and urban-type neighbourhoods (residential, commercial, etc.) whose locations and sizes are planned so as to control sprawl and development. What comes to mind is akin to a pastoral English countryside punctuated by high-density neighbourhoods or towns, with smaller cities dispersed among farms and natural settings. This bucolic vision has become a reality near some of the large urban centres of the northeastern United States. The concept requires an extended, regional approach since a coordinated landscape of mixed uses must reach dimensions as large as thirty-five to seventy-five kilometres, perhaps more; such an approach, it seems to me, outpaces provincial-municipal jurisdictional arrangements. A working landscape is, then, a valid category and is well exemplified in numerous places in Europe.

Green, treed spaces that are visible in the residential landscape are considered more important than ever. Roger Hart, director of the Children's Environments Research Group at City University, New York, proposes that nature is an essential educational tool; a rational adult has a sense of responsibility for the environment, having learned to care for it, having grown up to feel a part of it. Hiss suggested that a close, visible relationship between the natural, the city, and the intermediate working landscape (arrangements of the open spaces of working farms, residences, and commercial/industrial parks) provides for vital connections within one's environment. Hart has a simple message: that there is a demonstrable link between private property values and public health – and equally strong links between these two factors and the ease of physical mobility within a region, the region's economic security, and the resilience and well-being of its natural environment.[71]

A predilection for the natural, long an element of suburban neighbourhoods and, indeed, their major bequest, has not only persisted but is finding support in modern research. So an idealism, but one unlike that of suburbia, remains. The new orientation is wider; in moving away from an exclusive focus on the family and, perhaps, being less tied to residence, it may involve less segregation and so provide a basis for broader, if looser, cohesiveness. As someone said, new towns are a moral and social crusade to improve the urban condition. The origins of such thinking lie in a perceived need for social reform. Its objectives are to restructure urban life to achieve harmony between nature, technology, and economic and social classes. The proponents of the managed landscape are addressing not only environment-related issues but also the matter of whether newer forms of communities can alleviate or avoid social problems, as the suburb attempted to do with some success. The managed landscape, with its echoes of suburban ancestry, is utopian.

The vantage point from which to view new-form neighbourhoods is their ability to influence the use of land. Councils, committees of adjustment, planning, and zoning, reviews, permits, and so on are all part of elaborate, usually compliant practices protecting local interests; the politics of the smaller exurban communities may be even more amenable to citizen pressure.

Meanwhile, the crime-prone age group is in a decline. The size of households has also declined in tandem with a drop in birth rates and the emptying nests of an aging population. In the United States, the average family size was 3.67 people in 1940, 3.33 in 1960, and 2.89 in 1976. Alonso emphasized that changes in family characteristics are part of a long-term, enduring, and significant social trend, not merely the trend of two or three decades. He suggested that it is unlikely that "the same mix of [conventional] housing units can accommodate this bubbling social soup that held the calmer broth of some years ago, although no one to my knowledge is in a position to make predictions."[72] In Canada, half of the families of the inner city were childless (one-third in outer areas) and twenty-two percent headed by a single parent.

To reiterate, it is important that the study of the police mission and the attributes needed to carry it out must focus on the cities in which police work is so profoundly embedded. Urbanization, its pace and form, has already greatly influenced policing along now-familiar lines. In recent decades, the emphasis on the intensity of disorder in troubled neighbourhoods provided the impetus to search for the more effective programs, such as community policing. The community-policing approach was first defined by its utility in the older central city, and, while less appropriate to the typical suburb of the past, the client is still the troubled neighbourhood or community of whatever type. The first police department was established for the "old" city at a time when the suburban form, peculiarly English, was finding favour because it embodied the idealism of the day in which the effectiveness of social control, formal and informal, was grounded. The police role was subsidiary but supportive. It seems, then, that the issue of disorder is a matter for wide civic attention and includes the design of neighbourhoods that can shelter some of the idealism that shapes attitudes and behaviour. The neighbourhood ethic is characteristic of order. But a hazy lesson emerges from this line of discussion: the first glimmerings of disorder, the first sign of infection, must be attended to or a slide into further disorder is inevitable. The "sickness" of a neighbourhood in this case is a matter for the resources of the city, of which the police are but a part.

Urbanization is a process, a shifting mix of attributes, ethnocultural, social, economic, and moral, and evolving neighbourhood characteristics. Modern technology and urbanization have teamed to shape the newer form of the sought-after neighbourhood, which surely calls for redesigned police programs as the suburban form once did. This dynamic milieu places pressure on the *status quo* not only in police organization and programs but in the occupation itself. Further, as urban society organizes itself along networks of wider interests, the delivery of police services on a traditional geographical basis, for example, promises to be insufficient. Communities of interest, tied not to some territory but to an issue of wide concern, are common and many seek police involvement. It must be remembered, as George Kelling observes, that "this is a radical departure from the past in American policing. It says that politics, neighbourhood politics, is not corrupting and that police have to link themselves to the moral will of the community, to gain the moral authority to act. Without the moral authority to act, without citizens saying we can't let things get out of control again in the relationship between the police and citizens, they can't act to maintain control. Because when push comes to shove, citizens will not support the police unless the police are getting their moral authority to act from the community."[73]

CHAPTER FOUR

Maintaining Order – The Neighbourhood Policing Function

If crime is perceived as a violation of any law, the police are faced with an almost impossible enforcement task. But if crime is perceived as law breaking activities that negatively impact a community's quality of life, then the ability of police to control crime becomes more manageable, and in the minds of many, more relevant to what the role of police should be. [1]

INNOVATIONS IN THE EXPERIMENTAL RESTORATIONS OF ORDER

As noted in the last chapter, the deterrent patrol on call, which dominated policing strategies of the postwar decades, was well adapted to the suburbs but ill suited to other communities, including the older, troubled neighbourhoods where frequent police failures are found. Necessity mothered some innovative thinking that is generally grouped under the label of community policing, now a popular catch phrase in policing and politics.

If the richness of ideas about community policing are retained and not shrunk to fit present organizational capacities, approaches suited to the tough urban social conditions under which police labour might emerge. What follows is a discussion of community-related policing in its urban contexts. Questions will arise about the neighbourhood as a participant and client of policing; police as community leaders and agents of social change; the political and contentious nature of community policing; and the underpinnings of authority in community policing. But first it is necessary to go back to James Q. Wilson's three styles of policing, one or another of which tends to predominate, depending on a city's culture, racial mix, political structure, and police-department policies and organization. [2]

The watchman style, it will be recalled, reflects a concern for order maintenance. It is a tolerant style that allows police-administration officers to ignore many minor infractions, especially traffic and juvenile but vice and gambling as well. Law-enforcement activity is a means of maintaining order rather than of "regulating" the conduct of some group on whose character "order" might depend. Juveniles, for example, are "expected" to misbehave and blacks are assumed by police to be more tolerant of disorder and petty crime in some home neighbourhoods. Some behaviours are seen as criminal only because the law says they are; of these, what violates community standards becomes a problem of order. Private disputes are treated informally or ignored. Much disorder is privatized; for example, the police may take youngsters home to their parents. But officers judge the seriousness of a matter not by the law but by consequences that differ according to the nature of the group and the person, as well as circumstance. Thus, the well-to-do tend to be seen as self-correcting, likewise adolescents and families, while unruly visitors to a convention, among others, can be handled without recourse to arrest.

The better officers in the watchman style are those who "manage their beats," "keep their noses clean," and do not "rock the boat." Departments are highly sensitive to complaints so officers tend to withdraw from adversarial incidents and doubtful matters are referred upwards. Even when a serious charge is laid, the charge is not as important as the court's support for the relevant police action and the absence of complications. There is an emphasis on appearances and manner, on correctness (in avoiding trouble), but not on assertiveness or verbal aggressiveness. Thus, the department favours keeping traffic tickets and misdemeanour arrests to a minimum, informal handling of juveniles, and tolerance of discrete immorality. There is little specialization within the organization (if there are few rewards outside the patrol division, there is little incentive to work hard to be assigned elsewhere) and no great emphasis on training ("You can't apply book learning on the street"). So watchman-style departments display, more so than others, the characteristics of a craft: apprenticeship, word-of-mouth indoctrination, and minimal deference to authority. There are remarkably few "watchmen" in staff positions. Their paperwork and attention to procedures – beloved in bureaucracies – are not scrupulous. When the emphasis is on order maintenance, on the self-correcting qualities of the community, and on tolerance, the strength of the community and the family norms it harbours are relied upon: should these prove weak in a given situation, an arrest will follow an incident. Cities with the watchman style tend to consist of stable neighbourhoods of working-class people, now more or less long established and often of European immigrant origin.

Legalistic-style departments are oriented to law enforcement. Traffic tickets are issued at a high rate, juveniles are treated formally and illicit enterprises countered vigorously, and many misdemeanours result in arrests. Laws are not regarded as equally important; the inclination to apply them is uneven and private disorders are viewed as just that – disorders. Police officers, in general, tend to underenforce the law, but in areas targeted by a legalistic department they attempt rigourous enforcement, albeit without full success. There is pressure in such departements to issue traffic tickets; with the likely creation of a traffic unit, the rate will go up and stay up in any event. Treating juveniles formally calls on other specialized services beyond a simple arrest. Arrests are frequent, the attitude being that this is the proper mechanism to use if one believes that a probation officer may do some good and that retail-store security people, for example, should seek arrests rather than the recovery of property.

The legalistic style, with its law-enforcement orientation, may be characterized as follows: either there is trouble and action is required, or there is no trouble, no infraction, and no required action, formal or informal. Police do not make the laws – that is a political process – but merely enforce them. Thus, legalistic police departments are distanced, publicly and in their own minds, from responsibility for the nature of laws themselves.

In contrast to the watchman style, where justice depends on the attributes of the person and similar persons are treated similarly, justice depends under the legalistic style on attributes of the act, and the purpose of the law is to punish. Thus, for example, arrest rates for blacks and whites will be equal in a legalistic department; in a watchman-style department, blacks will be arrested at disproportionately higher rates, since they are viewed as less restrained by community or family norms.

Finally, in a legalistic department, aggressive patrol practices are common – stopping to issue tickets leads to recovering stolen vehicles and property and so on – and the practice is reinforced by its occasional success. In a watchman department, the concern is immediate and direct (will a drunk be hurt?), but in a legalistic department, the goals are more distant (youthful vandalism will lead to a life of crime). Furthermore, it values technical efficiency, that is, more output for a fixed cost. Regardless of how valuable the output is, the motto seems to be: get the people to work harder. Zeal and courtesy will be emphasized, and it depends on who you are as a citizen whether the zeal or the courtesy is felt.

In the service-style department, enforcement and order maintenance calls are taken seriously, but, in contrast to a legalistic department, resort to formal responses in imposing sanctions is unlikely. There is agreement in the community on the definition of and need for order. The resulting public consensus and support ensure that illegal or immoral enterprises are easy to suppress, so other issues, such as the management of traffic, regulation of juveniles, and provision of services, become dominant. Few arrests or formal sanctions will be imposed for minor incidents and ticketing will be much less frequent than in legalistic departments. Suburbanites want to be left alone with their minor, nonintrusive indiscretions; they want undesirables to be kept away, juveniles attended to with a light hand, and peace maintained. Specialized units tend to be used. The service style is common in middle-class communities in which the police job is to protect orderliness against outsiders. Residents expect and demand service – that is, prompt responses and frequent, high-visibility patrols. Officers are expected to maintain self-control (in contrast to the watchman style, in which the officer maintains self-respect first and self-control, if any, second).

In discussing the "arrest" solution to disorder (for example, breaches of the peace), Wilson suggested that "a police department is more likely to take seriously, by making arrests, problems of order maintenance when it is directly exposed to community concerns for public order than when, by its size or detachment, it is insulated from them."[3] While watchman-style departments make fewer arrests than legalistic ones, they do make more arrests for police-initiated order-maintenance activities such as quelling a disturbance or breaking up a fight. Furthermore, suburban people take order in their neighbourhood seriously so that disorder receives attention, but while "village" or local police are apt to distinguish strangers in the neighbourhood from those who belong, the larger service department does not and may therefore make fewer arrests of the residents, hence fewer overall arrests. Generally, the "tolerable level of disorder" is quite low in smaller suburban communities and their smaller service departments have fewer options; thus, in contrast to the larger service department, arrest rates are high.

Wilson maintained that proponents of a service style of policing, one suited to suburban communities, advocate a redistribution of authority whereby officers are directed, or at least influenced, by the people whose order they must regulate. Where contention arises or directives fail, the resolution lies in a reduction in the scope of police discretion and authority and an increase in the influence of the neighbourhood groups most likely to experience injustice, fear, etc. He spoke, for example, of "suburbanizing" the central city – that is, permitting each neighbourhood to define its own style of enforcement, though the matter of devolving police authority is, of course, problematic. The politics are local and the arrangement achieves what the usual administrative/bureaucratic methods may not. For example, so-called professional police officers hold the institutional view that the law must be vigorously enforced lest the law itself be questioned. The argument includes the notion that community and family norms are the foundation of order and any weakness increasingly calls enforcement into play. The redistribution or devolution of authority also opens the district police offices to the influence of local politicians, and high crime and disorder provide so great an opportunity for corruption that only the strictest, most centrally directed department can survive untainted. In contrast, "the localistic police forces of small towns and homogeneous suburbs work satisfactorily largely because they need not handle profound social conflicts; little is expected of them except to perform in middle-class areas a service function or in working-class areas a watchman function." [4]

Wilson advanced a "communal" model based on the premise that the maintenance of order requires different skills and resources than law enforcement does and so requires a different organizational form. Neighbourhood tolerance for disorder varies. Often, Wilson said, what seem to be weak norms are simply different norms. The subculture of one neighbourhood is no threat to another. "In this regard, community norms need not be changed so much as understood, and they are best understood by police officers who are not isolated from them. This requires hiring officers who are Negro, or Puerto Ricans, or whatever, even if they do not measure up fully to the standards of professional police departments," and assigning them accordingly. The issue becomes not one of corruption but of humanizing the officer cadre. [5]

The question who the clients of policing services are is pertinent to the issue of order maintenance. In thinking about policing in isolation from its milieu, one has no sense of who the clients may be. A community tends to be taken as a given, it becomes faceless, even though the "community" in community policing presumably means something specific and not merely the people as a whole; there is, as it were, no address to deliver services to. Without a known or even satisfied consumer, the maintenance of order loses emphasis to conventional practices. I will return to this topic.

The literature of urban policing tends not to acknowledge that among manifestations of civic government (street maintenance, garbage and litter controls, land-use regulations, by-law compliance, tenant services, and welfare support, among many others), police are in the foreground even though they alone cannot control or attend to the web of factors leading to decline or disorder in a neighbourhood. The participation of other municipal agencies – the array of available, largely citizen-centred resources – can be significant; so, too, the misdirection of a police program from its relevant civic/neighbourhood destination can be avoided. It is a matter of focus. Robert Trojanowicz and Hazel A. Harden noted that "foot patrol is only one method of dealing with community social problems. The community must have a commitment to solving problems like inadequate housing and education, unemployment, and racial tension. Foot patrol officers can only affect social policy in a limited way." [6] Foot patrols, they found, do not resolve deep-seated social or racial problems but tend to be seen as public-relations efforts that gloss over other the failures of other municipal agencies to address them.

Patrol officers are dispatched to or come upon incidents in which the behaviour of the participants is as variable as human nature itself. Consider as an example a late-night call about a fight on some corner in a neighbourhood known for its rowdiness: an inner-city neighbourhood made up of a changeable mix of residential, commercial, and entertainment uses such as all-night fast-food shops, a tavern or two, rooming houses, older apartment buildings with units further subdivided, and houses, many physically neglected. A small crowd watches a brawl between two people outside of a tavern. The immediate goal of the two officers on arrival is, of course, to gain control of the incident and separate the brawlers, before coming to any conclusions about the outcome.

At this point their discretion is considerable. Should one of the brawlers be seriously injured and the victim of an unprovoked attack, then the outcome will be one of law enforcement, the crime being serious and the evidence at hand. The officers then follow what are to them familiar procedures regarding arrest, charging, evidence, and so on. If the brawl was brief and without injury, and the participants, while inebriated, are disposed to go their separate ways with no more than garrulous dispute, then in the officers' discretion the matter will be one of maintaining, of restoring, order. The two will receive some form of admonishment. Between these two possibilities lie innumerable variations, each calling upon the discretion of the officer. The rapid-response patrol program blends the two functions into one approach, with priority given to enforcement. Simply put, the maintenance of order becomes a nonprogrammed "leftover" activity based largely on discretion but with the transient goal of restoring order in any given situation. Within the neighbourhoods of a city, then, restoring order is an uncoordinated program, while community policing is about planning and coordinating those numerous, disparate, order-maintaining activities in a systematic, problem-centred, and goal-oriented way.

Most studies of community policing come from the United States and are sometimes of little relevance to the Canadian urban scene and its seemingly nonpolitical system of police management. In Canada, municipal governments continue to be highly limited in their authority; in supervising policing, for example, they are closely overseen by provincial governments with their multiple tentacles of authority.[7] Canadian urban police differ in this and other, sometimes subtle, ways from their United States counterparts. The salient difference is the absence in Canadian urban-police history of local political control, its corrupting influence, and the weight of a reform-movement reaction to it. Canadian police, I submit, are less bound by reform products, such as the defensive war-on-crime reaction, and the exaggerated notion of a police department under an aloof, politically untouchable police general.

Police officers are acutely aware of the limitations of law enforcement when a pattern of crime is somehow intertwined with particular neighbourhood social circumstances. The resulting demand on resources has tenuous results. A short city block from where I write is a large social-housing development of mostly low-rise apartment buildings. There are no through streets but there are wide walkways and open areas with playgrounds, a wading pool, and so on. The pool area is ideal for the drug trade: approaches can be monitored, nearby apartments, stairwells, and hallways can be used as bases, and the area is well known to "shoppers." As a result, the pool area is often busy through much of the day and night; residents avoid it and the pool is unused by children. The development, even with a private security service, is well known to police, who patrol with increasing frequency. Still, the local trade flourishes. The area is cleaned up from time to time, but only temporarily, in spite of the concentrated action of the police – a senior police officer said, however, that there was little more they could do to clean up the pool area – and of security patrols and tenants who had formed a Tenant Action Group to "win back the neighbourhood building by building." The mayor, according to one news report, in a belated spasm of concern, urged the residents to band together to rid their neighbourhood of the "malignant blight" of drug trafficking.

Similarly, "a sprawling, tawdry apartment complex," Mayfair Mansions in Washington, DC, was a notorious open-air drug market, usually bustling day and night with crowds of gun-toting dealers." In April 1988, according to a column in the *Toronto Star*,[8] the residents, dismayed by police ineffectiveness (though in just under a year, the police had in fact made more than 1,300 arrests and executed fifty search warrants), took matters into their own hands through a program that involved round-the-clock Black Muslims patrols that video-taped and otherwise intimidated suspicious-looking people. Some violence occurred, drawing unsurprising charges of vigilantism and allegations of beatings largely from people unfamiliar with the plight of the development but including the police chief.

Both cases were marked by the absence of a persistent police/community program and effective law-enforcement "solutions." The teeth of the law abiding are missing, it seems, and the teeth of the unlawful have yet to be pulled.

One study in Canada found that when calls for service came from the part of a neighbourhood where the offenders themselves lived, there were larger numbers of multiple-unit residential buildings and nonresidential (retail, commercial, warehousing, light industry) buildings and, among residents, low educational achievement, single-parent families, and a longer length of residence (since the better off had moved from this leftover area to suburban neighbourhoods). Such areas had higher crime rates, though significant numbers of offenders tended to commit crimes, mostly "break and enter," in areas other than their own.[9]

In the Neighborhood Foot Patrol Study in Flint, Michigan, the benefits achieved by the program varied with the neighbourhood. Overall, however, the disparity between black and white attitudes towards police was reduced to negligible levels.[10] Trojanowicz said that the process involved foot patrol officers learning about and becoming responsive to the culture of the neighbourhood. They were able to distinguish between people on their beat and between normative behavioural patterns and threatening or dangerous acts. As a result, for example, unlike motor officers, they were less likely to conduct the usually demeaning "pat-downs."

The Houston and Newark fear-reduction experiments were conducted in areas whose rates of disorder, fear, and crime were high enough to single them out for attention. In Newark, the selected area contained 4,500 residents in 1,500 living units, and in Houston, 5,000 in 2,300 units spread over roughly one square mile. Most but not all residents were black, of low- to middle-income levels.

Houston, a newer city, is less densely populated while Newark is older, with more disadvantaged residents. Among the programmed activities in both cities were a monthly newsletter; the establishment of a ministation at which crimes could be reported, information obtained, and meetings held; efforts to create a neighbourhood organization; and a program to reduce "signs of crime," that is, to attend to the outward evidence of decline or disorder along the lines of Wilson and Kelling's "broken window" thesis, which holds that the early, minor signs of neglect or disorder – the incivilities that disturb people in a neighbourhood – need to be corrected lest they encourage a deterioration into further disorder and, perhaps, crime."[11] Patrols were directed to maintain order on sidewalks and corners, conduct radar checks, ride and check buses, enforce state disorderly-conduct laws, and conduct extended foot patrols. Overall, efforts to organize and communicate were of greatest benefit to white, middle-class homeowners and of least benefit to black renters. Generally, once respondents became aware of the ministation, saw officers in the neighbourhood, or were contacted by police officers, fear was reduced and their satisfaction with the neighbourhood rose. Newsletters had no beneficial effect apparently because it was difficult to establish communications with renters, and black residents tended to be renters though no other characteristics were given. The failure of the "signs of crime" activity was attributed to a low level of effort, a dearth of physical improvements, and random implementation made without extensive citizen contact.[12]

Two Toronto neighbourhoods, each characterized by the Metropolitan Toronto Police as having persistent policing problems that required "distinctive service strategies," were surveyed to determine residents' attitudes towards police, crime, and disorder. [13] One neighbourhood, in the Jane-Finch area, was fairly recently developed and is characterized by high-density (double the city average), publicly supported housing, a number of racial groups, a high proportion of living units in row housing and highrise apartment buildings, and more young people than average. The other neighbourhood, Parkdale, is largely inner city, also racially mixed, with more mixed-use buildings, a slightly older population, and more boarding houses. There were intergroup tensions and, in both areas a higher-than-average crime rate. Both had the same proportion of employed as Toronto overall and a much higher proportion of renters than owners.

An analysis of the survey data indicated that there were clear differences between the problems of the two neighbourhoods and between the neighbourhoods and Toronto itself. Residents of both areas identified more problems as "big" than people in the rest of Toronto; these included the presence of the drug trade and drug users, groups loitering in the street, inadequate building maintenance, and noise. Problems in the Jane-Finch area tended to be perceived as youth centred: the absence of recreational programs, truancy, and poor police-youth contacts. Those particular to Parkdale included vagrancy, begging and panhandling, prostitution, and drinking in public. This was a useful study, suggesting as it did that socioeconomic characteristics are related to distinctive problems; that there are sets of varied, complex, but distinctive syndromes pointing to differing social ills, and, with further knowledge, variable sets of ameliorating responses.

The riots in England of the early 1980s attracted considerable attention to certain inner-city neighbourhoods with their unemployment problems, the dead-end lives of their residents, drug-trade issues, high crime rates, fear of crime, and aggressive police tactics.[14] The riots were associated with racial minorities, although in one district where a "race" riot occurred, only six percent of the residents were members of a visible minority. The socioeconomic histories of these neighbourhoods went largely unreported. The police were intent on law enforcement and some aggressive police practices tended to alienate residents; in one case, a stop-and-question tactic itself set off a riot.[15] Yet London is also a city with extensive high-density residential tracts, most of them stable and ordinary.

A Canadian study reached the tentative conclusion that integration into the community (ownership, length of residency, membership in local organizations, and numbers of local acquaintances) was inversely related to the perceived level of crime.[16] In a United States project, high-crime-rate neighbourhoods were examined according to income level and types and rates of crime, and no area was designated for treatment "until analysis reveals that it contains 'good people' who routinely maintain their rent or mortgage payments, maintain their property, respect neighbors' right to peace, privacy and quiet and are willing to assist police and housing officials."[17] Thus, there was a base (of reliable people) with which to work. This neighbourhood-rehabilitation project, a most successful one reporting a significant reduction in crime, was a joint effort initiated by housing and other civic officials but soon came to include police.[18]

These comments illustrate the point that many communuity variables are significant in diagnosing the nature of disorder, hence the nature of civic response, policing included. The point is central to community policing.

THE OLDER CITY AND NEW POLICING

In a pioneering work about urban policing, Herman Goldstein, held that policing practices would be more effective if focused on specific community problems.[19] This implies, he noted, a new way of thinking about policing. Research over the past two decades has addressed the troubled neighbourhood, particularly in the United States, where inner-city problems of high crime rates, violence, and the social turmoil of the 1960s gave the flow of needed research money its particular direction. Persisting problems of order emphasized the appropriateness of focusing on troubled neighbourhoods, in which the ineffectiveness of deterrent-patrol/rapid-response programs more suited to the suburbs was more sharply visible. The people of such neighbourhoods need to realize that they have some problem of disorder if they are to participate and move beyond passive dependence on an official response. Community policing, with its focus on a particular neighbourhood, represents an intimate approach. Its suitability to suburban areas, to "modern, low density especially residential communities where people are so spread out," has been questioned, along with any attempt to create an artificial sense of community where none exists.[20]

Community policing represents a fundamental shift in the direction urban policing can usefully take, particularly a shift in function and purpose and in the nature of police resources. The need for the redevelopment of policing into a knowledge-based endeavour follows and is frequently advocated.[21] This newer notion of policing offers a double promise: first, to establish policing programs appropriate to a community, and second, to provide the incentive for police to experiment and innovate, to gain and use knowledge and thus to achieve greater occupational maturity.

Community policing has acquired a disparate range of meanings, some of misleading simplicity, in and out of police departments. The British Home Secretary commented that it "means essentially that police officers should know and understand the people whom they protect and serve."[22] In contrast, one United States writer suggested that community policing implied steady, low-level involvement by a resident police agency with law-abiding citizens in the interests of effectively controlling the law breakers. It is currently the fashion in departments to use the language of community policing. Few senior officers will represent themselves as less than committed advocates, and none can readily resist using the slogans – often the stuff of desirable media notices – of closer communication with the people of a community or attentiveness to its concerns.

As the community-policing notion has gained prominence, an often thin understanding of police issues is revealed in some "progressive" programs, which might nonetheless satisfy public concerns. But some projects that may be loosely grouped under the community-policing approach have yielded valuable knowledge, including many Canadian projects. This is the first path, the pragmatic business of accumulating and extending experience and thereby doing much to define the community policing concept. The second path generalizes on this experience to develop a way of thinking about urban policing and its experiments in neighbourhood order. Both go to the core of policing: its competence and functions in complex urban settings.

In spite of these and other variants, Albert Reiss, Jr urges us to recall that "what distinguishes community-oriented policing ... is that it represents a substantial shift in the organizational model of policing, one where police strategy and tactics are adapted to fit the needs and requirements of the different communities the department serves, where there is diversification of the kinds of programs and services on the basis of community needs and demands for police services and where there is considerable involvement of the community with the police in reaching their objectives."[23]

Community policing is receiving wide and active attention in Canada.[24] As a new philosophy about maintaining community order, it will do much to redefine the functions of urban police.[25] Community policing requires experimentation to determine what works on a case-by-case basis. You know it when you see it. Reiss's encapsulation describes a change from the criminal law/crime fighting orientation of policing towards a social responsiveness deriving from a client-centred occupation. Implicit is a professional flexibility and ability to cope with the contingencies of, for example, policing newly emerging types of exurban neighbourhoods – the landscape of a twenty-first-century city.

Community policing is a dynamic rather than a static enterprise; it will always be a more informed way of approaching problems, coupling often difficult diagnoses of problems of order with an inventiveness in selecting and implementing solutions. This dynamic quality is necessarily shared at all levels of responsibility in a police department. It also involves receptivity to community involvement and therefore, of power sharing with the community (an important issue that will be addressed in its different forms).[26] In Reiss's term, it is the "doing-with" rather than the "doing-to" approach.[27] The priorities are those of the community and not predominantly those of criminal justice. Community policing is tailored to the defined character and needs of the neighbourhood and thus reflects the notion that an equitable distribution of services does not mean uniform distribution, for there will be variability in order-maintenance needs and practices. (The uniform deployment of resources, particularly the patrol force, has come to be seen as a characteristic that makes a department resistant to external influence, i.e., every neighbourhood gets an equal share, and through the mere addition of those uniformly dispersed numbers, it is a frequent justification for claims on funding; an equitably distributed service, on the other hand, is based on need.) The focus is on order maintenance so police practices are tailored, anticipatory, and aggressive.

This sphere of policing involves public leadership by the police officer within the community, for the objectives are those of the community and not some purpose exclusive to a department. The police chief becomes, explicitly, an actor in the political arena and a senior municipal officer, being in this role one who both makes public policy and implements it.[28]

The ingredients of community policing may be characterized as follows.

- Its goal is a neighbourhood good, an improvement in quality through diminished disorder and enhanced stability.
- The specific objectives to be achieved are subject to neighbourhood influence.
- Local resources, especially participation, are committed along with those of the department.
- The commitment of senior officers to developing their programs over a period of many years is essential; it is a matter of profound, long-term change, a point that must be recognized at the outset.[29] As Commander Roach said, every police force must begin from the beginning, there being "no short cuts, no panaceas and no models" that can be taken off the shelf and simply imposed on a community.[30]
- Police capacity and leadership are needed to achieve and sustain both community involvement and police receptivity to it. The goal may not be the control of crime but the reduction of a troublesome fear of crime, something more personally felt and tied to neighbourhood.[31]
- There must be openness to change at all levels in a department and the recognition that no fixed solutions are available, for none have been found to be widely relevant.
- In its various programs and seemingly modest goals, it is a process of experimentation and thus calls for courage and persistence.[32]
- Community policing can be considered a philosophy of policing involving the commitment of police at all levels of responsibility, a philosophy that recognizes the officers' occupational maturity and accepts and relies on their competence to innovate, provide local leadership, and exercise discretion.[33] Hence parallel changes in the structure and capabilities of police organizations and the capabilities of the police occupation itself are required.

From these characteristics, one can see that community policing is a diffuse notion rather than a set of precise prescriptions; it can be said that it is a direction to take in experimentation and innovation. In the telling terms of Assistant Chief Thomas Koby of Houston, "This is a big-time change for the police culture. We're changing police minds and the whole bureaucracy. We're driving down a dark road without headlights on all this. We'll hit some bumps. But we think we can stabilize some pockets of the city and then it will spread, something like a good cancer."[34]

By the logic of the concept and through the reality of experience, officers of all ranks, not the least those at line levels, find community policing requires individual autonomy and responsibility, initiative and a capacity to be innovative. Greater latitude of discretion is clearly a part of it and so the orientation is one of trust and collegiality in an organizational climate that eases delegation. Indeed, project success is found where there is reliance on these attributes.[35]

There are large gaps in what we know about this new concept of policing, though knowledge continues to be extended by the many programs now underway or planned not only in Canada but elsewhere. Implementation throughout a department will take years, perhaps a generation; it will also be plagued with difficulty and even thwarted, as it has been twice in the Metropolitan London Police.[36] It runs counter to strongly held attitudes at the core of Canadian officers' beliefs of what policing is all about.[37]

The rationale for community policing lies in interneighbourhood variability; the older neighbourhoods differ from one another, as the various successes and failures of experimental police programs have demonstrated. Some caution in drawing conclusions from studies and experimental programs is in order. With notable frequency, they tend to be reported and perhaps implemented without detailed attention to, or specification of, the relevant range of community characteristics. *The Ontario Community Policing Manual* suggested that in "getting to know the community," information to be gathered should include the demographics of age, gender, marital status, household and family structure, level of education, occupation, labour-force participation, average household income, ethnicity, and period of immigration.[38] While this list is comprehensive, there are other relevant characteristics such as density, home ownership, multiple-unit residences, the area's stability, zoning, and actual uses. Still other avenues of police intimacy with a neighbourhood and its people may well be appropriate to the different neighbourhoods scattered across the greater spaces of exurbia and may call for some further, unknown variation in the nature of police-citizen contacts.

THREE PROJECTS

I noted above that community policing is definable through an accumulation of the knowledge that various projects yield. The characteristics of an experimental program, a successful one, for example, are the markers by which police practices become classifiable as community policing – definition follows usage, as the following projects show. Many of the innovative experiments reported in recent years, such as highly informative studies of the reduction of fear of crime, are not necessarily concerned with community policing. Other well-known projects including crime prevention, victim services, and neighbourhood watch creep into the community-policing dialogue but are not in themselves at all characteristic of it.

The Victoria Community Police-Station Project

The Victoria police developed a community police-station program to deliver crime-prevention projects in five city districts. Victoria is one of eleven municipalities in the metropolitan area, with a crime rate 85 percent to 180 percent higher than its suburban neighbours. Under then Chief Constable W.J. Snowdon, long an advocate of proactive, or preventive, tactics, the program focused on crime and the fear of crime.

The roots of the program are interesting if complex. First, in a singular achievement, the chief constable demonstrated that a non-crime-fighting orientation can, in time, become part of the attitude of department personnel. However, the recession of the early 1980s did much to curtail the resources going to prevention projects at a time when crime rates were rising. The mayor of the day and *ex officio* chairman of the board of police commissioners insisted, in a typical resort to law-and-order political views, that the crime rate be given priority in the allocation of resources, and he challenged the police to apply their law-enforcement ability to reducing the rate. Then a new, far less orthodox mayor supported the police view that the solution lay in crime prevention rather than in crime control. The objective remained a reduction in crime rates through prevention, by mobilizing the wider resources and commitment of the people of the city. An earlier storefront police office in Victoria, a similar experience in Toronto, and the Detroit ministation program led to the implementation of the neighbourhood-station concept being implemented.

The authors of the report made much of rising crime rates, suggesting in a somewhat misleading comparison that rates were inordinately high in sedate Victoria. (Such allegations no doubt bolstered the impetus to set up this innovative program.) In 1985, Victoria registered 212 crimes per 100,000 people, Vancouver 162, and Toronto 86. The rate for Toronto embraces the metropolitan city served by the one large department and includes vast stretches of low-crime-rate suburbia; Vancouver proper does not embrace all adjacent suburbs. In contrast, the Victoria rates are limited to the small central part of a large metropolitan area of mostly lower-rate, middle-class districts served by other departments. The migration of those seeking the exclusiveness and stability of a suburban neighbourhood had already occurred. The crime rates per 100,000 people reported by the authors for three of the suburban municipalities were 114, 91, and 76. Averaged out, it is probable that metropolitan Victoria's rate was quite low.

Community meetings were held to determine how residents viewed policing in their neighbourhood and how it might be improved to meet the neighbourhood's law-enforcement needs. What emerged was that the police were simply not visible, that citizens could not communicate freely with them, and that the presence of familiar neighbourhood police was desirable. On the other hand, the police administration realized that officers could not cope with rising rates alone, but needed community cooperation and assistance in freeing up police resources by redirecting noncriminal calls for service to other community resources.

The program called for the establishment of five stations in the five major communities of Victoria, including the downtown area. Each was manned by one well-selected and trained constable and a group of volunteer citizens, from fifteen to twenty, trained and coordinated by the constable. The station constable, supported by a volunteer coordinator and an administrator, implemented crime-prevention talks and projects, school liaison, and target hardening, among other duties, and oversaw the training of the volunteers who were to maintain the office, hand out prevention materials, take reports of minor incidents, make referrals to appropriate agencies, and so on. [39]

Tailoring services through community-station activities was part of the operating thrust. Within the department, community policing was stressed as the program's "operating philosophy." The themes of the program were community cooperation and involvement, increased accountability to the community, and improved service. Its goals included a reduction in crime, increased citizen perception of safety, increased satisfaction with the police service, and a reduction in calls for police service in the suburbs, thus allowing for increased police effort in the downtown core. Obviously, the community-station program was coordinated with the patrol and purely law-enforcement functions of the department, but it was organized as part of the department's crime-prevention section and set apart from the operational activities. The familiar crime-prevention projects – block parent, neighbourhood watch, bike registration, and antidrug education in schools – were folded into the experimental context. An expected backlash over police inability to stem the increase of crime did not materialize during early meetings with the public in any of the districts. But the basic vote of confidence was qualified by insistence that more civil-disorder and maintenance issues be addressed, along with noisy parties, vagrants, panhandlers, skateboarders, and traffic-movement problems."[40]

Evaluating the program was problematic and the results ambiguous at best. Nonetheless, there is no indication that rates of crime or fear of crime (measured by resident's reports of self-restricted movement in their neighbourhood) were reduced, nor any indication of greater community awareness of, or participation in, police activity.[41] As a test of the delivery of standard, often minor, crime-prevention projects through the efforts of an on-site police officer with the help of greater police/public contact, this experimental program, relative to its highly ambitious goals, was not successful.

The Edmonton Foot-Patrol Experiment

The Edmonton Neighbourhood Foot-Patrol Program was a pilot project designed to test the effectiveness of specially trained foot-patrol officers, each assigned to one of twenty-one beats (six downtown and fifteen residential). The objectives included reducing the number of repeat calls (callers tend to be repeaters), improving public satisfaction with police services and job satisfaction of constables, gathering more intelligence, and solving community problems. The overarching goal was the prevention of crime and creation of a "better state of society," which included police involvement with the community in solving problems. The leadership and initiative for the experiment came from then Superintendent Chris Braiden, an officer well versed in community policing. The beats, each with its own storefront office, were located within the busier areas of the city based on an analysis of about 153,000 calls for service. The nature of the residential areas was not described.

The beat officers, in addition to dispatched calls, received numerous walk-in complaints and telephone inquiries that under other circumstances would have become calls for service. Thus, through the use of discretion, the officer handled calls according to the nature of the call rather than to some administratively set disposition procedure.[42]

The project was successful. The officers' visibility and their contacts on the beat enhanced their knowledge of the area and citizen satisfaction. The use of community-liaison committees was seen as the least useful part of the project, especially in the downtown areas. The use of volunteers was variable since it was not widely accepted by the constables. The problem-solving initiative was notable in alleviating, for example, parking problems, problems associated with absentee landlords, drug and liquor problems (in one case the offending bar closed), juvenile crime, and, by referring individuals to helping agencies and working directly with schools and children, family violence.

The Flint, Michigan Foot-Patrol Program

The Flint, Michigan Foot-Patrol Program best exemplifies community policing. The experiment began in 1979, a time of very high unemployment in a city of some 150,000 people. Citywide neighbourhood meetings identified three issues: the absence of comprehensive neighbourhood organizations and services; the lack of citizen involvement in crime prevention; and the impersonal relations between citizens and officers. Twenty-two patrol officers were assigned to fourteen areas that held twenty percent of the population. The program was a marked departure from traditional foot and motorized preventive patrols. The officers were based in neighbourhoods to serve as catalysts in forming local associations to identify matters for police priorities and activities, and for community programs. Officers were to work in partnership with the neighbourhood to deliver a "comprehensive set of services through referrals, interventions and links to governmental" and other service agencies.[43] They were expected to become intimately familiar with their assigned neighbourhoods, focus on the social-service aspects of their job, bring resolutions to local problems, and mobilize citizens in order to create the means by which many problems could be dealt with. While they provided law-enforcement services, their day-to-day patrols and other contacts brought a degree of familiarity with residents that resulted in an effective cooperative relationship of trust and increased communication. Robert Trojanowicz has said that the usefulness of officer-citizen communications cannot be overstated. Mobile patrols on call obviously provided the swift response that foot-patrol officers, who in any event were not usually on duty beyond day-shift hours, could not provide.[44]

The experiment was an impressive success. Among other benefits, calls for service were reduced by forty-two percent as citizens began handling minor problems themselves or through the mediation of the patrol officer; citizens felt safer, were satisfied with the program, and improved police-community relations and some reduction in crime were the result. The people of Flint passed an increased tax rate to extend the program to the entire city, so far the only city with full foot-patrol coverage, though by 1986, more than two hundred cities had some variation of the program in place.

Further, it was found that the more contact there is between police and citizens, the more communication and trust. The flow of information increases. The marked contrast between this approach and O.W. Wilson's – mobilizing police resources around the centrally despatched and controlled patrol car – makes a fruitful subject for reflection. It will be recalled that Wilson's overall objective was to insulate police services from the corrupting influence of local politics. Today, traditional police executives continue to react negatively to the concept of the foot patrol, seeing in it either an obsolete practice or the threat of citizen involvement and the undermining of police as community advocates.

To sum up, the pioneering program in Flint involves the following aspects of community policing:

- the function of social engineering that Reiss pointed to, of working towards the establishment of local organizations and changing of social habits in coping with disorder and determining the community-specific capacity for tolerance;[45]
- at least in part, a tailoring of services according to neighbourhood need; the issue of quality of neighbourhood life was not restricted to disorder or crime, but extended to other services and troubles;
- an accountability to the community for the quality and relevance of services, as the well-supported tax-rate increase indicated;
- the acknowledgment of a working distinction between the place of law enforcement and prevention, order maintenance and service in policing;
- to a lesser, but still apparent, degree, the adaptable or experimental features of any community policing program.

A political process can be described as the development of a policy based on public support and the use of public resources in its implementation to achieve a social outcome. There is a qualitative difference between disorder, defined according to neighbourhood culture and conditions, and enforcement, defined according to the particulars of an act. Thus, order-maintenance policies and practices aimed at the problems of a neighbourhood are political. Insofar as their implementation involves people in a joint effort to change a substantial aspect of a neighbourhood, they can also be described as social engineering, however modest the objective. The Flint neighbourhood foot-patrol program shows that police accountability to the neighbourhood results in a reciprocity of trust between officers and citizens. Police are not only street-corner politicians in handling single incidents but neighbourhood politicians serving a specified constituency. One obstacle to change is an orientation of officers that favours law enforcement bolstered by well-entrenched attitudes of the police subculture.

Politics has to do with differentiating among various public-sector interest and often favouring one or another. Politics is by definition partisan, whether practised by elected or nonelected officials. Here, in the competing juridictional claims made by elected and nonelected authorities, lies the potential for conflict – open conflict in the United States, quieter and less competitive in Canada. The admission of the "political" nature of community policing invites the attention and, no doubt, intervention of elected authority, just as it invites the participation of the public. As shown later, the police, having achieved protection from political intervention, view the prospect with understandable circumspection.

"Engineering" as a police initiative may necessarily include engaging the participation of other departments of local government. In writing about a "mature city," Leanne Lachman and Anthony Downs [46] suggested that of the salient issues in strategies aimed at arresting physical and social decline in a neighbourhood: how to identify or create neighbourhood organizations aimed at preservation, and how to establish effective working relationships with central city staff and administrators.

A city council and its bureaucracy may favour uniform citywide strategies over the local. Neighbourhoods, in aggregate, are prime consumers of services, so if one or more each merit tailored services, the larger community seems threatened with jurisdictional fragmentation and jumbled accountability. Similar jurisdictional qualms arise over the issue of police accountability and orientation. One can appreciate police reluctance to become embroiled in the traditional tension between central authorities and local entities. The question who is responsible for determining whether a community has the skills to identify and resolve problems of order or what civic resources and leadership should be tendered is problematic. It is arguable that neighbourhood people seeking help can and should be able to influence the direction and shape the nature of accountability. (One element in the success of the Flint foot-patrol project was that many beat officers became well known and popular, local heroes with an informal political base, because of their capacity to listen, act, and often involve civic agencies. Yet neither a local hero nor the department is an all-purpose social or administrative agency.)

The consensus needed for police legitimacy – that is, public recognition of and support for the police role and how it is fulfilled – is often quite narrow: what the police do may be contentious, for there will be different views of what constitutes neighbourhood order and what behaviour may be tolerated, views that vary with socioeconomic and ethnocultural backgrounds. Current public attitudes tend to endorse policing that focuses on violent crime, so that if the order-maintenance purposes of community policing are not connected to a reduction in the crime rate, matters of consensus may arise. At this time, the better claim is that the purposes of order-maintenance programs are connected to a community's quality of life.

According to George Kelling, order maintenance has always been a sticky issue for those engaged in municipal-government reform.[47] It is difficult to define, but it carries a generalized basis of police authority to act in the face of minor disturbances and thus harbours the potential for abuse. It is difficult to manage and it raises issues of individual rights. Furthermore, a tougher standard of behaviour challenges officers either to be civil and orderly themselves or, where law enforcement is concerned, to observe procedural propriety. Police manage the response to serious crime well and can defend their actions, but in the amorphous area of order maintenance, their goals are often ambiguous and their defence less sure. Order maintenance, it is charged, targets minorities and the disadvantaged while those committing white-collar crime are spared. James Q. Wilson observed that police strategies do vary according to public morality, which in turn varies with different racial groups; an incident that is not tolerated by a patrol officer in a suburban neighbourhood may well be overlooked in the central city peopled by immigrants.[48] So the maintenance of order is indeed a sticky issue. Restoring order, which may involve aggressive patrol practices in troubled neighbourhoods (often the home neighbourhoods of minorities and the disadvantaged), must become suspect when questions of possible racism arise.

Neighbourhood order is violated by a youngster skateboarding on a busy sidewalk, or by the noise of a ghetto-blaster, littering, a deteriorating building, or many crude incivilities the residents of a bustling city centre are familiar with. Whether a police officer has the authority to act to restore order in the absence of a disorderly-conduct law is relevant. Whether it makes sense to translate acts of disorder into acts of crime, thereby invoking the judicial process, is also relevant. Kelling maintains that there is a need for legislation that subjects a range of minor acts to regulatory law in order to widen a patrol officer's legal capacity to keep the peace.[49] But disorderly acts have innumerable, often very minor manifestations and the risk of "criminalizing" unwanted numbers of residents is considerable. The legalistic approach, empowering police to regulate a range of behaviour not otherwise criminal in nature, was not and is not evenly supported – liquor laws are a case in point – and often proves difficult to enforce, as the various attempts to regulate prostitution indicate. Albert Reiss asserts that care must be taken in imposing variable prohibitions or regulations in different communities to avoid confusion among citizens about what activities are permissible. But disturbing the peace, disorderly conduct, loitering, and vagrancy all remain in the Canadian code, and in most United States jurisdictions, an officer has general authority to act to preserve order. Obviously, there may be no authority for actions against minor incivilities such as skateboarding or carrying a noisy radio.

So at the heart of community policing lies the recurrent problem of discretion. For example, officers will have a sense of the neighbourhood consensus on a given behaviour, but if not, they may insert their own and tend to ignore the reality that a consensus does not exist. Further, alternatives to the legalistic approach to consensus (in which enabling minor laws – disorderly-conduct laws – are in place) are rarely, if ever, considered except to note a reliance on the discretion of police officers in minor cases of disorder – the use of informal, often invisible practices, curbside justice, "kicking ass and taking names." Certainly, the prevailing attitudes in the police subculture are not reassuring as a basis for widened discretion.

Needless to say, society has gained some experience in the application of disorderly-conduct laws against acts, public and private, that may be innocuous but are for various reasons otherwise viewed; in the United States being black in a white neighbourhood could once be construed as an offence. Where it is based on consensus within a community, order and the acts sustaining it will be partisan in intent and impact, which again reflects the contentiousness of the issue. Regulatory approaches heighten that contentiousness. As with order-maintaining activities in general, deciding whether an act was likely to disturb the now antique and always mythical King's Peace was, for an officer, highly discretionary and open to abuse. Still, there is no victim of such an act except perhaps the accused and the order of a neighbourhood. The experience with minor laws aimed at regulating behaviour and maintaining local order amouts to well-tradden path that might have been appropriate in its day but now holds diminished promise; the remaining police authority to act against disorderly conduct, for example, is used with some effect, but the case for extended authority does not seem to be strong. Still, without graduated powers similar to Victorian laws, the police are restricted to weaker, consensus-based methods. In the absence of such powers, constables resort to "extra-lawful" acts, the source of abuse in authority incidents. As a caution, Reiner noted that giving the police further powers may reduce the incentive to develop other means of resolution and erode the emphasis on variable policing programs.[50] So the authority of the police, in concert with people of a neighbourhood, to act in situations characterized by serious disorder and crime in decaying areas is a central matter.

The powers of police to regulate minor acts that may affect the tranquillity of a neighbourhood, and indeed their obligation to do so, is an issue that one anticipates will be worked out as community policing and other newer forms of policing are fashioned. "The key idea here," as Commander Lawrence T. Roach of the London Metropolitan Police has observed, "is that of consultation. As I have already stressed community policing requires that policing policies, practices, planning and decision making must all be open to the influence of the community affected by them. If that is not the case then whatever is being done by the police cannot qualify as falling within that approach. It might be good policing, it might even be effective policing. But it is NOT 'community policing'."[51] Joyce Epstein and Sheila Vanderhoef have commented that the firmly entrenched notion that the consumer of a product or service is to be represented in some way in its development is applicable to policing.[52] The consumer's influence may manifest itself as police yielding authority to a neighbourhood, which accounts for some police resistance to the full implications of community policing.

The apolitical status of police and their resulting quasi-autonomy do not accommodate themselves to the variable needs of neighbourhoods. The familiar reactive police programs are presumably politically neutral and safe; apprehending offenders and responding to citizen calls for service, because they are crisis-based, do not stir up political dust. In contrast, the neighbourhood foot-patrol program involves, as Trojanowicz noted, a policing practice by which the community *collectively* decides what the local problems are and what resources are to be used to address them.

If we ask, however, how the experience of community policing to date aroused this knee-jerk fear of interference in policing, we find that police resistance is grounded not in the actual results of these experiments but in the standard police opposition to public input into their activities. Harold Pepinski, who takes the position that current policing in the United States clearly suffers from class bias,[53] proposed a model that could reduce the bias inherent in law enforcement: the initiative "must come from the private community and the police must merely follow."[54] He suggested that, "by rotation ... patrol officers in the district would come in to negotiate mutually agreed-upon criteria for police performance. In open meetings, the group and other community members would tell the police what services they wanted, and the officers would tell the citizens what they could and could not reasonably do. From the onset, it would be established that the agenda for discussion included only what the police could do for citizens and how police performance might be measured, not what the community could do for the police."[55] He indicated that the program initiates police responses rather than police initiating community responses to problems. Community representatives, it was proposed, would suggest objectives and the procedures for measuring police progress in meeting them, with both subject to approval by police and community members alike. So as much initiative and independence of decision remain in police hands as the community's. (That police responsibilities in a community will be circumscribed by an officer's determination of "what police could not reasonably do" is sure to collide with the attitudes of community members. It should be pointed out that Pepinski's process takes the police establishment, its organization and programs, as givens in his analysis, while a modified policing establishment may be implicit.)

Herman Goldstein first described the problem-oriented approach for improving police effectiveness in 1979,[56] and it has been widely tested since then. Reminiscent of community policing, the concept is a new way of thinking that has implications for every aspect of police work. In Goldstein's words, "the most commonly articulated proposals for improving policing do not go far enough. They concentrate on means, rather than ends. They dwell on the structure, staffing, and equipping of the police organization, with the assumption that such efforts will eventually result in an improvement in the quality of policing. To develop a form of policing uniquely equipped to fulfil the complex needs of a free and diverse society, police reform must have a more ambitious goal."[57]

Rather than a single incident, a problem is a cluster of similar and recurring incidents of substantive community concern, a cluster that is arguably a matter of police business. Incidents may range from the more serious crimes such as sexual assault to minor incidents of disorder, so it is important to recognize that problem-oriented policing is concerned with the particular outcome of problem resolution whether or not it is a criminal-justice outcome. Incidents may be grouped as follows: by behaviour, such as noise, the sale of drugs, or spouse abuse; by territory, such as an intersection plagued by alcoholics or prostitutes, or a tavern that attracts trouble; by persons, as with repeat offenders; or by time, date, or occasion, as on Hallowe'en or during certain concerts. Recurring incidents signal the presence of a problem. A problem may be of citywide or neighbourhood concern, or be so highly local that one officer on the beat may examine and resolve it. The attention a problem attracts does not necessarily depend on its being a law-enforcement matter as long as it poses a significant threat to the well-being of the city as a whole, or to one neighbourhood, locale, or set of people.

It has been noted elsewhere in this book that policing has been oriented primarily to law enforcement and to the methods associated with it. This perspective has not only distorted our thinking about the police role but has disproportionately influenced its operations, organization, training, and staffing. The problem-oriented approach, if used in all its complexity, promises to dislodge this distortion and influence the typical police organization, its personnel, and its operations. The basic elements of problem-oriented policing can be summarized as follows.

- Incidents are grouped as a problem. Incidents are usually handled as isolated, unconnected, self-contained events, perhaps on the assumption that responsibility for the underlying problem lies elsewhere. If incidents are taken as symptoms of a problem, then the people, the relationships among them, and the behaviour involved require in-depth examination.
- A substantial problem can be defined at different levels and in different ways. Shoplifting can be defined as citywide or localized within one shopping mall; other problems may affect the people of a neighbourhood or an apartment building. Furthermore, as Goldstein noted, citizens tend to define a problem as a police problem rather than more accurately as a "community problem." The latter implies that the community should recognize and perhaps contribute to a definition of the problem, thereby ensuring that it is more fully understood.
- The focus is on effectiveness as the ultimate goal. Since problems are usually intractable, effectiveness might mean reducing the number or seriousness of incidents; designing better methods for handling them; and removing the problem from police consideration. Reducing numbers and their seriousness reflects a valid police role in managing deviance; an arrest following spouse abuse, for example, does tend to reduce the number of incidents, especially repeat offences.
- A systematic attempt is made to identify problems that are not restricted to those of crime, and to gain the widest possible understanding of a problem through the literature, inquiries, surveys, and so on.
- Problems are disaggregated and accurately labelled, pulled apart to avoid generic labels such as categories of crime. Statutory labels help to indicate the department's traditional response (detection, arrest,

and charge); the challenge is to diagnose or define a problem unencumbered by extraneous information or customary, possibly irrelevant, categorizations and definitions.

- Problem analysis includes identification and analysis of the multiple interests involved. The customary interest in a crime problem has been that of the "law," now considered inadequate. The community may well have multiple interests, some conflicting. Goldstein pointed out that the business of assigning priorities to problems in the light of various interests raises difficult, value-laden questions, including who should make the decision. Significantly, he noted that without an in-depth analysis of what the police are expected to do, the questions, important as they are, are not being raised in the first instance. The police can be in an excellent position to raise them.
- The process involves identifying and critiquing the current response, which may be effective, although the critique could indicate improvements or alternatives.
- There is an uninhibited search for a tailor-made response. This involves breaking out of the law-enforcement mould. It is but one of a wide range of often informal methods used in doing the job and others can and should be invented. A search will recognize the innovative potential of line officers, especially those that mobilize the community.

Three benefits of problem-oriented policing may be anticipated: a reduction in calls for service; improved effectiveness in responding to citizen concerns by addressing the underlying problem; and a reduction in the negative consequences, for department and officer alike, of being call-driven.

Ambitious community-policing projects make the community a "coproducer" of policing services in that a careful cultivation by police of a community results in the community taking initiatives itself. Similarly, with problem-oriented policing, if after careful study the conclusion is that a problem may be significantly reduced by some form of community engagement, then that participation is obviously to be cultivated. Given the outspoken habits of police executives and unions, the suggestion that police should be more assertive in defining their mission may seem a little odd. But we have seen that officers occupy a little-used frontline position from which to gather insights about emerging social ills. The intelligent management of this police resource requires more outspokenness coupled with an advocacy role in the community, a course fraught with pitfalls. This role, like much of policing, is political in nature; problem-oriented policing implies that the police will develop a more active partnership with other public agencies.

Such open, strengthened decision-making processes bear on the issues of discretion and accountability. In the effort to structure and control discretion and increase accountability, the common practices have been to increase the use of written policies and regulations, assign more explicit (in the United States) accountability to elected officials, and resort to a variety of methods for controlling the police, including civilian review boards, judicial review, and vulnerability to both criminal and civil actions (again, more common in the United States). But the imposition of external controls tends to make the police more defensive and strains relations between the police and the community. Under problem-oriented policing, wider community participation in policy decision making looks for open discussion and mutually acceptable guidelines. The process educates the community in the capacities of the police.

Improved accountability can be obtained by having police executives assume greater responsibility for decisions that are theirs to make, by default or otherwise. They have – or should have – the staff and resources needed to conduct problem analyses and implement decisions, including the latitude to determine what is to be delegated to officers on the street. This entails a recognition of the policy-making role, a political role, of police executives and of the risks entailed and underlines the significance of careful data collection, the processes of analysis, and the significance of openness in the process.

The typical system of recording police activity and crime data is not geared to providing information on the nature of problems; reports will include all the information needed to support an arrest and to demonstrate that the officer acted correctly. But police have a first-hand view of inadequate government services and the failure to meet vital needs and are well able to make the connection between these inadequacies and the problems to which they respond. The practice of connecting with other government and private services in devising and implementing a response to a problem is manifest in problem-oriented policing and in the leadership it demands.

Community and problem-oriented policing projects are properly considered to be controlled experiments, the conduct of which requires rather complex skills. New and more productive relationships with academics and government agencies must be developed, along with specially suited research methods. Project evaluation, sufficient resources for confident, routine end-product evaluation, and publication of results are all essential to the process.

The disparity between critical examination of a problem at a high departmental level and at the patrol-officer level, however, directs attention to a more intractable problem. Street-level processes of problem identification amenable to the rigorous collection and analysis of data require skills that are rare in the typical police department. Departments generally do not have people with the necessary analytical skills, even for defining the precise nature of a problem; where such people do exist, they are not provided with proper organizational status and support.

Goldstein suggested that the police are preoccupied with management, including internal procedures and efficiency. When police speak of problems, they usually mean matters of internal management and resources – lack of personnel, among others. When police are "instructed on the meaning of 'substantive' problems and are then asked to focus on them, they are apparently so conditioned to thinking in terms of the problems of the organization that they frequently slip back to identifying concerns in the management of the agency. *Thus, focusing on the substantive, community problems that the police must handle is a much more radical step than it initially appears to be, for it requires the police to go beyond taking satisfaction in the smooth operation of their organization; it requires that they extend their concern to dealing with the problems that justify creating a police agency in the first instance"* (emphasis in the original).[58]

As Goldstein further notes, the power of the police subculture to resist change presents a formidable obstacle. "Powerful forces within the police establishment have a much stronger influence over the way in which a police agency operates than do the managers of a department, legislatures and courts, the mayor and the members of the community."[59] Similar conclusions have been reached in Canada. The orientation of a department to this problem-centred approach through a universal change in personnel attitudes is probably feasible. But such change, echoing the difficulties of implementing community policing, requires careful planning, "a long time frame, consistent and persistent efforts facilitated by a gradual turnover in personnel. It is hard to sustain."[60] Certainly, a clear statement of departmental values and mission is required under a renewed leadership that is openly committed to the approach, along with revised criteria for recognizing performance.

The organizational and managerial changes that are required include modification of the top-to-bottom nature of supervision by an insistence on a supportive role – one of guiding and coaching as well as partnering. Line officers are often treated impersonally; they are not well informed of department policy changes and issues and learn that rewards go to those who conform in appearance, deference, and paperwork. In addition, centralization of control, a characteristic of the reform in the O.W. Wilson tradition, must be reversed so that officers are in a position to capitalize on their knowledge of the community, particularly in the service of their own initiatives. Decentralization is fostered as much under the problem-oriented as the community-policing approach. The first step towards reform is a thorough analysis of current police circumstances, which brings us to the existing structure and resources of urban policing.

CHAPTER FIVE

The Structure and Resources of Urban Policing

PEOPLE AND FUNCTIONS

In the context of urban policing, the term "structure" includes the configuration and development of personnel, their certification of competence, and the resources of the occupation, particularly the available knowledge and skills, wether used or not. Finally, the term embraces occupationwide organizations and the common practices through which standards of performance, ethics, and police interests are generally attended to. "Structure," then, means police in a corporate sense.

The police occupation has been shaped by convention, politics, and history, and by a turbulent urban society. Conventional thinking is strong and phrases like "enemies of society" and "law and order" are commonplace. Law enforcement has an apparent meaning and a salience in the public mind, especially when serious crimes are committed. But the policing role, especially its desired outcome, implied by law enforcement is inadequately known and understood. We may ask the police for relentless enforcement, but however zealous they may be, this and other remedies for crime can only be partial and tentative at best. So this chapter, like the previous one, takes the view that the more complex function of serving a community so as to sustain its quality of life can have achievable and manageable purposes. The ability to sense whether resources are adequate, for example, is dependent on such a perspective, which does not, however, deny the validity of the crime-detection role, the apprehension of criminals, and the resources devoted to these activities.

Our conservative society, by deeming an act a crime, renders a moral verdict. The police participate in this verdict, but seldom acknowledge the confused, ambiguous situations from which the crime arose. The constable is not readily subject to close direction and regulation because the maintenance of order is highly variable and its outcomes dependent in part on his discretion. Maintaining order is antithetical to the either/or clarity of law enforcement; difficult to regulate, it implies less control over line personnel. Diminished control challenges claims of effective, professional management, and in accident- or corruption-prone departments, the predominant place is still given to the more easily regulated law-enforcement activities. The belated "discovery" of discretion within policing is understandable in this light. That discretion is necessarily exercised by line personnel is a given in this chapter. One point to bear in mind is the relative success (i.e., ready acceptance by residents) in the suburbs of the rapid-response patrol strategy – a success that, in my view, has tended to obscure any need for change and further entrenches the law-enforcement program in the police and public mind.

THE PERSONNEL STRUCTURE

When police officers are recruited, they are usually young people for whom education has held no strong attraction. Full high-school graduation is not a requirement in all provincial police forces, though it is specified by many departments. Stable personalities, clear records, and physical fitness constitute the fundamental qualifications. This in-at-the-bottom means of common entry is a fundamental feature of the police personnel structure. It is part of the policing ethos, entrenched in the attitudes of police officers, and seemingly ineradicable. It shoulders aside options for more variable personnel policies and practices; it pre-empts consideration of prerequisites beyond "apprenticeship" minimums. Its roots can be seen in Sir Robert Peel's attempts to dispel public anxiety by recruiting "apprentice" constables from the working class.[1] This design, repeated in Canada, was successful not only in helping to overcome public fears but in achieving a strong measure of public support that persists and reinforces the apprenticeship-entry strategy to this day.

One hundred years ago in Canadian communities, education levels were low, illiteracy common, and training resources meagre, at best. Informal and formal apprenticing provided a common means of attaining skills. For much of police history, however, there was one exception. In Canada and Britain, until the immediate post-war years, those in the senior ranks were usually retired military officers rather than officers experienced in policing itself, which suggests that there was little of a technical nature in its operations and little depth of competence in its ranks.

It is difficult to imagine the patrol function without an in-at-the-bottom system, or to picture this system except in the context of the low-status, general-duties/patrol function. Even today, a uniform signals the position of the wearer, the patrol or general-duties officer being indistinguishable from the rookie, a performer of largely routine or simple duties. In the priority of recruits' ambitions, the first is assignment to plain-clothes work.[2] The position of the constable on patrol is still the lowest formal recognition of worth. Nevertheless, it remains a visible position, challenging and intrinsically satisfying in its order-maintenance aspects, as well as the means by which a department integrates itself into the community and achieves public support. Challenging it may be, but its low status and the messy, ambiguous nature of order maintenance provide the incentive to seek an exit. This internal contradiction in the personnel structure of policing is often admitted but rarely acted on.[3]

The in-at-the-bottom dynamic also helps to channel attitudes and values into that of a brotherhood and this it does in swift fashion. The military are not alone in realizing that induction, if a singular and tough rite of passage, will entrench a commonality of attitudes and a strong *esprit de corps*; this seems to be doubly true of police. I can recall speaking with a class of police recruits early in their training, and even then they described themselves as a beleaguered and dauntless few against the "them" of the public at large.

Much indeed can be attributed to this settled characteristic, some of it positive. In-at-the-bottom apprenticing established a cohesive policing craft and a resilient personnel structure that was adequate until policing entered the postwar decades. It promotes strong in-group attitudes and perspectives, so that regardless of rank, there is a recurring, internal reinforcement of attitudes and goals (though scant discussion of wider perspectives).

A uniformed patrol division is the bedrock of a department. All other apparently more specialized duties were once thought to be ancillary, but law-enforcement specializations have since been accorded higher status.[4] Uniformed work has been downgraded to a pool from which to promote the "best" and to which failed specialists are returned. One result is that an aggressive self-image is fostered among the group; the car chases, "combat," and excessive zeal that bolster this image are taken as indicators of its status and prestige and are not always seen for what they are.

All of this invites comparison with occupational standards in other fields. If an occupation is to maintain a trusted place in society, the valid certification of a new member's competence is essential. For police, this certification is made after about one year of probation under the supervision of an officer-coach, following about twelve weeks of training – an exceptionally brief initiation into demanding duties. Advancement to first-class constable requires, typically, three to four years of experience. (There are provincial variations; in the US, only about a third of the states have training academies.)

Policing is a craft. Officers on the street know they are members of a subculture, that it is the subculture of a craft that conscientiously values mastery of skills and takes pride in it. Still, a craft is an endeavour of narrowed focus: the mastery of skills is exercised for one demanding incident, one immediate problem. And the most valued skills are those of law enforcement. On this the certification of the novice's competence rests, and progress through the classes of constable follows.

Membership in a craft implies a high level of certain experience-based competences, shared attitudes, and values, and intragroup esteem that grows directly out of a shared position. For police, these attributes flow from providing a critically needed service, from meeting the crises society has charged to them.[5] Participation in the tougher, dangerous incidents is sought because it defines one's place in the craft's "true" role; fraternity manifests itself not only in the possession of unique skills but in the critical occasions to exercise them. The informal skills called for in maintaining order – the easing skills or "recipes" – are not "in the book" but are shared among experienced officers and rapidly learned by neophytes. As a result, the use of all skills, including these supra-official, unrecognized, and unobtrusively practised skills, contribute to the aura of exclusiveness, to the belief that the public does not understand their work, and to the common conviction that senior officers have lost touch with the risks of the street.

The general reliance on the apprenticeship system has shrivelled over the past hundred years but particularly during the immediate postwar years, when education/training institutions multiplied as the more cost-effective means of training for various occupations. For police, however, essential knowledge and skills are still to a large extent acquired and refined in the master-apprentice mode of the craft.

The qualification deemed necessary for a career in policing is early success in general duties. The minimal-entry prerequisites imply that the job is not demanding, and what is learned during the typical twelve weeks of training and during early performance on the job suggests that such duties were not deemed to be onerous. Having said that, "street duties" remain an effective teaching mode. Once a constable is enrolled and working, opportunities to upgrade fundamental qualifications are few and far between. Experience-based skills upgrading occurs, perhaps through some special-investigation work. (With one exception, recruit training itself, largely provided by the provinces, dates from only the mid-seventies.) It bears repeating that one reason for officer effectiveness is the early acquisition of a uniform set of attitudes and values that must be displayed if acceptance from one's peers is to be gained. It is a matter of measuring up. The pressure is informal, but their cohesion, marked by the three Ss of secrecy, silence, and solidarity) is traditional and impressive.

This is a thin accreditation system for an occupation providing a vital public service. Training courses for experienced officers, invariably of a brief, often intense, technique-oriented nature, are now commonly available, particularly at provincial and United States academies. Formal entry hurdles have not greatly advanced beyond the simple matter of being sworn in. There are two consequences of note. First, performance problems on the street, in the case of an individual officer who has attracted a complaint or attention, are frequently diagnosed as correctable through the disciplinary process, or, with more common occurrences, by a revised regulation or, in more recent years, by a change in the training syllabus. These responses, given the weakness of supervision, are superficial in contrast to an officer's quick and intense acquisition of vital skills and the equally intense experience of induction into the police subculture. That the attitudes and cohesion of the subculture are a potential resource that can and often should be harnessed, goes unremarked in managerial and supervisory thinking.[6] Second, the craft model does not lend itself to acquiring new skills and practices either through internal experimentation or through the entry of people who possess wider skills or knowledge. But police are not alone in this; there are very few, if any, tightly bound occupations that are at ease with the intervention or introduction of outsiders.

Promotion is the one significant, prized career-development practice; it is employed as motivation, as a misplaced reward, and as the solitary recognition of status and worth. Rank within police departments is arranged not in a pyramid but in a large rectangle of constables surmounted by a thin steeple of administrators, typically one for about every four or five constables. With low levels of turnover in the administrative ranks, opportunities for promotion are scarce. The ladder is crowded at the bottom, so the career constable has become commonplace. Promotion, then, is as elusive as other recognized means of attaining recognition and achieving personal growth.

It was not always like this. The heady days of postwar expansion created ample opportunities for advancement, but in the absence of pressure, other personnel policy options were never developed. An important feature of those years was the inexperience and youth of officers on the street, the more experienced of whom tended to be candidates for promotion. Two separate components of an effective personnel policy – motivating competent performance and fostering talent – became tangled. When only a job well done can secure a promotion, the rank and file get the message that reward has completely eclipsed qualification or talent for development as a key to advancement.

The identification, attraction, and training of people with different talents and qualifications, and their subsequent occupation-centred development, require extensive time early in a career as well as the commitment of resources that police departments have traditionally lacked. In Canada, resources available to urban police for professional development have been paltry when compared to their responsibilities, to the military, or to most European countries. In the Netherlands, personnel are recruited and trained for four years at a police college for the rank of assistant inspector and up. They are then assigned command responsibilities. Denmark recruits lawyers, and West Germany provides lengthy training if the officer is not yet thirty-five years of age.

In keeping with most crafts, an officer's ability to use the common range of skills on more difficult tasks is a near singular mark of distinction. There is little recognition that other knowledge and skills need to be developed and used; those who might possess such skills usually go unremarked.[7] The Calgary Police Service is something of an exception. It has divided its assessment system in two: one side with a focus on current performance improvement and the other on suitability for promotion to a particular position. This suggests that the craft-induced lockstep need not be so rigid.[8] The lateral movement of police officers among departments and of qualified civilians into a department at more senior levels has often been advocated by nonpolice observers who detect a need for fresh thinking, for opening up windows. Despite the concern, these proposals offer little in the way of concrete professional-development opportunities.

In terms of rank, teeth-to-tail ratios suggest that four levels of responsibility are adequate and appropriate to the collegial approach of community policing.[9] Large Canadian departments with more than 750 sworn personnel average nine ranks, including constable and chief. Departments of about 250 people average seven ranks. The typical department of about 100 to 150 officers boasts six. (The rank of corporal is excluded from these figures.)

We live in an age of specialization. Specialization is characterized by narrow areas of study and work and the use of knowledge and skills particular, though not necessarily unique, to it. We think of specialization as requiring considerable investment in training or education of those identified as having scarce or needed aptitudes. In contrast, twelve weeks of new-entry training is usually the longer period of training in a police career. Thus, general police duties could be classified as specialist but for three factors. First, patrol and investigation are general duties in police eyes. Secondly, specialization is a frame of mind; specialists believes that they are specialists and acquire the orientation and attitudes of their area. Thirdly, specialists are commonly regarded as such by others in their organization.

As the content and complexity of specialization increase, so do the time and cost involved in specializing. If specialist ability is available on the job market and not unique to an employing organization, it is usually more cost effective to hire an outsider who already has the necessary qualifications rather than undertake expensive in-house qualification programs. However, if it is unique to an employing organization, there is a need not only for training programs but for developing and maintaining that body of specialized knowledge within the training system, however costly. Finally, those people at executive/senior-management levels where overall operations and administrative policies are set are *ipso facto* generalists, with the attending common values and attitudes.

Faced with a need for (nonpolicing) specialized knowledge and skills, a department tends to employ either a police officer with an added-on veneer of entry-level specialist qualification (as in personnel administration) or a civilian, who is often hired at a junior level of qualification because any specialist activity is assumed to fall outside of police experience, while also being subordinate to it. In-house advice from a nonpolice specialist, must be filtered through that experience to be valid. Furthermore, the erstwhile specialist police officer, perhaps in an administrative role, will usually be reassigned to dissimilar duties after a few years. Hence the disincentive to developing specialists when the time and cost this entails can only be justified by longer-term employment in one role. Regardless of their qualifications or length of service in a specialist position, officers will still consider themselves generalists first.[10] Thus, internally developed specialists do not seek higher qualification advocate new perspectives and approaches because of their commitment to general or common attitudes and rewards.

The growing complexity in policing functions, both law enforcement and, especially, order maintenance, is apparent. The thinking behind community policing, that the police are competent to make diagnoses or conduct experiments in response to community problems of order, suggests the difficult nature of the task. In law enforcement, one need only point to commercial and computer crime and fraud investigations, explosives disposal, youth and family-abuse programs, and drug-related crime, among others, all of which take officers beyond standard policing skills into the esoteric. That many policing areas, particularly the investigative, are highly specialized is reflected in the longer-term employment of the officers engaged in them; individual competence in such areas derives largely from experience. Policing tasks by nature, they not only retain the generalist cachet but take on added lustre. From this perspective, it is possible to discern opportunities for formal career-enhancement policies other than promotion. (Much, though by no means all, police capacity to respond in these tough enforcement areas is based on knowledge and skills generated in other occupations or forums.)

This brings me to a critical point. The fragmentation of urban policing into hundreds of large and small departments makes it difficult to generate, systematize, and transmit knowledge in the form of training. Policing is inherently a consumer rather than producer of technical knowledge. The combined resources of the federal government and the RCMP were needed to put in place crime-detection laboratories, central information and identification banks, and a college. But acknowledgment of the need for wider policing resources is not common within the occupation.

Even large urban departments cannot readily develop extensive in-house specialist training. But options exist. Recruiting, selection, training, performance-improvement systems, individual evaluation, career development, administration, labour relations, and contract administration constitute a complex area for managerial attention based on specialist advice and staff work. It is the stuff of consultancy and advanced education programs. The issue is recognizing the need for senior specialist administrators who are not necessarily required to have police experience. One regional police department employs civilians in finance, administration, and labour relations and retains accounting firms, among other consultants, as a reservoir of expertise for commercial-crime investigations. As one police executive put it, "they have brought into the force improvements in recruitment, selection and training methods, an independent source of counselling, cost centre and program budgeting concepts, improvement in computer storage and analysis, advice on benefits and compensation and new perspectives in labour relations."[11] This departement is an exception. But the employment, on a lateral-entry basis, of civilian members even at the executive level in these nonpolicing fields is not only feasible but desirable.

Senior officers without direct experience of successive levels of law-enforcement duties will not have, in the eyes of their peers and other officers, the essential brand of a generalist. In this organizational climate, officers will tend to see little value in any qualification beyond the self-confidence that comes of being deemed suitable for "getting there" – signalling that someone, endowed with the right personal attributes has gained the qualification of experience, the two ingredients that are both necessary and generally sufficient in an occupation where the fund of know-how is shared by senior and junior alike. If executive effectiveness depends on effective employment of staff, then police staff who are highly qualified with regard to their duties are, with some exceptions such as criminal investigators, largely unknown in policing. (This includes the RCMP, even though it employs many civilian specialists with impressive qualifications in the "new" technologies.)

Comparison with military practice is illuminating. Historically, the military has incorporated into its ranks, as its own, people of high but disparate qualifications, adding further substantial qualifications early in their short careers and ensuring that senior officers, in addition to their primary qualifications, are sophisticated managers who often have high specialist qualifications themselves. But, as I have said, police tend to lack the mid-managerial level of competence wherein policy advice, evaluation, and planning originate and into which advances in police-specific knowledge might be integrated and exploited. Here, I am referring in part to the knowledge that stems from research conducted primarily in the academic community (the birthplace, one might add, of community policing and neighbourhood foot-patrol programs). This knowledge is not usually familiar to the police generalist.

Senior officers who make decisions bearing on police operations need a rare mixture of knowledge that embraces policing at its leading edge; knowledge of its problems, clients, and environment, and the concepts and skills of management. They must display a capacity for political leadership. Neither effective policing nor effective management alone are up to it. But this combination, challenging as it is to develop, is still but part of what is needed. The terms generalist and specialist are less distinct in an increasingly specialized working world. The specialist, hypothetically, can be said to be the one to whom the greater part of a department's training resources is devoted, and who employs increasingly specialized, hard-won skills in one or another increasingly narrow area of police responsibilities. Community-policing experience suggests that different types of officers, ones with differing orientations and specializations, should be identified and encouraged.

The utility of requiring that officers have years of general police experience before they qualify for advanced assignment to newly emerging duties is questionable. Many duties are becoming so intricate and intimidating that other bases for qualification will be more economical and time effective than the traditional crucible.

In summary, an examination of police characteristics and resources reveals the hobbling effect of the bottom-entry personnel custom, with its inducement to conformity and the clearly secondary role it assigns to qualifications and knowledge gained outside. Police themselves have been slow to recognize the progression of complexity in policing jobs and the need to rearrange personnel practices and internal resources to provide substantial qualifications. Organizationally, the strengths that should be maintained and built on are the zeal and initiative of most line officers, the intrinsic challenges of general duties, and the nonmanaged but cohesive police subculture. To acknowledge such traditional virtues is one thing; to adapt them to changing circumstances is quite another. The mutually reinforcing, familiar rationalizations of a narrowly qualified corps of executives forecloses on the searching examinations that might be possible with people of differing and wider perspectives. Upper-level managers in such organizations are almost certain to be constrained by their own narrow perspectives and those of their peers.[12]

THE SKILLS AND KNOWLEDGE RESOURCES OF POLICING

The following comments on the utility of advanced knowledge and skills are something of a brief digression into the nature of knowledge as part of the ethical basis of a vital public service. A distinguished police executive, in discussing leadership some years ago, said that the first attribute of an effective leader was integrity, and that the foundation of integrity was persistent effort across a career to ensure not only that competence, often a matter of practice, was maintained but that new learning occured, expanding on experience. It is known that one of the important motivators in the workplace is the opportunity for personal growth in meeting challenges of increasing complexity, each more satisfying to master than the last. To this process, new learning is a major contributor. The same police executive pointed to courage as a further attribute of leaders, not the physical courage of the officer on the street, but the courage of persisting in achieving the goals one believes are worthwhile in the service of others. It is also important, and I think urgent from an ethical standpoint, for people who have the capacity to affect the vital interests of others as police officers do to master their duties, including exploiting newly available knowledge resources; others have noted that knowledge derived from day-to-day performance of a vital role is insufficient to allow one to continue to perform that role for an indefinite time.

Mastery comes from effort and logically precedes responsibility; high rank is not a certification of competence. The qualities of police experience are valuable but do not extend to advancing one's knowledge so much as providing the occasion for testing it and learning how it may be applied.[13] Training tends to be consigned to the early stages of a career, while learning is a central human characteristic. It is not surprising that a select panel, well versed in the particulars of Canadian policing, drew attention to a body of knowledge specific to policing and pointed out that learning was a career-long process beginning on the first day of engagement.[14]

Resistance to occupational reform is systemic and historically based. Formal training is a fairly recent practice in Canadian policing. Widespread concern in the postwar era about standards in quickly growing urban departments led to the eventual establishment of seven provincial police commissions (in Alberta, a senior-level provincial office). The first acts of the commissions included the provision of formal training for police recruits, which dates from 1962 with the establishment of the Ontario Police College. The other provincial police academies (or upgraded urban-department training facilities) followed in the 1970s. Similarly, the initiative for the Canadian Police College, which opened in 1976, originated with RCMP concerns about urban-police effectiveness in combating organized crime. The list of specialized demands made by modern urban centres is long and varied: for tactical units, specialized investigative techniques, explosives, barricaded persons, juvenile work, and so on. The sources of training are now varied, but few, if any, involve public educational institutions. Training is brief, oriented to skills or technique; yet with some exceptions, it is effective. While this increased reliance on training and its availability is in itself recent and notable, departmental resources committed to training remain small in comparison with other major institutions and organizations, even bearing in mind that in policing, people must first be hired and then trained. Training, be it for recruits or the more experienced, is usually geared to law enforcement.

It is useful to point out that training-course content often consists of the knowledge and experience of the officer-teacher, little of which is systematically compiled for ready access, expansion, or reference. Police officers are tough students; their patience is strained when the relevance of what they are learning is not apparent. Having experience in their own right, their judgment of the validity of training can surface quickly and often with merit, so they too influence content.

The full range of knowledge and skills available to police, particularly that derived from advanced research, is not incorporated into their development – they are not, either as individuals or as an occupational collective, devoted students of it. This knowledge, for example of cities, and its application is substantive, research-based, and hardly compatible with the training-academy approach.

The viability of an occupation depends in part on recognition of the exclusive nature of its knowledge and skill, hence of its service. In one analysis, Barry Swanton placed each police activity into one of seventeen categories and found that in five English-tradition countries, including Canada, only three activities were found to be exclusive to policing: the maintenance of order, the resolution of conflict, and what he called the provision of police assistance – those services rendered through the authority and twenty-four-hour availability of police. He identified eight "coercive" functions in addition to order maintenance, three of them being apprehension of offenders, prosecution of minor offenders, and regulation of noncriminal conduct (as by security guards in shopping malls). Performance of these three functions is shared with other agencies in all countries. The remaining five – preparation of cases, traffic control, law enforcement, enforcement of traffic laws, and intelligence gathering – are shared with nonpolice agencies in four countries (Britain, the United States, Australia, and New Zealand), but in Canada are performed exclusively by police. Other noncoercive and service functions are shared in differing degrees with other government agencies (at the federal level there are about forty-seven), as well as with private police including those with extensive legislated authority such as railway and harbour police, volunteers, and private security agencies, among others.[15]

Swanton's analysis indicates that the customary knowledge and skills of policing are widely shared and not at all exclusive. The shared functions tend to fall into the law-enforcement area though matters central to serious crime remain police "property." It is significant that the maintenance of order and conflict resolution remain exclusive functions. It would seem, then, that it is there that police will find recognition, legitimacy, and potential in their occupation.

In contrast, however, Swanton suggested that the future of the public police institution depends on a much more narrowly defined law-enforcement function, as well as narrowed responsibility, lowered prestige, and diminished public recognition.[16] Klockars's conclusion is similar, that American police may be best left as is, restricted to familiar enforcement functions in the absence of a capacity to achieve the necessary occupational development. He gave three reasons: the inability of the police to attract and develop people with the talents

required for order-maintenance policing; the fact that order maintenance requires a "professional" administrative structure that is collegial in nature and suited to the job and those who perform it; and the
lack of professional status and the deference and respect that goes with
it, which is essential to order maintenance.[17] Canada, however, has not
been so burdened by the rigidities of law-enforcement ideology and
the legacies of the reform movement. The need to formulate policing
policies will be met, not always effectively, by proxies for police and by
the typical combinations of politicians, lawyers, and public administrators, all of whom function at a distance from emerging research findings and related innovative work. The assignment to private agencies
of only the familiar, less complex functions of keeping watch can be
done fairly easily without extensive political and legal change, except
where the issue of accountability is concerned, but the trend towards
private security has not run its full course. The restriction of policing
to law-enforcement responsibilities will raise the question where the
order-maintenance function, now exclusive to police, is to be assigned;
the consequence may be the creation of another public institution
rather than a revitalized police occupation.

Lest the burden of responsibility fall too heavily on police departments, however, let us recall that most occupations receive considerable
public support to train their people. The programs for prospective
tradespeople, technologists, technicians, paraprofessionals, and professionals constitute long lists in the calendars of community colleges,
institutes of technology, CEGEPs, universities, etc. The military-training
establishment is a huge education/training endeavour. Further, using
professional-school programs as an example (whether nonscientific
as in law or highly technical as in engineering), the money devoted
to scholarships and research comes largely from the public purse.
The repository of that knowledge, its maintenance and dissemina-
tion through technical and university libraries, is based on public
money, and the costs of tuition are paid in the smaller part by the stu-
dent (twenty percent in the case of dentistry). Billions are spent qualifying Canadians for work and for furthering occupational knowledge and skills, and rightly so. Yet policing as an occupation has
neither asked for nor received more than minuscule amounts of this
largesse; it has remained dependent on its own traditional system and
has not sought out other avenues of occupational development.
Clearly, given the quality of police services provided, the country has
received a bargain.

As an occupation with insufficient links to higher education and the
advanced knowledge required to cope with urban problems, policing
exists in a kind of time warp. The knowledge exists, the costs are paid,

the university classrooms are in place, but few, if any, police programs exist and few people attend them. The corporate world of policing and its political superiors do not believe that the innovative skills that are so critically needed are born in the disciplined acquisition of knowledge, a distinguishing mark of a mature occupation. Swanton understood this when he noted that many institutions that deal with matters relevant to police development are not integral to (police) science. These external institutions reflected, in part, the concern of interested parties and some police in the nature of police occupational development and performance.[18]

A 1976 report stated that of the US chiefs of police it surveyed, ninety-five percent thought education to be important, while thirty-five percent of these thought it very important. So virtually all chiefs were in agreement, but among small-force chiefs (fifteen officers or less), forty-five percent felt a high-school diploma was acceptable as opposed to large-force (over one thousand personnel) chiefs of whom half thought an undergraduate degree suitable.[19] Given this ambivalence, it is not surprising that several commissions have bemoaned the relatively low educational achievements of police recruits. It is useful to recall that an advanced education program with substantial police-specific content has, in my view, only recently become feasible. But in prior years many recommendations for advanced-level police education have been proffered. For example, in 1980, an Ontario task force on the racial implications of police-personnel practices expressed the belief that education, rather than regulation and prescription, could provide the best assurance of an officer's competence to exercise discretion and responsibility in diverse tasks.[20] In 1967 the President's Commission on Law Enforcement and the Administration of Justice recommended that all police have baccalaureate degrees. (Subsequently, the Law Enforcement Education Program, or LEEP, was set up to permit the educational upgrading of United States police.)[21] A British Royal Commission on police made similar recommendations in 1962. The Royal Commission stated that even though police play a vital role in society, it was deplorable that "police today are not securing a sufficient share of the better-educated section of the community."[22]

One of the characteristics of the postwar decades has been the so-called knowledge explosion. The development of policing knowledge is recent, substantial, and growing; it is well founded on scientific methods and available in scientific literature and major libraries. As this book indicates, its range is considerable. While education itself is no panacea, police tend to avoid the institutions of education that provide the means to generate knowledge, the occasion to exploit the work of scholars and researchers, and the locus of the reference systems that could constitute an occupational memory.

A constable requires no great fund of knowledge to quell a disturbance, resolve a dispute over noise, or intervene in a family fight. Discretion informed by training and experience suffices. Law enforcement needs the added knowledge, also tempered by experience, of the Criminal Code, the central place of individual rights, and procedural requirements. Nothing in such activities themselves justifies the costs of higher education; we have ample evidence that simple skills-training requirements are effectively addressed in police academies. That possession of a university degree will result in the more effective performance of a constable's traditional street or patrol duties has not been demonstrated.

In general, the debate concerning the goals of education is by no means settled, and for the most part the issues are beyond the scope of this discussion. The substance of policing knowledge is growing, and the arena of its application is increasingly recognized. Conventional wisdom tends to support the notion that both constable and chief constable would benefit from an advanced education. It is often said that a department's make-up should reflect the community; police do not reflect educational levels typically found among educated urban residents. Moreover, a liberal education fosters a more profound recognition of the place of power and service, police and government alike, in Western democracies and thus enhances the understanding and sense of propriety that imbue tolerance and temper the edges of authority. It may be argued that educating the police was a precondition for achieving the broad perspectives needed in the context of policing an urban society. Judge Marin, reflecting the prevailing wisdom, said that if police officers are left with their many difficult tasks of social control and the exercise of broad discretion, sometimes involving life and death, the need for officers who are mature and knowledgeable about social and political conditions is apparent. But this need is unlikely to be realized unless the educational level of candidates is upgraded.[23]

Programs devoted exclusively to occupational skills harm students and occupation alike by producing technicians or technocrats rather than educated professionals. There is no particular accumulation of wisdom over years of police work. The authority of rank and experience will be increasingly challenged in modern society.

The general purpose of an advanced education is the attainment of applied knowledge through which the instruments of urban policing, of which community-policing programs are examples, can be replenished or renewed. Members of the police occupation, it seems to me, must become familiar and comfortable with experimentation in the production of evidence and, thus, knowledge. The purpose of this aspect of education is not to turn officers into researchers so much as provide them with a grasp of how the pieces of policing knowledge are achieved, evaluated, systematized – fitted together – and used.

Police education at the university level is of longer standing in the United States than in Canada, and some of the more recent US programs offer insights, among them the hugely expensive lessons of the the Law Enforcement Education Program. LEEP was established in the wake of the riots and disorders that convulsed US cities and compuses in the late 1960s and early 1970s. Critics said that the police had overreacted, aggravating situations they were supposed to defuse. The liberalizing effects of advanced education, it was expected, would remedy the problem. "Police-science" programs flowered in the hundreds at community colleges and universities. But by 1973 funds were restricted to programs directly related to the narrow focus of law enforcement within an approved curriculum. Between 1969 and the late 1970s, about $265 million was provided by the federal government for police-science education. But the program was a failure and funding collapsed. It is impossible to evaluate according to its vague goals (for example, reduction in crime), but among several analyses that were made, one of the most searching was that of Lawrence Sherman.[24]

First, the programs tended to be narrowly based on so-called police-science material and were thus training-oriented; that is, they emphasized skills, rules, and procedures at the expense of substance and the rigorous processes of learning. Second, the establishment of separate programs segregated students from the wider academic milieu, thus minimizing the broadening effects of the experience. Administrators favoured, at least implicitly, the education of serving police officers so that the effort tended to be piecemeal and part time in nature. The challenges of the discipline of learning – grasping and understanding principles and developing critical faculties – were missed through part-time, short-term participation in acquiring insubstantial matter. Commentators would point out that the broader aim of higher education should have been the primary purpose.

Two of these points merit elaboration: first, that the programs were narrowly based. The major qualification of course teachers was police experience, not scholarship. This was nothing new; O.W. Wilson, in establishing the first police program before the Second World War, emphasized the practicality of technique rather than the theoretical approach typical of other professional-school programs. He valued experience over academic attainment in his faculty and his programs were challenged, as a result, for their lack of substance.[25] Reliance on experience in the tutelage of apprentices permeated not only the law-enforcement programs of colleges and universities in the United States but also the law-enforcement and security programs of community colleges in Canada.[26] One result is that police tend to have a weak grasp of relevant knowledge found in wider academic and scientific circles and show few signs of using it. Little is done, corporately, to participate in or contribute to the production of that knowledge. It is significant that in Canada, most of the institutions producing knowledge relevant to policing are external to policing and reflect the interests largely of social scientists and political and legal scholars. Goldstein argued for a police educational institution sufficiently independent of police administration.[27]

Finally, education proceeds according to a somewhat basic scheme. As rational beings, people have a basic trio of abilities: to acquire knowledge, to retain it, and to manipulate it. These are, as Patrick O'Flaherty observed, the building blocks of intelligence: "The mind is not a bucket that can hold only a fixed quantity. It is like a muscle that is strengthened and expanded by the kind of exercise that reading implies."[28] Similarly, a select panel assembled in 1979 to advise the Canadian Police College on senior-officer courses noted that, while there is a body of knowledge unique to policing and shared among all ranks, it is less a quantum of information than a process of testing and evaluating it, of clarifying basic premises and incorporating new insights. The panel commended "cognitive, intellectual skills that enable one to identify problems, define those problems accurately, and generate alternative solutions all within the context of the basic function of the organization."[29]

So learning is a continuous, disciplined process that extends beyond graduation day. Its value is evident in the success of new police programs which require independent, innovative thinkers, while many of the traditional qualities of a patrol officer totter into obsolescence.

THE MYTHS AND REALITY OF MANAGERIAL PROFESSIONALISM

On becoming the commissioner or civilian chief, of the New York Police Department in 1895, Theodore Roosevelt, an early reformer, viewed as his main task the rooting out of police corruption.[30] One hundred years later, the issue is still relevant. But corruption aside, Canadian police share particular characteristics with their United States and British counterparts. It is relevant to consider how these characteristics came to be.

A useful starting point is the evolution of the US police occupation. We have seen that policing matured during periods of industrialization and extensive urbanization under the sway of local politics, then later of civic reformers and emergent professional municipal managers. Importantly, ineffectiveness in the face of rising crime rates, violence, and the riots of recent decades did much to change the direction of police thinking. At an earlier time, the police had been decentralized and politicized. Influential civic authorities and practices, some corrupt, were informal and local. Policing began as casual labour whose management was nonélitist and vulnerable. The city-management reform movement, paced by urbanization and its attendant pressures, influenced the nature and goals of police reorganization. Policing became bureaucratized, converted into a closed, hierarchical structure given direction and uniformity by regulations, procedures, records-keeping activities, and tight internal disciplinary practices, all presumably objective and all contributing to an upsurge in police unionism.[31]

The depoliticization occasioned by the reform movement narrowed the scope and orientation of policing towards apolitical law enforcement. This exaggerated emphasis, and the insulation from wider community concerns and narrowed accountability that followed, were the conditions under which the ethos of the "thin blue line" was forged, becoming hardy and tenacious in its hold on members. George Kelling said that the war on crime or the war on drugs demand an all-out attack on criminals – no quarter given – but in fighting an unwinnable war, police assume wide responsibilities that belong more properly to politicians. The path Canadian policing has taken differs, occupational characteristics are less sharply set. But for all that, they are enforcement-oriented and shelter behind similar apolitical formula and government structures.

It has been seen that the characteristics of urban police are unquestionably confining and may well drain any potential for improvement. The condition is, as Klockars said, an accident of history, perhaps an unfortunate accident but also one of consequence. It thus merits further comment.

Policing has not produced another leader and innovator of the stature of O.W. Wilson. He had a distinguished career within the academic and police communities, culminating in his appointment, aged sixty, as superintendent (chief) of the Chicage police. His 1949 textbook on municipal police administration, for example, had run to a third edition by 1974, having sold over 200,000 copies in five languages.[32] That his legacy remains dominant is evident in the publication of a fourth edition in 1977, five years after Wilson's death.

Born in 1900, he became a police officer at twenty-one, then a chief in a small town. He was asked to resign within a year for being radical, and at twenty-nine he became chief in Witchita, Kansas, where he stayed for eleven years. There too his capacity for innovation was evident; in 1936, for example, he set up the first cadet education and training programs. Wilson was the father of the Law Enforcement Code of Ethics; he inaugurated the first systematic approach to combating juvenile delinquency; he hired the first woman police captain; he set minimum standards for police officers and initiated psychological testing for selecting and promoting them; he invented the idea of roll-call training and pioneered state-sponsored training courses.[33]

In 1939, he became the first full-time professor of police administration, this at the University of California, where he remained for twenty-one years, moulding a degree program into the School of Criminology, of which he became dean. The program was oriented to administration and by about 1947, it featured core criminal-justice-system subjects as well as those relevant to the career path (such as corrections and "criminalistics") and status such as department administration and law enforcement. It was pioneering work, for at the time, the relationship of education to policing was uncertain. Yet Wilson's practical orientation was challenged by senior university officers, who thought that is lacked the academic substance professional programs required, that is was too vocational. Some of the courses, patrol deployment among them, were indeed shallow. Wilson had decided that criminal law, identification, police-patrol practices such as deployment, criminal investigation, evidence, traffic control, and police administration were appropriate for university study and made them part of his police-science program. He emphasized the practical over the theoretical in his professional-school model and the value of experience over academic attainment for the faculty.

Among Wilson's attributes were a loyalty to law enforcement as a whole and not to a particular department; a belief in the development of people through movement among departments; a strong penchant for orderliness, which alienated otherwise competent officers; organizational development along military lines with narrow spans of control, a rigid chain of command, specialization, interchangeability, close supervision, and an iron fist. At least the first three remain as principles in some departments, including the RCMP. Wilson was also a pioneer in adapting modern business records to police work, including computerization, record keeping and communications systems. Through this, policing shifted a degree from craft to bureaucracy.

Wilson did recognize that the qualifications of leadership – those needed for promotion – went beyond competence in the job, but much of his work was aimed at rooting out corruption and promoting managerial competence so as to insulate departments from partisan politics. He had, however, a narrow view of subordinates; he tended to distrust line officers and granted them little leeway. This influenced the development of his widely accepted managerial and supervisory systems. As Bopp noted, it was ironic that Wilson, who contributed so much to policing, would be the one who ultimately hindered its success with of his cynical view of "the human condition" and his zeal for orderliness.[34] Wilson's notion of professionalism derived from the reform mainstream of municipal governments, whose outline could be seen by the 1930s in a police bureaucracy that was under centralized, hierarchical control, and in its regulations and record keeping, characteristics that coexisted with a tightly knit, inward-looking police subculture.

The policing strategy Wilson pioneered was that of preventive patrol, which proved, as already noted, well suited to the suburbs where a more traditional presence would be expensive and ineffective over the greater distances of sprawl. The strategy also had the benefit, it seemed to Wilson, of insulating line officers from the corrupting temptations involved in close contact with citizens. Out of a history of police venality, patrols as we know them were devised as the primary means by which line officers were controlled. Wilson and the chiefs of the day, including J. Edgar Hoover, successfully promoted the war-on-crime analogy, the notion of public enemies, and remnants of their legacy remain.

With the greater part of police work reduced to the routine of response, and with little delegation of responsibility or recognition of discretion, Wilson located professionalization in the managerial competence of the more senior in rank. In addition, such competence supported the war-on-crime posture, that is, the effectiveness of senior police professionals, providing they are unencumbered by political intervention.[35] The consequence has been an exaggeration of efficiency; good management as an end in itself regardless of the ends of policing.[36]

Wilson set the stage for the postwar decades. While Canadian urban police were successful in meeting burgeoning postwar demands for service, they were staffed by officers who were relatively untrained or inexperienced in the management of large organizations at a time when modern managerial competence was deemed necessary in other growing civic departments. Those decades saw the rise of professional administrators and the growing prestige of the newly established university schools of public administration and business. Educated managerial competence became the common mark of executive respectability and, therefore, the talisman of senior police officers. The qualifications they sought, however, were not those of serious education.

By way of illustration, the two Canadian Police College flagship courses for mid- and senior-level officers, each lasting only five to seven weeks, were devoted exclusively to the techniques of management. Neither material related to the functions of policing in modern society nor research on the effectiveness of police programs was requested by police executives, the RCMP, or the college's advisory body. The managerial qualifications among police are thin compared to those acquired through the years in business or public-administration programs demanded by other occupations.[37]

Wilson downgraded, if not eliminated, matters of trust. Rules and supervision diminished discretion and placed emphasis on conformity rather than guidance, on regulations rather than coordination and support. Others have noted that police bureaucratization hampered professionalism by limiting the autonomy of the line officer.[38] This bureaucratic-professional characteristic is an important one, for in a closed structure under tight supervision, any occupational development springing from pools of less-fettered talent is crudely stalled, with the result that police unionism and other outlets for frustration are encouraged.

Perhaps Wilson's most important legacy is that the deterrent-patrol program is now known to be ineffective in controlling or suppressing crime. As one writer noted, a consequence of patrol research was the frequent managerial response of tightened control to improve the unimproveable. In neither law enforcement nor order maintenance does it contribute at levels commensurate with the resources committed to it. Beyond this, the deterrent-patrol function fostered, even entrenched, the law-enforcement orientation in policing and, I submit, in the public mind.

O.W. Wilson was not alone in his thinking, August Vollmer, an earlier policing pioneer who was active primarily the 1920s and 1930s, held the view that

centralized, scientific and consolidated policing was linked logically with a close concern for monitoring crime and crime control ... he strongly advocate[d] the role of the police as non-specialist crime fighters, combining apprehension and crime prevention undertaken in conjunction with local community agencies with centralized communication and record keeping ... The criminal, in his eyes, was a cunning, mobile enemy who had to be pursued

using modern sciences of all kinds and the latest technologies such as the radio, the automobile, and modern record keeping. These developments are
clearly linked to the differentiation and dispersion of modern populations
across wide city areas ... and the availability of property.[39]

Kelling claimed that the reform movement under August Vollmer
and O.W. Wilson shaped police in particular ways:

They changed the source of police legitimacy, police tactics, and technology,
police management, and the standards by which police were judged. Legitimacy derived from local political leaders and close ties to neighborhoods was
rejected in favor of law, especially criminal law, and police professionalism.
Foot patrol was replaced by preventive patrol in automobiles and rapid response to calls for service. Determination of beat structure on the basis of
neighborhoods was replaced by mathematical formulas developed on the basis
of calls for service and reported crime. Police administration moved from decentralized police units closely linked to neighborhoods and local political
units to centralized patterns incorporating "scientific" management characteristics of the Progressive era: improved recruiting, supervision, training, management, record keeping, and methods of accountability.[40]

O.W. Wilson blazed a particular and eventually well-trodden path in
the search for legitimacy and support. In general, the key managerial
proficiency exercised through a bureaucratic system, in Moore and
Kelling's eyes, could be sustained only if the scope of police responsibility was narrowed to "crime fighting."[41] For example, reliance on
routinized bureaucratic flows of information by those monitoring the
activities of line officers and regulating (that is, diminishing) the scope
of discretion is feasible only under the more procedure-bound practices of law enforcement. The everyday effect has been to harden attitudes within policing and shape practices accordingly. In Britain, the
Unit Beat System of patrol (the assignment of constables to home areas or beats for closer police-public relations, but with Panda-car back-
up) was intended to be ground breaking in bolstering relations with
the public and improving the officer's lot. It did, for a time, transform
the police organization of the 1960s but mainly by emphasizing technology and managerial professionalism. The constables' action-cen-
tred perspective, "accentuated by the technology of fast cars, sirens
and flashing blue lights" of cars on call, in time defeated its good intentions and the fire-brigade style of reaction, still common today, persisted.[42]

Wilson's initiatives, which in part aimed at controlling the conduct
of line officers, can be said to have failed in this regard: they were

based on distrust and on an inability to recognize that discretion cannot be regulated out of existence. The issue remains.

Intelligent and hard-working officers fill the ranks of Canadian policing, and the more competent are generally identified and promoted. There are different definitions of competence, and the different talents underlying that competence merit development. That they are not always developed is tied to the state of human resources in policing during its more recent history and their failure to maintain the internal currents of occupational transformation.

In the stable, low-growth years beginning in the early 1980s, promotion opportunities available to constables became even more limited. Now, the race is for the few; it favours those with experience in law enforcement and not necessarily those with the "talent, ability, imagination, and leadership that police administration requires"[43] in different areas of responsibility. O.W. Wilson argued, without effect, that the qualifications of leadership are not necessarily those of job competence.[44] The preferred view, it seems to me, is for a leader with general attributes, including integrity, honesty, judgment, and common sense, as well as demonstrated administrative skills. This emphatic narrowing of attributes to the obvious, with its emphasis on administrative over policing knowledge and skills, has been a persistent pattern; for example, the list of qualities recommended for inclusion in performance evaluation by a 1989 Canadian Police College report did not reflect advanced knowledge of policing, the one knowledge requirement being that of the job held.[45] The model for redevelopment of the Senior Police Administration Course at the same college made no reference to leading-edge thinking and research, including that of community policing.[46]

Herman Goldstein observed that police managers, in identifying people for promotion, look for attributes cultivated in the performance of enforcement-oriented tasks and demonstrated administrative or supervisory ability.[47] The emphasis is on a candidate's suitability for the target job, while suitability for longer-term development, a common consideration in other organizations, is generally overlooked. The limited nature of the search is perhaps understandable, given that the police must focus on rising crime rates. Suitability for promotion to the available position suffices. No distinction is made between administrative and leadership skills, and there is little concern for wider-ranging abilities. In contrast, a Canadian study recommended a management continuum, sketchily realized at best, characterized by involvement of the lower ranks, such as staff sergeant, in "engineering" decisions – scheduling and related short-term deployment of people, overseeing operational practices, and ensuring adequate responses to events. The middle-level manager focuses on economic matters – the effectiveness and costs of policies, operational and personnel, among others – while the more senior addresses the political matter of developing suitable strategies that are acceptable to the department's various constituents.[48] As stated earlier, "in-at-the-bottom" entry practices and the priority given to gaining law-enforcement experience leave little or no time in a career for substantial post-entry qualifications; inadequate organizational incentives are offered and peers are not supportive of those who wish to attain higher qualification. Put another way, policing as an occupation does not seem to recognize the need for people with attributes other than the management/law-enforcement qualifications. Goldstein suggested that, in the United States, the singularly competent people are accidents of the system who suffer in this milieu and tend to seek early retirement.[49]

The near-exclusive focus on demonstrated administrative expertise persists regardless of the challenges urban police face. In one major Canadian city, the board of commissioners employed a consulting firm to assess applicants for the position of chief. Consultants no doubt know about managerial ability and the nature of public administration, but they know nothing about the issues facing urban police, including personnel deficiencies, or about emerging trends such as community policing.

It is an occupational characteristic that in the development of its people, police departments offer little or no opportunity for broadening experiences suited to the ambitious, in lateral moves into other organizations, or even among departments. In British policing, candidates for the position of chief constable must have served in another department in either of the two next-lower ranks. Earlier in their careers they will have spent at least a year at the police staff college at Bramshill. In Canada the lack of interdepartmental movement is usually explained by the nonportability of pension rights. This is not an insurmountable problem; it has been overcome in other areas. But to my knowledge, the police have made no attempt to do so.

Line officers, a closed group, are adept at ensuring that little of their activity – discretionary activity – comes under the scrutiny of rule makers. The administrative/bureaucratic mode, in this context, tends to translate effective performance of duties into adherence to rules, including an emphasis on well-executed record keeping.[50] Requiring procedural compliance lessens the need to trust others in the performance of their duties and to be trusted by them. Against this background, the "discovery" by both the research and police communities that operations officers exercised substantial discretion was a fairly recent event. Wilson emphasized law enforcement, which is more amenable to rules, while order maintenance, being relentlessly variable, demands the use of discretion. While guidelines – for example, a departmentwide approach to family disputes – may be appropriate, close regulation does limit and drive the exercise of discretion from ready supervisory observation. The Wilson tradition is reflected by one Canadian police writer, who stated that firm administrative control is needed for several reasons, one of which, perhaps innocent in itself, was that "discretion ... exercised by an individual policeman without the scrutiny of someone with higher authority" leads to "uneven enforcement of the law and possibly even to corruption."[51]

These tight patterns of personnel supervision and administration, with their command/disciplinary orientation, push a craft into the arms of a bureaucracy; they will be resisted by line officers, who will perceive them as a failure of confidence in them and a withdrawal of support. The stress on record keeping, rules, procedures, and appearance is among the roots of the inherent distrust by line officers of police management.[52] According to a comprehensive Canadian Study, line officers believe that adherence to the administrative proprieties – paperwork, appearance, adherence to protocol in the presence of superiors – facilitates promotion more than effective performance of duties. Many patrol officers can serve effectively within this model, but most react to it, and the effect is stifling and narrowing in its perpetuation of the *status quo*.[53] Conformity, accepted and visible, is perhaps the safer stance in a hierarchical, chastening occupation; the in-at-the-bottom legacy intrudes once again. Yet in evaluating a set of policing experiments, project leaders found unexpectedly that successful programs relied on the autonomy, initiative, innovation, and responsibility of individual officers in developing and implementing programs that best responded to needs identified by citizens. These programs include the various neighbourhood foot-patrol projects and the Newark and Houston fear-reduction studies discussed in the previous chapter.

ORGANIZATIONAL COMPETENCE

Policing is civilian work carried out in a civilian environment by a quasi-military organization. Centrally organized and directed units under "HQ" and a clear rank-based chain of command are its more obvious traits. The command view of law enforcement sees policing as "a response to universal law-breaking elements of a monolithic society, rather than as a situational and moral activity at least sometimes involving clashes between different, but possibly all legitimate value systems.

The police officer with a strong sense of 'what is right' has an equally strong sense of 'what is wrong' that is appropriate in clear-cut cases of criminal activity," but inappropriate in cases where value and attitude systems clash as in the case of racial-minority disturbances and crime.[54] "Inappropriate" actions are often seen as an abuse of authority. The command posture, then, fosters a dependency on the generalist concept in what may be an attempt to mask differences and conflicts among policing roles; the sense that dependency on generalists promotes sensitivity to and understanding of another's tasks is valid. It is the tribal approach to easing internal conflicts and creating a sense of common purpose and cooperation, if not coordination. So it seems to me that this uniformity of resources and their organization into a command system that characterized even the first police department was a better means of deciding who got what part of the work and then dividing it to get it done. The chain of command was thereby facilitated and remained intact. And the direction of operations was routinized.

The type of information processing favoured by a law-enforcement/command orientation involves whatever is high profile about criminals, crime, crime rates, and citizen complaints. It does not typically use the varied but valid sources of information that an intimate familiarity of neighbourhoods provides under order-maintenance functions. It can thus be said that while police perform the most local of all functions, parallel needs for information go unrecognized. Within the patrol division, the allocation of limited resources according to some problem of disorder will obviously affect performance capabilities in other parts of a department, so that information about probable effectiveness is of considerable utility. But such allocations tend to be granted in reaction to a matured problem, often in the wake of public/political agitation. Research that might help both to anticipate problems and affect their outcome has rarely been a priority.

One major area of organizational competence centres on the management of a patrol officer's behaviour, and in this respect, much turns on guiding the exercise of discretion. As James Q. Wilson asked, how can on fulfil the demand for guidelines that leave little discretion to the officer and direct acts of discretion along desirable lines, while avoiding collision between the ambiguity of an officer's responsibilities and the law?[55]

The enforcement emphasis on procedure has been noted, as have "observables," propriety of appearance, paperwork, and so on. These seem to have become proxies for, or evidence of, competent work in ambiguous situations where supervision is hampered, ineffectual, or avoided. Other signs that appropriate work is being done – for example, a satisfied citizen (complainant or victim), an absence of public complaints, and the issuing of suitable numbers of traffic tickets – can also be seen as proxies for a more substantial proof of competence.

This aspect of the use of procedure is easily exaggerated. The chain of command is a downward channel of directives and dispatches; not surprisingly, where managing discretion relies on disciplinary methods for their observance, culpability is invoked, culpability that need not be shared by supervisors. The amorphous nature of order maintenance defies the effective use of rules and infractions, but it still shapes accountability, the onus for which is rarely found at even the first and second levels of supervision. Careful consideration becomes impossible for the constable, who must move from one tangled incident to another. The ability to exercise discretion thus wisely is developed over time, and they will develop most successfully under supervision. This important mechanism is available for the guidance, coaching, or practical schooling of constables, but it is simply not used, as an excellent Canadian study attests.[56] This is a significant weakness in policing, which brings me to the question of reactive administration.

A police executive is quoted as saying: "The original concept of policing was to prevent crime and protect the people. Before the Second World War this was done using the watch system, often involving only one man patrolling the area. However since then, there have been rapid technological advances which rapidly improved the levels of prevention and protection. Policing got better, and police were asked by the public to do more. The police accepted these requests, until we are now in a situation where policing is very expensive, citizens are complaining about high taxes, which leads to financial cutbacks, and citizens are still demanding the same services. It is much of a circular process."[57]

The computer is a case in point; it is a threat. It promotes routine, is amenable to procedure, facilitates some aspects of oversight and quantification of work, and perhaps erodes operational-level initiative. The computer is to the police function what radio, telephones, and cars were forty years ago in the development of the patrol philosophy.

There has been much in the police literature about the "reactive" nature of police management and about the need for usually ill-defined "proactive" programs. The two terms, originating in the management sciences, entered police literature and enjoyed a brief turn at centre stage a decade or so ago. The diagnosis of typical departmental management as reactive in terms of management principles was not far off the mark but the recommended resolutions, more exhortative

than practical, were ignored. One example will suffice. It was commonly urged that goals, defined as measurable and achievable, be set
as a means of achieving efficiency, if not of managing future events as
they came about: a proactive orientation. For a complex political/pub-
lic institution, this attempt to squeeze an amalgam of political and social goals into a simple grid of what is measurable or readily countable
is hardly satisfactory. Much of what policing is all about has been disre-
garded; the maintenance of order, with its unqualifiable outcomes has
been equally neglected.[58] Response time, for example, is a questionable measure of effectiveness but it remains popular, since it caters to a
generalized public fear. To their credit, police executives did not adopt
much of what was then being advocated.

Victor MacDonald, in suggesting a somewhat similar approach to
management, pointed to the different characteristics of three models
of operation: reactive, proactive, and intermediate. With the reactive,
the central organizational purpose involves acceptance of some form
of the traditional, institutionalized role of upholding the law and de-
tecting criminals. The intermediate, in contrast, has a more diverse
purpose that embraces differing sources of citizen demand and situations differing in urgency.[59] The reactive organization generally defines its objectives in terms of the activities performed – for example,
reducing response time or monitoring the numbers on patrol at set
times and places – all in the context of a highly structured and proce-
dure-based setting; in other words, ends are replaced by means.[60] Others have indicated similar differences under the labels of command
and management. Police executives who identify with the activities of
their line personnel will then attempt to oversee the details of their
performance and will thus reflect a command, rather than management, approach. The command tendency precludes examination of
what functions or reconfigurations of personnel will place members in
more advantageous or effective positions. It dilutes an appreciation of
the crucial role of developing choices among departmental features,
i.e., of cultivating organizational flexibility, in achieving goals. But
choices are rarely easy and the past is no guide in the absence of relevant experiences or knowledge.

As a visible sign of competence, efficiency, the dominant public-service virtue (fostered by a reactive police administration), wards off intervention particularly from municipal officials who, when setting tax
rates, are vote sensitive. O.W. Wilson's influence and the doctrines he
advocated are understandable in view of the severe pressures in the us
for municipal reform, as is his emphasis on the functional aspects of
policing – the patrol program and managerial modernization – for the
freedom they brought from political meddling. His general focus on

administrative efficiency was rational and appealing, offering as it did a haven strengthened by renewed public support for apolitical law enforcement. He was not alone in the direction he advocated, though he, more than others, epitomized it. The patrol strategy he devised was also rational, given the suburban nature of growing cities, but it was reactive to events. Being call-driven, demands for patrol service were, and to some extent still are, beyond administrative control. The placid days of prewar, semirural Canada did not stimulate debate about the adequacy of justice-system programs, nor did the pinched days of the Depression. So with postwar growth, police had in preventive patrol a program that was readily standardized and therefore amenable to central supervision and expandable in uniform increments – in all, a manageable and suitable design for growth. When a standardized service is performing well, there is no pressing reason in the public mind why it should be done any differently. The other half of the Wilson design – the exaggerated place of law-enforcement functions – constitutes an equally prominent legacy, though perhaps hangover is the apt term. But newer problems and orientations have surfaced.

Reactive administration also stifles leadership, which is difficult to define even in a specific context. Here it means, in Philip Selznick's general terms, a blend of commitment, understanding, and determination that requires, among other things, a clarity of direction and goals (a virtue of leadership, for it prevents the institution from drifting) and the professional realization of the utility of knowledge and skills.[61] This is a challenge for the future since, as Goldstein implies, it is nearly impossible to build a proactive approach on the current structure and programs. (In the past the call was for a proactive "style," the catchword of the day, rather than more fundamental reform.)

The seductive nature of reactive administration eases both policy and operational decisions: the characteristics of a department's resources and how they are organized or mobilized; the system of controlling those resources including utility in the assignment of tasks; the immediate utility of decisions; and the feasibility of implementing a program. Is a goal well defined and practical so that, if selected, attaining the desired outcome is probable – will, for example, a programmed use of radar with an increased rate of ticketing reduce the rate of speed-related accidents? Can the program be implemented with available personnel resources within an existing or modified organizational framework, and within the context of public attitudes? Usually, the entrenched mobilization of resources in a patrol division of high mobility under central control, but with weak supervision, will effectively influence how the department defines a community problem (usually as one of law enforcement), and how it may be resolved. For an internal problem, a "command" approach might emphasize the reaction of discipline and regulation.

So, at any one time, a tactic becomes a commonsense matter of defining a problem to fit familiar resources and systems of control and not necessarily the exigencies of the problem itself. Obviously, any tactical benefits are diminished. For example, the appeal of crime-prevention programs was tempered by an approach constrained by the nature of the organization; such programs become the bureaucratic add-ons usually of the administration rather than the operational elements of a department. The police-administration climate sketched thus far also has what others have called a penchant for "low risk technological fixes," many economical and productive; of the pioneering examples of this phenomenon, the centralized Canadian Police Information Centre is one example.[62]

Albert Reiss put the case in different terms: "Police departments are organized primarily to react to inputs from their environment rather than to generate them by their own mobilization strategies. Nowhere is this reactive stance more apparent than in the preoccupation of police practitioners with the 'in basket' or 'daily input' and a concentration on the day-to-day responsibilities. Police administrators are crises managers and invariably they give priority to the more minor crises of today rather than the anticipated ones of tomorrow".[63]

Consider the twenty-year history of experiments in team and zone policing – the assignment of "teams" of officers from the patrol division to specific districts, each team charged with achieving detailed knowledge of the area and its security problems, for example by examining patterns of crime by type, area, and time, and by liaising with citizens in an attempt to anticipate local problems and target policing activities accordingly. All but the most minor investigations as well as investigations-support functions and the central despatch of patrols remain centralized. The program, then, of zone-assigned patrol personnel adapts the existing organization by spreading it out without changing it or its traditional programs of crime-oriented police services. The program also retains traditional practices, such as the mobilization of resources around centralized despatch suited to less-troubled suburban districts. This type of policing experiment was costly and, with its limited success, did not merit extension. Durable programs, I suggest, were to be found in departments with more competent, or perhaps venturesome, managers and people who were more comfortable with change and innovation and thus better able to work out and smooth over the tenacious problems of fit, organizational and goal faultlines, and flaws inherent in a project. (This is not a critique of the "ministation" projects set up under the more novel, reoriented approaches to community policing.)

The problems with zone policing stemmed from the attempt to commit basically the same resources to both local and central levels within the confines of a traditional operating system. Zone policing can be said to be an educational, if flawed, precursor to the more innovative notions of community policing. It also illustrates the diminishing effectiveness in meeting current needs of the typical, rigid organizational structures that served so well in the past.

As I have mentioned, a police executive will understandably tend to shape initiatives or the response to a major issue around the way resources are organized and controlled. As with zone policing, this is often to flirt with failure in the long run. The feasibility of a proposed innovation or experiment will tend to be assessed, internally, in the context of departmental structure, with its uniform set of attitudes and beliefs and its system of control that tend to resist variation. Control systems, for example, that retain central authority or a detailed command orientation will be challenged by the delegation of responsibilities to local levels and the greater use of discretion this implies. Adding constables (or at least putting more on the beat) entails a reorganization, a change in the approach to specialization, and the capacity to be innovative. "If organizational purposes and goals are not subject to review by people with a variety of perspectives, narrow and probably self-centred rationalizations may influence internal decisions, e.g., roles and personnel systems which stress the satisfaction of people within the organization at the expense of organizational effectiveness. While such decisions may be based on what appears best for the organization or the incumbents, a broader social and/or client or customer perspective may be missing."[64]

In policing, goals are set in a reactive planning mode, which amounts to a look into the near future so as to estimate the levels of resources needed to cope with an anticipated change in the level of customary demand. In a proactive mode, the plan aims at changing the future, for example, to manage the level of demand for service or shape the nature of demand; this tends also to change, incrementally, the basic nature of police capacities. The more vital aspect of planning, both in private and public endeavours, goes beyond these well-trodden areas to look at what transformation may be called for in the organization itself. Reiss put it that police planners are inclined to look to the future for what it tells them about their proactive and reactive capabilities, "rather than in terms of what those capabilities might become."[65] Political endeavours have a diffuse set of purposes such that it is difficult to assess effectiveness; policing is not so easy to define. As a result there is little interest in planning or in the development of planning practices. The utility of taking a close look at the policing environment to determine what may be instructive in planning organizational change does not seem to have registered. Among the changes indicated by community policing, as Reiss noted, is the creation of new roles for community-service and police-service personnel and a significant role for civilians rather than sworn officials.

A probe into what longer-term strategic planning involves gives an idea of what the future direction of police management might look like. It includes identification of distinctive new goals, such as giving the police a role in promoting social change and addressing the reality of it rather than just reacting to it. A sense of the utility of knowledge and ex perimentation as a function of successful change also derives from planning for social change. Similarly, the capacity to experiment and use results may, in considering the long-term planning process, provide a context in which the characteristics of the occupation can be probed.[66]

There are two categories of organization: the first contains reactive organizations that can adapt to changes in demand only through a built-in capacity surplus to current needs that relies less on forecasting and planning as on an ability to adjust by increments as the need arises. Priorities may be set in stone, in part because of the not-unreasonable assumption that the ends of criminal justice should be, and are, relatively stable.

The other type of organization is one for which the future is for less certain and for which adaptations are not an appropriate response, the environment of the organization being an unstable one. This type of organization is designed to cope with changing conditions. It has the ability to sense change early; it experiments to determine possible responses; it has the capacity to modify both its internal structure and the nature of its resources; and it recognizes that goals need ongoing assessment. Such an organization is oriented to its environment, to demand management, while the first is oriented to supply management of relatively unchanged services. Police organizations seem unprepared to shape the kind of supply they can offer or to determine how to organize themselves to cope with change.[67]

In terms of demand management, the pertinent role of police, indeed the central issue, is to anticipate, respond to, and shape social change, which is ubiquitous and accelerating. In other words, police may either perpetuate the *status quo* or serve as agents of social change in communities. In catering to the *status quo*, i.e., serving the interests of government and of dominant sectors of the public that support its policies, the police tend to be "lightning rods" attracting hostility away from government. In this way, Reiss has suggested, demands for reform of government implies demands for reform of the police. In urban Canada, this tendancy is evident in problems arising out of pluralism and various other social characteristics.

In turbulent communities, there is a dilemma of order policing whereby attempts to change situations, to remedy grievances, and to bring about new conditions may conflict with the business of sustaining the *status quo*. Conventionally, the police are not a revolutionary agents of change but protectors of state or central interests, however defined. The police are bureaucratized to ensure their political neutrality and a so-called universal application of the law. Reiss indicated that it is important to recall that the *status quo* itself does change, and it is equally important to acknowledge that police uphold the changed interests of a reset *status quo*. "The police ordinarily are given little part in changing the *status quo*, since they are responsible for enforcing it. Yet they are called upon to enforce changes that some elements of a local population support, while others do not. Therein must lie their political neutrality."[68] It seems, given the logic of Reiss's argument, that neutrality and support for the *status quo* are the two sides of the political coin, for police executives traditionally expect, and are expected, to react to social change rather than anticipate it. In this way the roles of police may be limited in a democracy since the thrust of police management has been to insulate the occupation from politics and the exercise of political influence. Reiss pointed out that police advise on the capacities and means of policing in the development of legislation, but not on the more political question of ends.

Reiss has pointed out that models of social change are in any event too general, while the rate and complexity of change defies any explanation of reality that is scaled to locality. Large-scale changes cannot be used to explain reality, which will be more changeable and turbulent. Forecasts both of broader social change and of local changes are important, but the two cannot necessarily be related one to the other. Variability across a large urban centre, for example, is considerable. The analogy to weather forecasting is apt; broad weather patterns may be predicted but the need to assimilate large amounts of evolving and often incomplete data invariably leave them open to change. Broad patterns do not often apply locally. It is the local community that places demands on policing. Even when some forecasting is possible, the planning that follows is reactive, applying some modification of what has traditionally been done, or adding on a project or office of minor scale; Reiss called this reification of the *status quo*.

Under these conditions, the future may be addressed in one of two ways: first, one can attempt to ensure that forecasts come about – if only by letting them happen, determining whether they did come about, and being able to explain why they did not; or, second, one can envisage the future environment and the organizational response by which it may be changed, and attempt to bring the desired change about (obviously, within the limits of reality). The latter means making the organization malleable to change; how to build the future is the rub. One or more forecasts, difficult to make and uncertain as they are, will be of less help than the knowledge of how things change and where they are going – something less than an explicit forecast, less than an explicit theory, and more a working out by increments. Reiss describes the police as agents of social change; he says that to bring about social change in this way requires knowledge that is largely unavailable.

Planning has to do with deciding what an organization is to become and what it is to do, then implementing the changes needed to achieve these ends. There are important constraints; some factors may be beyond change, such as the law-and-order attitudes of the public, certain legal aspects of police work, and political contingencies. More relevant in the United States, and still applicable here, is that decisions affecting the demand for policing are made externally in the community (the 911 system is an example), and police are dependent on the level of that demand for their resources. So the supply-and-demand problems faced by the police are largely political. Reiss suggested that even when departments know that changes in the community affect workload demands, police priorities in the handling of various community problems are not often addressed when mayor and council hold sway over resources; the police, and city councils, rarely address police priorities in the context of other concerns such as zoning. So planning even in terms of increments to workloads and resources is often not undertaken in the United States.

Police tend to pursue the traditional mission rather than explore the possibilities of a mission transformed to meet a transformed future. They are unlikely to turn to strategies that involve research and development in areas that have nothing to do with hardware. Yet in Goldstein's view, R&D could well become a core function.[69] At the least, it is as critical to the future of policing as it is to industrial and commercial enterprises. "Were police organizations to accept a research mandate seriously, they must both anticipate (i.e., forecast to some extent) the future and plan for its change, particularly by setting forth new goals based on research. That is the core meaning of research within organizations."[70]

As a closed society, policing tends to employ internal, researchers who are indifferent to external standards of accomplishment; those with adequate credentials are not attracted. It is generally thought to be safer to assemble a research unit from police officers with some bent for the work rather than risk exposing the workings of the department. Research is perceived more as a gathering of information than as the conducting of controlled tests to gain knowledge. Police researchers, use only policing knowledge and experience as the relevant variables in an otherwise scientific process. So the issue becomes whether and how police departments might become experimenting departments – how R&D might be institutionalized in the policing occupation. One broad strategy, at least, is known: link R&D to planning in the context set out above.

Reiss sums up the broad topic of planning, styles of management, social change, and research in this way: "Serious consideration must be given to the moral and political implications raised by police participation in shaping social change. To what extent can the police become agents of social change, as well as anticipated change, and adapt to it? Any consideration of the role that the police might have in social change confronts issues about what are their roles in democratic societies – indeed, societies where the very concepts and nature of democracy are changing. The extension of citizens' rights is but one example of the way that democracies are changing in the twentieth century. Can democratic societies cope with the dilemma of an activist and accountable police?"[71]

ATTITUDES AND VALUES – THE
SUBCULTURAL FRAMEWORK OF
EFFICIENCY

Robert Reiner observed that "an adequate approach to police reform must be grounded in an understanding of police culture and practices, not a simplistic view that if only the right authorities were in charge all would be well. But both police and popular culture embody views of policing and its purposes which are at odds with the reality of police work."[72] Distrust of management, a sense of isolation, and solidarity are the three intertwined facets of the police subculture that demand attention in any study of policing. It is not often that the ideology and subculture of any occupation command scrutiny, but those of the police amplify and strengthen much of what characterizes policing or occurs within it (strikes/job actions, rejection of criticisms, the rigidity of its structure, and the persistence of the *status quo*, including the law-enforcement orientation).

Police attitudes and beliefs, best exemplified by patrol officers, rest on a strong sense of mission that includes that perennial law-enforcement duo of protection and apprehension. Rapid response and the dangers inherent in arriving at an uncertain scene reinforce both the primacy of protecting people and well-placed police convictions of the critical nature of their role, all of which buttresses the lore of the police department. Victor MacDonald's study of three urban Canadian departments contains this summary of policing tenets: [73]

- a sincere commitment to a role in society broadly based on enforcement of the criminal law, protection of the public, and the maintenance of order;
- a concern for the maintenance of police authority and for public respect for that authority (the need for this respect is understandable; it eases the task of defusing incidents and gaining control. This concern is widely – and mistakenly – thought to mask a request for more powers under the Code, for example, powers of arrest, stop and search, and extended rights of entry without warrants);
- an entrenched conviction that the public has no say in influencing policing policies, programs, or activities;
- a general belief that society and the court system are too lenient;
- a general belief that the press is unfair;
- a strong action orientation, including a belief that police must act to resolve anxiety and reassure people under stress;
- a commitment to mutual support when needed (the failure to back up a fellow officer breaks the foremost commandment of the subculture. But noninterference in another's actions and secrecy as to those actions are equally important);
- a general belief in the appropriateness of whatever action police may take coupled with a limited concern about the abuse of authority;
- a general distrust of top management's understanding of the complexities of street policing and its priorities, and a distrust that management will stand behind line officers when needed; and
- limited tolerance of deviance from broad social values; a rigid definition of right and wrong coupled with a sense of the utility of stereotyping to simplify events and categorize people by an easy formula.

I might add that even among officers from different countries a sense of brotherhood spontaneously arises.

Allan McDougall has noted that the more cohesive the group, the more its members, executive and constable alike, will adapt their own attitudes and perceptions to conform with those of the group. Thus, in learning the tools of the craft, a member will temper or discard attitudes that conflict with those of the occupational group. "If specialists belong to a self-conscious group, their mutual reinforcement will justify the necessity of such actions [such as abuse of authority] on the grounds of the importance of the function they perform for society."[74]

Major incidents that are critical to a citizen's vital interest define the central functions of policing for officers, even though they are relatively rare. Again, it is in law enforcement rather than order maintenance that police officers discern the challenges and achievements that define the core of their work and their satisfaction.

Police officers are pragmatic. A down-to-earth approach to reality is as typical of constables as of chiefs. Once on the job facing myriad contentious and sometimes dangerous incidents, they learn workable methods for handling them that soon become tried and true techniques. The ruminations and prescriptions of others are irrelevant before this personal knowledge has been acquired and become matters of indifference afterwards. In this light, the difficulty of overcoming resistance to a different set of behaviours dictated by a different type of policing program, becomes understandable.

This pragmatic approach points to the origin of the police conviction that outsiders cannot understand the nature of police work, since they have no personal experience of the job. This aspect of the police subculture is not anti-intellectual or antieducation or antianything, but rather an inclination to rely on what they know through experience works. The search for and reliance on the successful technique becomes an enduring habit of the police mind at any level of experience and responsibility.

This may be described as part of an ideology, an "orienting philosophy for police activities which fosters stability, mutual understanding and communication among officers. It also represents a source of inertia which allows officers to resist changed public values and managerial interventions ... In short, the police ideology (although not comprehensive) provides a guide to action and the evaluation of action for operational officers."[75] The ideology is shared by officers of all ranks, though line officers usually do not believe that they hold it in common with management. (The cleavage between junior and senior officers cannot be discounted, however. MacDonald has observed that the major functions of a department would be carried on in the absence of any senior direction until shift and other schedules failed.)

The achievement of desired outcomes in the incidents patrol officers attend to rest on forbearance, equanimity, wisdom, training, and experience in the use of discretion; such mature discretion is the professionalism of the officer on the street. General police duties are intrinsically motivating in the challenges they pose and in the swift realization of benefits to the citizens. However, they are not extrinsically motivating; that is, performance of duty brings no particular formal recognition or status. The diffuse nature of order maintenance does not provide a foothold for detailed regulations or guidelines or even for desired outcomes. Supervisors tend to believe that "good" street work can be recognized when seen. Yet the need for an officer to impose his will in bringing an incident under control almost inevitably generates antagonism, which often escalates into hostility. The constable's notion of what kind of order is to be restored may not correspond to that of his superiors or of citizens on the scene. Peter Sallman noted that, as a result, most officers take refuge under the umbrella of police solidarity and indulge "in a 'siege mentality.'"[76]

A related and complicating effect is distrust of the public, which does not always applaud patrol work. Being a police officer singles one out socially and has an isolating effect, which police solidarity alleviates. One study, for example, found that after about the sixth year of policing, officers' friends will be almost exclusively other officers.[77] The police recognize that the public has a vital interest in policing and they prize favourable press, but line officers are adamant that the public and its political representatives should have no say in the decisions and activities of a department.[78] The public should trust the police, and criticism or scrutiny implies a lack of trust. The statements and actions of the chief of police *vis-à-vis* the public are viewed as pandering to popular clamour and as a weakening in the face of public relations. It threatens line officers. (Executives, however, tend not to share this attitude, having realized in office their unavoidable dependency on wide support.)

As noted above, a crucial issue arises: how to make an impact on the working rules of the rank and file, how to influence the use of discretion. Otherwise put, how are the ramparts of solidarity and silence just described to be breached?[79] Police administrators keep aloof from this subcultural, self-directing approach to performance. Most first-line supervisors (sergeants) are coopted into the subculture and included in its solidarity; they do not represent a management-line officer point of interaction.[80] In this situation, the executive's capacity to take a department's activities in new directions is limited indeed.

THE INDISTINCT OCCUPATION —
DEPARTMENTS, ASSOCIATIONS,
AND UNIONS

One salient characteristic of the police occupation is its fragmentation into numerous departments of under fifteen people and into the few of considerable size. In Canada there is no typical size. There are well over four hundred municipal departments but fewer than fifty employ eighty percent of the officers. The many departments of up to fifteen, perhaps even twenty-five, employ officers requiring no more sophisticated skills or experience than that of being "watchmen," even if they are academy trained. (Two patrol officers on duty around the clock roughly implies a department of about fifteen people.) The immediate occupational focus remains, unavoidably, the department; there is no overarching commitment to the occupation, at least no tangible or formal one. There are no occupationwide institutions. Concerns about functions remain, understandably, bounded by the department but so too are horizons. There is nothing to distinguish among police officers, either formally or by responsibility, qualifications, or common recognition. Their singular entry into the occupation ensures acceptance as equals in competence and in their authority under the law. This is, in part, an aspect of the rigidities of the police personnel structure discussed earlier in this chapter, but much is tied to departmental fragmentation.

The International Association of Chiefs of Police has a professional orientation owing to a large membership base in the United States. Its initiatives are supportive; it offers, for example, certification programs for senior officers, training services, and publication programs. However, the association is often troubled by a large-department/small-department split in approaches to policies and concerns. Interests obviously differ so the divergence is understandable but the problems are built in. There is a tendency to uphold the fiction that the nature of responsibilities, functions, and purposes is the same in any department, regardless of size; hence a need for adaptability is not tacitly admitted. Departments are held to be similar in function and orientation; officers' duties are considered unvarying, so training needs are identical. The fragmented arrangement of police by department is accompanied by a sensitivity, derived in part from size and the challenges it presents, about the status of one's department and, therefore, its members. In practice, however, the smaller department is less oriented to law enforcement and tends to have a "watchman" style.

This situation suggests that there is a place for different categories of police personnel, based on their roles and qualifications, within and among departments. The circumstances that larger departments must face tough urban conditions indicates where the leading edge of certain kinds of competence is to be found and points to the need for more sophisticated policing and police officers. But having different categories of personnel should be a function not only of departmental size but of the diverse nature of police functions, the qualifications and career paths each entails, and entrance policies that encourage diversity.

The authority to regulate entry into policing certify competence, or define an officer's area of work are among the characteristics of an occupation that is coming of age more or less free of the vagaries of employing organizations. However, policing, as a less-developed occupation, is subject to external, provincial stipulations supervised by provincial and local boards or similarly charged offices. The occupation lacks overall leadership.

It seems that policing has an anachronistic place in the array of modern occupations, with its fragmentation into numerous disparate departments, its fragmented or shared functions, uncertain leadership, and dearth of occupationwide institutions with a strong and responsible mandate.

An occupationwide association provides a corporate mechanism by which to consider and further the development of the occupation (qualifications, standards of entry, maintenance of competence including the generation and transfer of knowledge and skills, specification of the areas and standards of work, etc.). An association is a hallmark of maturity in any occupation. Thus, some comments about the Canadian Association of Chiefs of Police are relevant. Membership, as implied by its title, is restricted and department-based (though membership is also available to senior officers). The membership reflects a one-time distinction between "rank and file" and the appointed chief constable, once a senior military officer in Britain and Canada. Further, police developed along the bureaucratic rather than the professional lines on which rank or status would be less relevant.

The association can be classified as thin in its representation of policing as an occupation. It addresses itself to issues identified within a set of committees assigned to functional areas (usually related to law enforcement) in which members are well informed and experienced. A consistent approach to policing issues is achieved through an advocacy role at government level, for example on Criminal Code provisions. Since membership numbers are limited, so are the association's resources, and some reliance on public money, with all its entanglements, seems to have been unavoidable. There are no available reports about provincial associations, but some observers suggest that they are more intensely concerned with provincial and local issues, occupational and functional, and consulting with provincial authorities. These processes thus bring relevant policing expertise into government ministries. Police unions also tend to be consulted.

Police unionism in its present form is a modern institution and is still developing rather quickly, in various ways. (Most departments have an "association" but the use of the term union avoids some confusion.) Dennis Forcese has alluded to growing pains experienced, for example, in the highly aggressive adversary tactics seen in the frequent resort to job actions of earlier postwar years. The traces linger. Senior officers, at one time comfortable in nests of traditional so-called management prerogatives and inexperienced in labour relations, also contributed to this state of we-them confrontation.[81]

In the past, police unions proved to be more competent than management not only in protecting but in furthering members' interests. They were the more able and better prepared bargainers. The evidence is impressive: truly high rates of pay for even junior members where educational qualifications or other individual investment is minimal; significant gains over other occupations in terms of wage increases between 1967 and 1980;[82] influence over manning decisions such as the restoration or retention of two-officer cars; sick benefits comparable to any; and, in general, the erosion of so-called management prerogatives in many areas affecting employment conditions, such that what is now not bargainable is usually a matter of discipline under provincial codes of conduct.

Neither management officers nor line officers, who comprise the majority of union members, recognize that the more profound attitudes, beliefs, and knowledge of police work are shared, and each group tends to see itself as the better custodian of this heritage. The line officer's view that senior people are "soft" in responding to public and political interests is illustrative, as is union belligerency towards intrusive public influence, including review boards. Union perspectives have heavy ideological/law-enforcement biases that reflect line-officer beliefs. The solidarity of line officers carries over into the union, giving it impressive cohesiveness and strength. Further, the union will hold tenaciously to outspoken and often antagonistic positions that give vent to line officers' distrust of management. Allegations of racial bias and the publicity surrounding those allegations, for example, may well invoke union involvement, which at times can be as intemperate as it is forceful. It must be remembered that policing has no nonunion association in which members may participate and address issues of general occupational concern; it would require a collegiality among all ranks, the achievement of which is hampered by departmental fragmentation and rank-based claims of competence.

While political neutrality is expected of the chiefs association, the union, as a sometime political voice, will enter into open debate over some public policy, such as parole, department-manning practices, police weapons, and civilian review boards. Their input often reflects dogmatic views that are not uncommon in Canadian society; they might , for example, deplore current social tendencies towards excessive and indiscriminate tolerance. The conventional quality of police-union thought, its ideological freight, is shaped by the membership's close-up observation of life, but is still reflexive for all that.

Still, police unions make themselves heard. Few agencies or offices of government with responsibilities in the policing area do not now consult the local or provincial union. Much weight is placed on a union's political potential; general public support for "their" police is consistently high in any community. As unions grew and found their feet during the postwar decades, it was inevitable that they would come to represent the police viewpoint to society. It is a role that employment associations take by default, and it was founded in an absence of significant attention by chiefs to the occupational interests noted above. Given the spirited ideological nature of the police subculture, union positions will surely remain conservative, even rigid, seemingly unprogressive, and demanding of public trust. But the activities by which these ends are promoted are often innovative. Employment associations have the potential, perhaps questionable, to evolve into organizations, unique in their own way, promoting both occupational and employment objectives, as some teachers' associations demonstrate. But the matter has not been well investigated, so useful detail on this point is not available.

Working conditions, which are bargainable, are now broadly defined, which diminishes the latitude by which a department may be managed outside of the contract. That the focus of bargaining may involve a dispute over what the department should be doing is an aspect of the penetration of the labour-relations process into functions and purpose. At one level, the outcomes of the two-officer car, shift-manning, and scheduling issues affect not only costs but also the means of deploying scarce resources and, thus, the way tasks are attended to. Of some significance is the intrusion of labour relations into personnel policies, including those of training, promotion, seniority rights, or any related bargainable working condition, which all tend to protect the *status quo* and dampen occupational development.

These comments indicate that police unions, in their ability to command the loyalty and ideological commitment of their members, are an unavoidable part of the evolution of policing as an occupation. Unions assign high priority to job security and benefits. Police unions are no different, but they do go beyond this by their entry into public-policy debates. Further, as Forcese has pointed out, their success in bringing management rights onto the bargaining table does not limit command discretion so much as require a different, newer managerial approach, one of thinking twice, of checking with the union, and of attending to the concerns of the line officers.[83] They are not inherently a barrier to the development of the occupation, but as with the chiefs' association, their limited horizons remain inimical to the modernization of policing.

Profound consequences flow from this dynamic relationship between structure and subculture. The first is that the in-at-the-bottom practice of manning a department is reinforced by the attitude-based prescriptions of the subculture: no one may be accepted into the brotherhood without identifying with those attitudes and values. This singular entry lies at the heart of the police ethos; it is not merely a personnel policy of long standing. Flowing from this is the seemingly impervious, uniform nature of rank, which is an example, and perhaps a grave one, of the restriction on sources of talent and the impoverishment of existing human potential.

As with problem-oriented policing, community policing will redefine aspects of the street officer's job in ways that will undoubtedly conflict with typical contract provisions about shift work, job-assignment choices, overtime, criteria for advancement, and relationships with supervisors. Should line officers be involved in the decision-making processes and other initiatives of community policing, more complex processes will be inserted into such department-union matters as delegation of responsibility – bearing in mind that for many, if not most, officers, the work will be challenging in a different way that requires different support and direction; and the rewards will be more valued if the work is given status and recognition.[84]

Albert Reiss's summation is apt: "One of the issues for the future of policing, then, is the extent to which the current unionized model of resolving issues will come to dominate the nature of policing and its organization. The capacity of the police to experiment, to change, and to involve local constituencies can themselves become objects of collective bargaining. If so, then the future of policing may be determined more at the bargaining table than by management through research and development."[85]

CHAPTER SIX

Accountability and the Supervision of Policing by Governments

The public and their political leaders still do not fully appreciate the very great amount of discretion that the police do and must exercise and the fact that this discretion must necessarily be exercised by the relatively low ranks, who are far removed from the police chief in the large departments. Controlling such discretion to the satisfaction of citizens, community organizations, courts, police unions, and all those who are or suddenly can become interested in police conduct or activities is the most difficult responsibility in city government. [1]

THEMES, DEFINITIONS, AND ABSTRACTIONS

The subject of this chapter is the mechanics of accountability, not only where accountability is supposed to be located and paid for under provincial-government practices but also how it is cross-hatched by the autonomy and discretion possessed by chief constable and constable alike. The urban-police establishment has been variously sheltered and supervised during the modernization of government and the wider rearrangements of provincial and municipal relations, of which it is an inextricable part. The issues of police discretion, their wide-ranging autonomy, and the nature of their accountability, all of which are enmeshed in politics, are best seen in this government context. The discussion will thread its way through several rather broad themes towards the gritty topics of supervision by boards of police commissioners and accountability.

James Q. Wilson argues that only through a study of the way police are managed under different circumstances might something be learned about the way their behaviour may be changed. [2] This is directly relevant, he says, to such crucial matters as society's ability to manage social conflict and its prospects for maintaining the balance between liberty and order. At the police-department level, Victor Macdonald's study revealed a considerable gulf of mistrust between line officers and those in management; for example, line officers' sense of what constitutes effective patrol behaviour diverges from that indicated by managerial and supervisory practices and emphases. Problems attach to the exercise of discretion as a result.[3] Along with the urban environment of policing, then, this government environment has been critically influential in the evolution of policing and has also determined its current status and manageability in many ways.

It was pointed out in earlier chapters that Canadian, British, and American urban police achieved, in differing degrees, an apolitical form of autonomy or independence. It is useful to note that "autonomy" and the status of being "apolitical" are near synonyms, autonomy meaning independence from political authority in some degree. Determining the priority – and resources – to be given to each police activity (antiprostitution, traffic enforcement, serious crime, or order-related) is a political act, but since these are internal decisions, they seem, to the Canadian observer, to be made on some rational, perhaps technical, basis and are thus "apolitical." Nonetheless, as Patrick Murphy notes, here, as in the United States, the police executive's job is inherently political. Many mayors have told me that the police chief is protected from the rough and tumble of politics. But the reality is that politics is our way of life."[4] The same status armours police against interference in criminal matters, and properly so.

Police autonomy evolved from a history of ensuring that policing be free of interference by largely local political or improperly biased interests. In the United States, police chiefs enjoy considerable autonomy even though they are appointed by a mayor and can be readily dismissed. Much of police autonomy, while informal, is politically potent because it is founded on public support for an "apolitical" police force. Still, both the efficiency of police departments and their capacity to adapt to change with innovative programs that reflect government priorities are vital questions for elected politicians.[5] So the role of politics – as played out by elected offices and bureaucracies, or by citizens and their groups – must be a significant matter in the responsiveness of police and the nature of their accountability.

The current systems of police supervision – a mixed bag that was jerry-built over time – reflect the axiom that policing must be somehow "responsible" but also beyond the reach of partisan interests. How to ensure that policing is subject to democratic (that is, political) direction is presented as a perpetual administrative dilemma, but actually the axiom is a relic that obscures the central place of political processes in the provision of this, or indeed of any, public service.

When it comes to policing, an analysis of relations between provincial and municipal governments and how they have been worked out across this century is the essential first step to understanding the mechanics of accountability and access that has stymied so many citizens and politicians. A key problem for citizens is not whether administrative control is centralized or decentralized in the bureaucracy, but how they can be brought closer to the centres of political power. The matter of central versus local authority will be discussed later.

Equally at issue in this context is the junior occupational status of policing, which ensures, for example, that government attempts to give direction, to have the frontiers of innovation probed, are in effect more bureaucratic or regulatory than substantive, given the accupational reluctance to change and relative inability to adapt. As James Q. Wilson has observed, "[any] organization resists change, and the police role, with its vulnerability to legal sanctions, its (perceived) low esteem, and its absence of professional reference groups, produces a sufficient sense of insecurity to be especially resistant to change."[6]

It is difficult to avoid using the terms management and supervision interchangeably, but I tend to distinguish between them. Management encompasses purpose, resources, operating policies, their implementation, and concern for results. Supervision is an act of directly overseeing to ensure that what has to be done is done according to some formula or standard. Accordingly, I prefer the term "supervision by government" as a better reflection of what is actually done, excluding as it does matters of purpose and priority peculiar to an occupation into which government does not readily intrude. The term management is not often used here. Boards and offices of government are clearly not involved in managing a police department; police autonomy here and elsewhere is a matter of historical and present reality.

A related distinction is that between a departmental process and what that process was expected to achieve. For example, the process of consulting with some group about a prostitution problem is not outcome. The distinction brings the place of the process, the means itself, into perspective. A department may be held accountable for following some process and thus announce *that a highly desirable and publicly acceptable activity occurred regardless of outcome*. It is not at all unknown.

Two further observations are relevant here. First, accountability is not a blanket matter. Tradition has it that in applying the law, police are free of biasing influence such that, in general, they are not immediately supervised when deploying resources or exercising the discretion needed to pursue individual criminal cases, a "quasi-judicial" function. It is often said that the authority of the office of constable is original, to be found nestling within common law and not delegated, and that the officer is "answerable to the law alone." So by way of tradition, there is a law-enforcement operations area in which the police are relatively autonomous and do not yield to other authority excepting the judicial. However, as noted earlier, decisions to deploy publicly provided resources to serve the well-being of a community – particularly those decisions that give priority to one set of interests over another – are political. The second observation follows: the roots of the police attitude that the public may not have a say in policing (not only in law enforcement but by extension in the order maintenance) is found in this seemingly quasi-judicial autonomy; as noted earlier, it is a strongly held attitude shared by all ranks, though police executives keep wary ears tuned to public voices. There is no implication that any external authority should be involved in day-to-day decisions.

In a society such as ours, the well-spring of advances in major public services is public attitude. As society becomes postindustrial, it is also becoming increasingly well informed and, Daniel Bell observed, increasingly conscious of its fate, and in seeking to control its own fortunes, the political order necessarily becomes paramount.[7]

The public's attention, guided by the TV clip and headline of the day, tends to fasten on some incident of immediate gravity such as a violent crime. Where such incidents persist, public concern about police competence is unlikely to arise, given the conventional support for and trust in the police. There is, however, growth, if not a flowering, of postconventional attitudes tied to the nature of policing, not so much in relation to crime as to orderliness (or quality of neighbourhoods) in changing circumstances, for example, that include, changes in a local ethnocultural mix. Concern, triggered by some vague sense of unease, may not be easy to quell. It will reflect communal attitudes, less to the issue of protection as to acts and qualities of police themselves. As an example, a group may well seek heightened attention to its particular interests so as to gain official recognition; in gaining that recognition from the police, it gains the stamp of legitimacy, often a highly desired status, and possibly some latitude in behaviour; in failing to be legitimated, its negative reaction will be certain and vocal. As "the primary influence on the public's view of local government, law, and justice"[8] and usually the first visible representatives of government and established society in a community, the police unavoidably become involved in this social process of legitimation. They are inextricably involved in the dynamics of a demographically mixed citizenry jostling for recognition of its varied interests and problems. In this milieu, controversy is near certain and detrimental to police effectiveness. To be the centre of public controversy is to be politicized in a passive rather than an active sense. Similarly, members of some minority group will more readily complain not so much about some singular abuse of authority as about inadequate service and uncivil treatment. Incivility demeans, of course, and therefore abuse of authority is the more strongly felt. The point is that public attitudes are increasingly complex, informed, and sensitive.

The issue of the government responsiveness is of long standing. In the eighteenth century, Jean Jacques Rousseau argued that practical concerns should limit the size of government, for "administration becomes more and more burdensome as the distance grows greater." Further, he suggested that with distance the vigour of government declines, and the uniformity of laws made by a large, centralized government cannot suit the diversity found in large subjurisdictions. Such broad or uniform laws, in differing from those suited to local usage, "lead only to trouble and confusion among peoples which, living under the same rulers and in constant communication one with another, intermingle and intermarry, and, coming under the sway of new customs, never know if they can call their very patrimony their own ... The leaders, overwhelmed with business, see nothing for themselves, the State is governed by clerks." [9] Rousseau wrote before the advent of large urban centres with their diverse cultural communities and distinctive demographics. But his comments about ethnocultural pluralism and its values have resonance in late-century Canada. Both John Stuart Mill and Alexis de Tocqueville were of the qualified view that local self-government was desirable, if not absolutely necessary to democracy. The note was sounded in 1925 by Harold Laski who said that the individual tends to feel impotent before a vast administrative machine and that in large states the mere achievement of equality would be impeded without the maximum decentralization. In modern-day Canada, Higgins noted that "participation is more likely to be frequent, informed and meaningful when people are able to identify with and understand their government in terms of its structure, decision-making process, personnel and issues." [10] Similarly, John Sewell, a one-time alderman and later mayor of Toronto, regarded people "as the best interpreters of their own interests" who thus merit a voice in the decisions that affect them; in his view, the role of elected officials at the time was to represent those interests, especially if they are expressed through well-organized group.[11] He commented on the continual tension arising from the municipal/provincial split in the mechanisms of police governance.

Clearly, one of the tenets of democracy is that interests and problems are best identified and defined at the level of immediate concern and resolved accordingly. Smaller governments are said to invoke grassroots, hence more informed, participation while central authorities might dismiss local wisdom as parochial. So the problem of central versus local competence is ongoing and troublesome in all the practices of government, not only in policing.

Still, citizens and politicians are better schooled in local politics, where governmental processes are easier to grasp and issues are both closer and clearer. United States political history reflects the birth of its democratic inclinations in the once-dispersed communities of a largely rural population; local politics and town-hall meetings set constitutional preferences and patterns that reinforced local-level access and participation. The status of local governments in the US persists in the prolific numbers of local authorities and governments and the resistance to centralization in general.

A former RCMP commissioner, in discussing police accountability including that of the RCMP in its municipal and provincial policing roles, noted that the increasing social diversity that was "creating local customs and traditions in the process, can only work as long as the political arrangement allows for a high degree of local autonomy and local control over the affairs that press most heavily on the day to day life of the citizens in any given region." He went on to suggest that local police forces be responsible for "local" crime and accountable to whichever government had responsibility for relevant social policy and social control.[12] While restricting his comments to responsibilities for "crime" (in the traditional sense), he implicitly included peace-keeping responsibilities and thus advocated an element of community responsiveness. An Australian observer also commented on the inappropriateness of a national police department conducting a service that is locally oriented, and pointed to the centralizing tendencies of powerful bureaucracies as one evident problem. Swanton indicated that policing organized at a federal level is not necessarily successful. He suggested that a close look at the Royal Canadian Mounted Police, an otherwise highly competent body, reveals problems arising from the duplication of police agencies in this country and the stalled development of police services, such that, in his judgment, the RCMP has not been all that effective.[13]

It is useful to recall that the social diversity in cities has a significant geographical or spacial arrangement. People of similar ethnic backgrounds tend to cluster in identifiable neighbourhoods characterized by interrelated attributes of language, religion, age, occupation, income, education, type of household, social standing, financial status, and so on.[14] Categories based on occupation (the common designations are upper, uppermiddle, middle, skilled blue collar, unskilled blue collar, and unemployed) represent a further elaboration of the social and spacial arrangement of people, clustered in part according to varying housing costs. The relevance has to do not only with political representation and diversity of issues but with the pursuit of solutions to diverse problems. Because of the density of cities, these people in their separate groupings are unable to provide services for themselves and so are dependent on others, thus creating a complex set of interdependencies, a perspective that defines the urban status as a set of functional relationships through which people are able to satisfy daily needs. R.A.W. Rhodes suggested that there are two broad government functions satisfying daily needs: social investment, that is, the provision of the infrastructure of business, and social consumption (the provision of the services related to daily life such as health, courts, hospitals, schools, and so on). Obviously, the two overlap.[15] A somewhat different but telling emphasis arises in the further grouping of functions under the categories of social control and social support. Because of both population density and complex patterns of social interaction, cities are inherently disorderly places with a high degree of anonymity.[16] The threads of the social-control function run through these patterns since, in recognizing interdependencies and differences among themselves, people foster a balance between tolerance for individuality and the need for a level of social conformity that allows a diverse community to work.

The functions of social support and social control, moreover, merge to form a continuum for potential political-administrative attention. Not only the Criminal Code but "local bylaws, local courts to administer them, local police to enforce them, and local jails to deal with those who break them are obvious examples of public agencies of social control."[17] If social control is interpreted more broadly to refer to attempts to instil or sustain order, there are other examples: even local land-use planning and zoning can be regarded as manifestations of the city's control over socially corrosive proposals for particular neighbourhoods.[18] The many programs and practices of local government, then, seem to have various potentials for social control that can be adapted to the local, spacial peculiarities or arrangements mentioned above.

A common view of local government is that it is an agency of the central government created primarily to administer centrally developed policies. This view, as traditional as it is limiting, maintains that certain services are best administered at the local level. Thus, municipal governments have an administrative rather than a "grassroots" (democratic) value. These services are usually related to property (roads, sewers, water, and so on). Some provincial direction may be appropriate to mitigate or remove any unacceptable variation in the standard of service provided.[19] So in varying degrees, social-services policy and related administrative matters are retaind by the provincial government and distanced from the influence of municipal institutions.

A contrasting view holds that local governments have a policy value. In this broader perspective, local self-government implies the existence of significant decision-making powers, financial self-reliance, and the right to organize and administer services according to citizens' wishes (the exercise of varying levels of responsibility and discretion for "how" certain things are done and not for "what" things are done). In some areas, local-government power is relatively unfettered; in others, including policing, hospitals, and education, it is curbed, that is, allotted to local, semiautonomous agencies or supervised by the provincial government. It is this broader, less rigid view of local government that tends to conform to reality.

FOUR PHASES IN THE EVOLVING JURISDICTIONS OF CITIES

The First Reform Era

In the United States the local-government reform movement began in the latter decades of the nineteenth century; in Canada, it began and ran its course in the first few decades of the twentieth. The movement was prompted by inefficiencies in the provision of municipal services and parallel deficiencies in the management of surging city growth. Much was attributed to the corrupting grasp of US machine politics. The interests of the newly influential leaders of industry and commerce lay in well-run, stable municipalities and their attention to reform diminished once adequate measures were achieved.[20] The reformers viewed municipal government as something akin to a private corporation, with citizens as shareholders and administrative and line departments under competent, usually specialist managers topped by a board of directors (small numbers of elected councillors comparable to a private corporate board). The entrepreneur brought

technology and business practices together under managerial competence, thus providing the private-corporation model for the reform
of municipal government. In this "public-administration" approach,
elected officials (who were divorced from involvement in administration and day-to-day operating issues) were restricted to broad policy
matters considered at less frequent intervals, as with the private corporate model. It was in the reform era that city-manager systems and the
practice of incorporating municipal governments came into being.
With fewer councillors or aldermen, wards tended to be abolished and
officials were elected "at large" rather than from particular areas of the
city, which they had formerly represented. The trend was towards bureaucratic and depoliticized government, with early flickers of the long
process of centralization to come.

That the more significant reform influences in Canada came from
the United States is clear from the writings of early reformers in
Canada.[21] Canadian reformers, with their modest colonial mentality,
scoured Europe and America for ideas. They were strongly temper-
ance-minded, emphasizing morality and the promotion of a high
moral tone throughout society by means of, for example, a regulatory
approach (aimed at prostitution, gambling dens, observance of the
Sabbath) permitted by law-and-order practices. The label "Toronto the
Good," with its overtones of civic piety, embodies characteristics that
lasted beyond the Second World War. As a vision it was popular, reinforcing as it did the characteristics of growing suburban communities
that were deemed to be desirable. The reformers also trumpeted the
cost-effectiveness of "good government," including the efficiencies of
compartmentalized, specialized civic functions. The rationale, again
found in the private corporate model, emphasized newer technologies
in civic services such as water, sewage, road engineering, and municipal finance. Experts managed with only broad direction from a "board
of directors." Partisan interest was thus removed from daily operating
decisions; policy making and politics were equated. The impact on local government can be summarized in one word: depoliticization.
Small councils and citywide constituencies ensured that only the
"right" people would be elected, for who else could afford a citywide
campaign? These features from the first reform era still characterize
many local governments.[22]

Many features in the governance of urban police departments can
also be attributed to this early modernization of urban-service bureaucracies.[23] It was in the general context of government reform that
O.W. Wilson introduced the notions of managerial competence and
crime-fighting specialization with diminished local influence, as dis-

cussed in the previous chapter, enabling police department to seek the shelter of a "depoliticized" and compartmentalized civic administration.

A Half-Century in the Two Levels of Government

The earlier, fairly extensive autonomy of municipal governments themselves began to diminish under early reform rearrangements and was spurred through the centralizing tendencies of central bureaucracies (the fiefdoms of professional groupings) for greater provincial supervision. In time, specialists at both levels of government achieved well-defined spheres of responsibility and, in generating ministries and offices specific to their specialization, created what others have called compartmentalized government. Along with their counterparts in the private sector, these specialist ministries and offices achieved in large measure the autonomy of occupational self-management, thus protecting their specializations from encroachment. Certain emergent occupations specializing in some facet of government tended to acquire the same protective mantle of professionalization. It is instructive to look at a list of big-city boards and departments that are staffed by specialists and have provincial counterparts:

Boards/Commissions	Departments/Services *	
Health	Health**	Legal**
Police	Police	Fire
Education	Finance**	Public Housing
Transit	Community Services	Sewage
Housing	Urban Design**	Planning/Zoning
Library	Engineering**	Public Works
Electrical Power	Water	Social Welfare Wervices**
Parks and Recreation	Transportation**	Garbage and Refuse
Hospitals	Emergency Services**	

* Excluding purely administrative departments such as personnel.
** These employ people with professional qualifications typical in government administration, for example, road engineering, administrative law, public accountancy, in addition to the many already obvious in this listing.

Urbanization in the late-nineteenth-century United States (later in Canada) put understandable demands on government, highlighting the efficiencies of intermunicipal coordination, common municipal standards, the introduction of technological advances into local services, and the need for supervision of provincial financial grants. This centralizing trend reflected the persuasive notion that so-called modern scientific management, being rational, science-based, and objective, separates government from politics.[24] Professions have figured indisputably in the growing capacity of government to manage its increasingly technical resources. The responsibility for services compartmentalized along functional-professional lines crosses geographical and political boundaries, blurring both the processes of democratic representation and the reality that, invariably, there are policy-relevant interests peculiar to a locality that are often inconsistent with central conceptions of those interests.

With the introduction of more advanced administrative bureaucracies and the use of emerging specializations in both traditional and new public services (policing among them) came a set of professional bureaucratic complexes, or policy communities, each with personnel that shared an ideology, expertise, and a career structure, and each tending to span the boundaries of government institutions, national and subnational.[25] The centre of policy making shifted upwards in Canada as in Britain, where the trend was more evident, so local authorities were increasingly bereft of influence. Central policy making itself, while undiminished, became fragmented or compartmentalized; thus, in Britain for example, the well-known the problem of legislatures trying to control a powerful professional bureaucracy supports the argument for the decentralization of state functions.[26]

Each specialist group has a collegial interest in activities on its own "turf," both municipal or provincial, and in the interactions affecting its profession. The tendency is to shelter policy areas of importance from political interventions, and distinctions emerge between functional and political domains. In an Ontario-based study of occupational groups in government, Allan McDougall found that their structural characteristics include:

– protective provincial legislation that sanctions the authority of professional associations;
– a sympathetic minister;
– offices of government staffed by members of the occupation (physicians of ministries, commissions, and boards of health, lawyers in the offices of the solicitor general and the attorney general and so on);
– provincial associations, often with local or regional "colleges" or chapters, that govern an occupation;
– local, semi-independent authorities, where occupational-service variations merit, such as hospital boards and local boards of police com-

missioners, with one or more provincially appointed members (in other cases, in the effort to distance authority from the local political establishment, complete and separate authorities are set up, for example the school system, with its own elected officials, tax base, and bureaucracies); and
– an active occupation jealous of its autonomy, such as the medical and legal professions and, of course, the police.[27]

Given a sympathetic provincial government, favourable legislation, and elements of government specializing in its area of occupational competence, an occupation, McDougall says, will enjoy a position of security and autonomy. Not so the police. It has been noted that the ostensible purpose in the creation of provincial police commissions was to coordinate police services and provide support for local forces that lacked technical expertise – all in the name of greater efficiency.[28] Police commissioners tend not to be police specialists (though they are supported by police advisers) and are therefore exceptions to the general case in professions.

McDougall observed that municipal responsibility is segmented into small (functional) domains according to the administrative structure of a particular province. The functional link between such a domain at the municipal level and its counterpart at the provincial level may well be the occupation itself, which gives these bodies their longevity and influence. Thus, policy areas in provincial-municipal relations, each usually exclusive to an occupation's area of competence, can be and usually are examined and discussed separately. When they are, the perspective will tend to be administrative rather than geographical and political, a feature that has unquestionably impoverished thinking about police services. By way of illustration, provincial-government supervision of police tends to focus on issues that galvanize public attention, not on the suitability of conventional functions or of occupational competence; the recently enacted policing bill in Ontario, the Police Services Act, responds to public concern about policing with more government bureaucracy: enlarged and restructured provincial supervisory offices and agencies; municipal police-services boards (commissions); and new, local civilian review boards supported by a renewed, central public-complaints system – all semi-independent agencies. Incongruously, the legislation exhorts chiefs to inaugurate community-oriented policing. Further, when functional areas are the preserve of specialists (as with policing), there is a disinclination to share responsibility with others; coordination is a prominent victim. This weakness is not only one of turf and lack of knowledge: it is a structural flaw built into provincial-municipal arrangements.

When local-government politicians seek enhanced jurisdiction over some aspect of an occupation's domain, members of the occupation assert the technical nature of their work, its vital public value, and the detrimental effects of interference. The sheltering influence of a sympathetic minister is likely, as is the support of a kindred provincial agency and the occupation's association. "By 1957, after a number of court cases and subsequent amendments to The Police Act, the police achieved their goal. The courts declared that the police were officers of the Crown who enjoyed independent authority in the enforcement of the law. Municipal authorities were limited in their control of the police to the powers and procedures contained in The Police Act and its regulations. The police thus achieved insulation from municipal politics."[29] The influence of provincial associations of chiefs of police should not be overlooked. According to McDougall, until 1948, municipal interests were invariably consulted in the formulation of urban policing policy but not at all after 1958, except, for example, indirectly through municipal membership on local boards and through a municipality's membership in an association of municipal authorities. Further, public concern about the spread of gambling and organized crime led the government to establish the Ontario Police Commission to direct the fight against organized crime and "to take the police out of politics." The issue of organized crime was central to the strength of the police position, adding persuasiveness to the claim that a vital function was within their area of technical competence. Ontario municipal police thereby not only sought but gained a measure of insulation from direct provincial intervention, since the provincial commission occupied an intermediate position.

The provincial posture, then, to ensure that municipalities achieve efficiency in the delivery of local services, is both fatherly and nonpolitical; the municipalities are generally dealt with as not-to-be-fully-trusted juniors in terms of competence, a role they sometimes deserve. Likewise, the ordinarily considerable municipal power inherent in the capacity to tax and raise influential sums is now eroded through a growing dependency on provincial grants, two-thirds of which are conditional. On average, in 1983, fifty percent of municipal revenues came from municipal sources and the remainder primarily from provincial governments.[30]

An occupation's claim to independence from municipal authority is based, first, on the argument that its special area of performance is critical to society and so immune from intervention; this the police have consistently and successfully claimed. The claim also rests on problems within communities that fall within the occupation's area of competence: the more vital the community interests being threatened, the more the senior rather than the local level of government becomes involved. Another factor that tends to favour police independence is a tension between municipal and provincial governments. If the provincial government intrudes into police autonomy, the charge of interference in policing efficiencies in a way that is detrimental to the local good will be made, as will one of interference in the affairs of urban government. For their part, municipalities will invoke symbols of democratic government in a bid for greater authority over policing, but they are countered by provincial claims of the potential for undesirable interference in policing "as it attempts to fulfil the needs of society." Police autonomy shelters in the eye of this dispute, and their adroitness at finding shelter, in McDougall's view, perpetuates their dominance in the policy area.[31]

Public-service professionals tend to be able to define problems in terms of their own specialization and deny the area to others seeking to stake out a patch. The expanded embrace of law enforcement under the crime-fighting rationale is an example. Senior civil servants, ministers, and leading members of the establishment are the "strategically placed actors" among whom professionals negotiate claims to "ownership" of evolving public issues. As part of the current reform era, public-interest groups have emerged with whom such professionals may or may not ally themselves so as to be on the "right side" of public opinion, a desirable place to be. However, siding with popular opinion and public groups in too obvious a manner risks loss of the apolitical, objective image public administration requires – an image that community policing, for all the uncertainty of its role, projects very well. This alignment of professional influences seems to include the police, whose area of specialization is defined but only in criminal and related legislation such as the provincial police act.

It is possible to make too much of the role of nonelected officials in developing policy; the crux, however, is whether or not suitable policies are actually made and implemented and who is accountable for them. Policy suitability, in turn, given the attitudes of the current reform movement, depends on who has access to the process and whose interests then receive attention. The function and experience of specialists in implementing and administering policies invite their involvement in the policy-making process. The information that middle- and senior-level administrators and specialists receive through their training and their day-to-day contacts with others are as valuable as their competence in determining alternative approaches and assessing them from an administrative perspective. But if specialists constitute autonomous sources of influence on policy making and implementation, then ways must be found to manage them and to specify their accountability.[32]

The police occupation has not been caught up in the central thrust of government professionalization. Policing began with an uncomplicated set of duties and a late recognition of the vital nature of its service; in their early years, police departments were accepted as part of the rationalization of civic government and not out of evident need. In Ontario, it was social unrest to which the militia had responded that prompted the establishment of police departments; otherwise, the relative calm of those decades contributed to a tenuous grasp of what this new civic department should do, rather than a multiplicity of purposes, a diffuseness of purpose shaded by its moral and political roots. The chosen reform path was one of managerial competence and crime fighting, pioneered by O.W. Wilson and August Vollmer and characterized, as noted in the previous chapter, by centralized, command-oriented control with generalist rather than specialist officers slotted in.

The experience in the teaching was similar. As semiprofessionals, teachers brought so-called modern scientific management to schools and school systems, thus providing the "protective institutional buffer" that was often erected around nonprofessional occupations; the organization, then bureaucratized though not professionalized, could assert its monopoly of a given area. The Canadian education system is reputed to be the least politicized in the Western world. Similarly, policing was centred around managerial competence, and bureaucratized departments settled on the vital and esoteric practices of law enforcement.

Geography and Suburbanization – The PostWar
Rationalization of Urban Governments

The trend of the first half-century culminated in the upheaval of the fifties and sixties, in particular urbanization, a spate of municipal-governments reorganizations that transformed their relations with their provincial counterparts. The challenge was the spread of suburbs across municipal boundaries, which, along with technological changes especially in transportation and communications, widened the geographical scope of daily life and made further provincial intervention in the activities of local government politically feasible and desirable. Urbanization prompted postwar municipal reorganization in all provinces but one (Prince Edward Island), and this, in turn, enhanced supervision by provincial governments. The primary effect was to realign municipalities through, for example, amalgamations, resulting in reduced numbers of municipal governments and such bodies as school boards. This period of reorganization has run its course. The trend to regionalization and to supramunicipal authorities – agencies of narrower functional but wider geographical embrace such as regional planning councils – has largely ended.

No guiding precept shaped what the political responsibilities of municipalities might be. Rather, urban growth prompted a quest for efficiency and hence a jurisdictional realignment into larger municipalities for economies of scale; in this quest, some solutions tailored local-government structures, for example, into two-tier arrangements so as to cope with expensive-to-service suburban complexes, a practice that soon ran into strong political opposition. Some provinces tended to adopt regional, two-tier municipal arrangements. One supported a form of amalgamation through successive incorporations of contiguous suburban areas into the single-level, larger city. Still others permitted metropolitan urban areas to remain a patchwork of jurisdictions of increasingly denser populations.

Access to government is arguably more difficult to achieve as the jurisdiction – and population within it – increases and as authority is reserved to politically and administratively distant offices of second-tier governments, municipal or provincial. Thus, reorganization, whether by piecemeal annexation or regionalization, emphasized the administrative requisite of scale. The retention of lower-tier governments to satisfy the political requisites, particularly of representativeness, did not effectively eliminate all imbalances. In 1988, councillors in the second-tier "regional" governemnt of Metropolitan Toronto were to be elected from wards for the first time in three decades (the mayors of the six constituent cities are now the sole nonelected members) to introduce accountability to a specific electorate and thereby promote appropriate levels of service. It was felt that appointed members of a metropolitan council were "rubber stamping" decisions made by bureaucrats. Now, in spite of having a base in a ward, councillors are still accused of being out of touch with the community and unable to handle major problems like garbage disposal and housing. One councillor indicated that council has no hands-on effectiveness, and that effecting change is a slow business.[33]

Local boards, commissions, agencies, and special-purpose bodies, often quasi-autonomous, are fairly common. Many are mandated by the province and include boards of education, health, and police commissioners, parks boards, conservation authorities, library and museum boards, public-transit commissions, electrical-utilities commissions, emergency-measures agencies, and industrial-development boards. Boards of education came early, in the older provinces before 1850. Boards of police commissioners followed – in Ontario, at about the mid-nineteenth century – though with appointed rather than elected members. (The older provinces tended to set the order of precedence for the newer ones.) The now abandoned system of police commissioners in the United States was of long-standing, having been established before the turn of the century. The use of special-purpose bodies at municipal level is North American in origin rather than British. The range of authority of these bodies varies widely, for example from boards of education, which control their own finances and policies independently of the municipality, through those whose major decisions are subject to council approval, to those that have an advisory role only. Each "quasi-autonomous" body, then, has at least some influence on policy-making and unquestionable influence on budgets. They also fragment the decision-making process, which is political. The consequences and ramifications of decisions (including those that issue from bureaucratic compartments) cannot be known or anticipated because of this fragmentation so that the capacity to coordinate services, an essential component of policy formulation in government, is eroded. To Higgins, they confound accountability. Whether elected officials can be held accountable even at election time is questionable; the depoliticization of governmental processes has been that effective.[34]

The Contemporary Reform Period

The second reform movement was concerned with the internal relations and processes of local government. It began in the mid-1960s and has not yet run its full course. Regionalization had much to do with the land-use planning of the much larger spaces of suburbia and commuter basins. It limited the participation of people in decisions affecting the integrity of their neighbourhoods and of the city itself, including the potential and often real deterioration of city cores and changes in core land-use functions. The ongoing reforms of internal municipal relations and processes are focused on land-use planning and zoning, but not exclusively so. Among the objects of reform are the relations of city councils to local bodies, commissions, boards, and city departments, and the relations of bureaucrats to local publics.

It has been said that "the central question on which the two eras [of reform] focussed related to the word 'politics' and more specifically the issue of whether or not local politics should be 'political.'"[35] Current reform tendencies are marked by the notion that local politics are not only desirable but essential. Further, it seems, the deferred costs of administrative and policy centralization should be paid in the currency of local access to what are now provincial matters. The compartmental arrangement of functions is less acceptable to those who wish to hamper attempts to express local interests and concerns through administrative or political offices. Reformers believe that those who live in an area are best able to determine its land-use plan. But community access to policy making runs against the grain of administrative habits now hardened after many decades. "Whether they are elected members of council or not, liberal reformers find in their dealings with such officials as chief administrative officers, directors of engineering, heads of planning departments, and municipal solicitors that the terminology used and the type and volume of data are so daunting that the council in effect only sanctions decisions already made by staff."[36]

Innumerable community groups have attempted to open up city hall. First, a common concern was activated by threats to the integrity of neighbourhoods posed by redevelopment and rezoning. Second, council was widely perceived as a private club acting behind closed doors to serve the interests of their friends in the development industry – a situation exacerbated by the absence of wards in many cities. Third, appointed specialists in city halls, particularly those in planning departments, were thought to possess excessive power. "Planning had become the preserve of professional planners and the planning process tended to be monopolized by them along with pro-development councils. Planners had considerable job mobility, being able to switch back and forth between public and private sector employers."[37] Higgins suggested that there was a further ideological impulse behind the reform movement consisting of beliefs that were critical of the power structure of capitalism and its social effects, particularly in light of the growing disparities in well-being that are now more visible in cities.[38]

It will be recalled from an earlier chapter that neighbourhood-group participation in policing programs calls for the accommodation of some form of citizen access – influence – and neighbourhood groups are agents of decentralization. People organized around a neighbourhood or other common interest create a potential power base but where the interest spans neighbourhoods or districts, the potential tends to fragment. In more recent years, groups have been learning that networking, communicating among themselves, forming semipermanent alliances to add force to their voices, and, at times, acting in concert are all practicable techniques that yield access and command attention.

The Winnipeg experiment with local citizen-advisory groups indicates that people will not participate if there is little or no immediate point in doing so. It seems participation had not yet become a habit, in part because of the hands-off political legacy of earlier decades and a seemingly lasting antipathy to traditional political parties in municipal affairs. So now it is a near truism that interest and activism in local affairs will be high given some specific and immediate problem, of which there now seem to be many.

POTHOLES, POLITICS, AND ADMINISTRATION

Lionel D. Feldman and Katherine A. Graham noted that municipalities are perceived as purveyors of local services that are best carried out in an administrative rather than a political milieu. They suggested that political awareness at the municipal-council level has suffered, leading to a division of the local-government organization with important local responsibilities assigned to independent nonpolitical "agencies, boards and commissions," which function in a manner described as remote from the centre of responsible local government.[39] Such was the condition of provincial-municipal relations as the current reform period began to flower. It is my view that the climate of thinking that fostered the reform movement is making such reorientations as community policing possible.

Those relations determined both the approaches taken to the supervision of policing and the status of the police occupation itself. That worn phrase "The police are the public and the public are the police," which once suggested the conventional view that policing has a nonpolitical status – benign, unbiased, and, therefore, broadly acceptable – is an empty slogan. Similarly, in the British tradition, it was said that police are "armed with prestige rather than power," which in Robert Reiner's view forced them to seek a similarly broad-based acceptability,[40] a condition that is no longer contemporary: setting police priorities, allocating resources, and exercising discretion obviously involve more authority than prestige. Such practices are political, the nonelected status of police executives notwithstanding.

While the pattern-setting system of police boards was established in Ontario in the mid-nineteenth century, the present system of police governance is the product of twentieth-century evolutions in government administration. Thus, no matter how deficient a system of police supervision may be, it is part of that complex system of municipal-provincial relations with its tight hold on important municipal services. The issue, that arises is one of public access to policing policies, programs, and needed innovations, as the growing credibility of community policing indicates. The newer approach provided by the current reform movement promises outcomes that, while discussed above, merit reiteration. The new reform notion of what "politics" means is likely to influence policing programs well into the future.

Community policing, a function "lost" during the reform movement of the early century and the subsequent bureaucratization of government, encounters a more hospitable social and political environment in the present reform movement. The wisdom of the movement holds that administration and policy making should now be directly linked. It was once popularly believed that a separation of the two was dictated by the need to develop the professionalism of municipal administrators and depoliticize local government in the interests of "clean" administration. "There is only one right way to fill a pothole" was a popular slogan conveying the notion that political intervention in administration was merely costly interference in the work of specialists.[41] The slogan ignores policy questions, such as whether or not to fill the pothole, and reduces an issue to a rare level of simplicity.

Approached more broadly, there is a wider range of factors and interests that are obviously the responsibilities of elected, accountable policy makers. These people need to be attentive to disparate community concerns, to priorities, and to the coordination of programs among various departments and districts – matters of both policy and administration. The complex array of interests in land-use planning, for example, take it well beyond the competence and jurisdiction of professional planners. The point is illustrated by the budgetary process – the ultimate form of priority setting – which fosters innovative approaches in resolving local issues. Elected officials avoid their responsibilities if they merely react to those budgets already prepared and presented and do not themselves control the process.[42]

So the word politics no longer means what it did during the first reform period. In the present period, it means participation by people who are representing and promoting their own interests, policy makers and administrators who are sensitive to them, and public access, at least through procedures that ensure a hearing. Contemporary reformers view politics as competition among diverse interests "to achieve goals that may not all be mutually compatible."[43] The thinking is that it is not possible to have government without politics, and politics means mediating or arbitrating among interests competing for scarce public goods. Clearly, politics cannot be cleansed of this inherent and legitimate bias.

A useful distinction may be made between the intent and the impact of laws. While "the impact of the law and its enforcement in an unequal society will be objectively political even in the narrow sense of partisanship ... it does not follow from this that the law or its enforcement are partisan in intention. This would be a deviation from the legal ideals of impartiality and universalism."[44] Laws have a universal purpose, but urban communities are divided along class, ethnic, gender, cultural, economic, and other lines of inequality and difference, so that the application of the law, even if compliance is impartially sought, may well discriminate among people along the lines of one or another of these divisions. Thus, the impact of a law will be political in nature because of the inequalities in society. This is one way of saying that the political practices the first reform era sought to eradicate remain inherent in government. It is a critique of the partiality of impact that the police seek to avoid. The survival of the early reform model of policing, clean and bureaucratic, was thought to depend on narrowing the scope of policing to the enforcement of laws that have an arguably universal intent; i.e., the police engage in "crime-fighting" as "servants of the law." The law-enforcement image of policing fosters the public impression that police action is largely dictated by their warrant under law and supervised by the courts, an impression still compatible with what many believe their police should be.

The repoliticization of policing, making it clearly accountable to local political offices if not placing it under their immediate direction, has found its proponents. The report of the Waterloo Region Review Commission underlines the strength with which the proposition can be made. Reasons for keeping politics out of policing, it noted, are largely fraudulent, for however the system may be structured, the police governing body must ultimately be responsible to the public. This, the report continued, is both accountability and politics. Having the provincial government, elected through a party system, appoint the majority of commissioners is every bit as "political" and potentially more dangerous than having a local government composed of twenty-four elected individuals from different political parties appoint the police governing body.[45] (As we shall see, where the majority of commissioners are appointed by a municipality or where a committee of council exists, the approach will still remain one of keeping politics out of policing.) Police recognition of the political character of their job and of their local political responsibility for policing services will not, by itself, promote police responsiveness.

So the conundrum persists: how to arrange police accountability and supervision within a political mix of interests, local and central, while fitting these arrangements into the existing structure of government and the criminal-justice system. The time has come to discuss this conundrum from the perspective of professionalization. To begin, the meaning of policing is being revised in keeping with the times.

The failure of the criminal-justice system to control crime has thrown popular thinking about the role of the police as the front-line crime-control institution into some confusion.[46] Durable conventional attitudes still tend to support this combative role, particularly when it is directed at the violent and predatory. The criminal-justice system itself seems to be aimless, given its overall failure not only in controlling crime but in formulating a replacement rationale. This presents police with an occasion, incentive, and responsibility to contribute to resolution of the problem. Their meagre capacity to do so and to participate in relevant public discussions is in evidence.

One definition of policing is exemplified by the pre-eminence it assigns to law enforcement and the kindred, supportive law-and-order attitudes of the public. Such has been the police contribution to the general "There is only one way to fill a pothole" rationale of the first reform of government. The apolitical stance of the "impartial application of the law" made a good fit. Now, as I noted earlier, priority is being given to order maintenance, as the growing attention to community policing indicates, and here public access and police responsiveness are primary attributes. In tandem with the redefinition of politics, the order-maintenance function presents a corresponding redefinition of policing.

A core point of community policing is adaptability to distinctively different communities. As Philip Stenning said, "[The] decision to organize the police locally rather than centrally can properly be seen as a conscious decision that the policing function should be defined and performed more by reference to the characteristics and needs of the local community than by reference to the characteristics and needs of the wider community, 'the people as a whole.' "[47] From this vantage point, the many small-scale arenas of order-maintenance practice – especially police-citizen group interactions – are seen in relief, as is the role of boards, as it becomes clear that order can be the sum of many smaller, individually tailored endeavours.

Apropos of Stenning's comment, an agency will try first to satisfy the senior level of government to which it must account for its performance. Provincial concerns thereby gain in influence regardless of their real importance. Provincial supervision emphasizes internal discipline and reactions to public complaints, uniformity especially in administration, and no surprises or embarrassments. When a sample of police board members were asked who or which body exercised significant influence over their deliberations, the responses, in order, were the union and council (because of contract and budget responsibilities), closely followed by the provincial offices of the attorney general or solicitor general, and finally the provincial commission.[48] Similarly in Britain, the Home Office Inspectorate of the Constabulary certifies departments and grants are tied to those certifications; hence attention settles on administrative standards serving the bureaucratic interests of a central rather than local authority. The resulting loss of influence by the local authorities was described as the chief constable's gain; the postwar amalgamations in Britain reduced the numbers of departments by two-thirds, so that each tended to become, according to Robert Baldwin and Richard Kinsey, much too large for local responsiveness.[49]

SUPERVISION BY BOARDS AND COMMITTEES

One cannot usefully venture into the area of police boards (references to boards are meant to include committees of council unless otherwise indicated) by stating what they are mandated to do and then assessing their levels of success. Rather, what is possible is a description of what they actually do in an uncertain context.

Early in their history, while not numerous, the police had largely the same responsibilities and authorities that they have today. Police departments, as required by the province, were set up by fractious local governments in a society that was highly sectarian in its attitudes and where pronounced social distinctions were often the basis for overtly biased practices – this in the mid- to late Victorian decades. When in the 1850s, a time of some religious disturbances, municipal authorities in Ontario tended to employ police in partisan ways, the establishment of local commissions was required by statute. As McDougall pointed out, the modern public cry in Ontario for efficiency in the fight against rising crime rates was a cry for noninterference in the work of specialists and commanded public support; thus, autonomy, or insulation of police, can be seen as a durable condition. [50]

Much of the following is based on a singular study by Robert Hann and his colleagues[51] of the governance of urban police departments in Canada; it was a descriptive study, so the conclusions and speculations set out here are not theirs. Municipal boards of police commissioners, committees of council, or comparable supervisory offices such as city managers were established at different times across the country according to the pace of settlement and the kind of the policing to be found in different communities – the RCMP, for example, were used in many pioneer communities. The first Ontario municipal boards were established under legislation in 1858.[52] At the present time, there is great variation across Canada: municipal boards do not exist in Prince Edward Island or New Brunswick (though both have some form of enabling legislation) or in Newfoundland, where the jurisdiction of the Royal Newfoundland Constabulary is provincewide. Quebec does not have municipal boards and policing arrangements are all municipal. The authority for the two boards in Manitoba (Winnipeg and Brandon) is municipal but in the remaining four western provinces, it is provincial. The majority of members are appointed by the province in British Columbia and Ontario but by municipalities elsewhere.[53] Actual board practices, however, are surprisingly similar across the country except in Quebec. Generally, they are responsible for the terms of employment of police officers; they are the employers for purposes of the contract (in this, and in some other respects, chiefs and senior officers are not instrumental in negotiating agreements and thus avoid certain management/line officer divergences). Boards generally set hiring procedures, appoint or promote to more senior ranks, and, in smaller centres, select from among individual applicants and carry responsibilities in disciplinary matters. Boards are responsible for setting the police-department budget, which is typically first prepared in the department; in some cases boards have nearly automatic drawing rights on municipal coffers. They are also responsible for budget administration and for the general effectiveness of department administration. In these matters, boards stand between the department and municipal political authorities at large and provide a forum for citizens and citizen groups concerned with some aspect of policing.

One can summarize with the suggestion that, where boards impose accountability on the department, they do so in areas of administration and have been restrained, or otherwise held aloof, from more specialized or functional aspects. So accountability is but a partial thing; boards do not set policing policies or priorities so much as rely on the chief to ensure that these are in place and effectively implemented; they restrict themselves to the efficiencies of management and do not intrude into the policing area itself. Hence they act as a buffer and, by extension, emasculate the notion that police departments are formally accountable to them in responding to local concerns and problems. This is not to deny that boards provide a forum for public expressions of concern and interest. Their traditional mandat has been to monitor administrative performance, but also to provide a barrier to political influence and to act as a conduit for public interest in police policy.

Police executives and board members alike believe that a rationalized division of responsibility would be desirable, but it seems the rationale is too difficult to express. This aspect of police governance revolves around the issue of how one supervises such an endeavour; "how does one govern without meddling," or "how does one permit public voices to be heard without interfering" are erstwhile questions in the search for better means.[54] The provinces in their wisdom have set out no statement governing the division of responsibility except in very general terms. Active search for a rationale, again, is unlikely since chiefs risk losing degrees of autonomy and boards risk unwanted public and political attention. One board chairman, for example, said boards tend to believe that police independence is important because it allows police executives to stand up against "improper political interference." The discussion thus tends to be set in the language of good intentions, relying on often empty terms such as "improper" influence.

The Myth of Board Policy Responsibilities

One can say that in general, a board ensures that the police department is administered efficiently, that matters of the contract and budget are attended to, and that interventions, even of political policy makers, are avoided. These activities however, are specific and minimal and the question where the responsibility for ensuring that policing policies, priorities, and programs lies is not explicit. In other contexts, this would be a matter for a board of directors, but in the case of urban policing, it is left to the police executive. The integration of priorities, policies, and their implementation – in matters having to do with neighbourhood disorders, racial issues, or problems of security raised by women's groups, among others – by police is at least problematic. Whether boards actually have a superior responsibility, whether they are capable of meeting it and do meet it, was explored by Hann and his colleagues.[55]

The unhampered discretion of a police executive to deploy resources as expressed in British common law [56] has been questioned in Canada, but, it seems, not directly.[57] To speculate, it seems that executive latitude in law-enforcement policy making tends to embrace all police programs. For this reason, Hann and his colleagues discussed the matter of division of responsibilities in terms, for example, of a policy operations continuum, with boards apparently involved in the former but eschewing the latter. They also approached the question by distinguishing between long-term (policy) and day-to-day (nonpolicy) decisions.[58] But boards, it was found, exercise scant influence over either area. Policy matters of interest to boards are related to administration; boards are perceived by members and senior police alike as having a voice in over half of the important decisions of a department, but when matters of the employment contract, budget approval, discipline, and other matters of administration are excluded, board policy activity, or even any discussion of resource deployment and related considerations, is almost nonexistent.[59] In short, there was little in the record of a board's proceedings to suggest some clear boundary or underlying rationale for the police chief/board division of responsibility. None exists, and by default, the chief has it.

There is, however, an arrangement that supplies its own plausible, working rationale, an arrangement that is unlikely to be found in formal records of board chief of police relations. It consists in the fact that if needed policing policies are in place and effectively implemented, the major responsibility is met. "If" rather than "who by" becomes the important point; the question which authority carries which responsibilities is moot, if the responsibilities are met. It may be said that a *modus operandi* has been achieved, one, it is emphasized, that is largely informal and peculiar to locale. There are many informal understandings among police executives and board or committee members; they are shaped by minor day-to-day contacts and exchanges that allow for the anticipation and handling of concerns are anticipated and attended to before any internal dispute can erupt. Such an arrangement follows no pattern and resists categorization. It involves an unspoken division, born of habit and understanding, whereby certain responsibilities are tacitly reserved for one side or the other, with a kind of no-man's land in between. One board member remarked that members appointed by city council prefer not to become involved in police issues. The commissioners' concern is that funds, no matter how they are spent, be spent frugally. Even where the majority of board members are appointed by the municipality or where a committee of council for police matters exists, police autonomy appears to be stronger, as with the larger forces in Quebec.[60] In my observation, boards, even though charged with budget approval, do not corporately scrutinize the utility of policing programs and their costs in an informed way, though some members may do so individually. If so, they are scarce.

The Waterloo Commission report argued that police independence is predicated on law-enforcement activities that are based on the individual authority of the officer. But it noted that the greater departmental effort, especially patrol, is oriented to prevention outcomes and is thus eminently manageable and, one might add, accessible. The report of the Canadian study by Hann et al., expanding on the matter, pointed to the importance to a community of policing as a service, both on its own and in its interrelationships with other civic services, and cited a conclusion in the Robarts Commission report that current arrangements made it virtually impossible for the public and its elected officials to make an informed assessment of a commission or of the management and operation of the department.[61] The same report noted that modern political processes are not sinister and that councils are not unworthy of confidence.

A key issue is access, how citizens might be brought closer to centres of discretion that control priorities, programs, and the quality of their implementation. Current reform attitudes tend to view access as a right. Boards provide a somewhat passive conduit for citizen groups, while police autonomy survives behind its own operations bulwark. A board member in one metropolitan centre put it thus: the concern is who sets the agenda – who selects the winners and losers from among police programs.[62]

In reality, the need for a shield for police authority is a secondary consideration given modern reform attitudes, an activist public, and heightened public scrutiny through the media. The concern was dismissed by the Robarts Commission report, which, along with others, pointed to the political "hands off" attitude as a source of difficulty in the management and supervision of policing.[63] It tends to distort new policing programs, such as order-maintenance programs that work in partnership with neighbourhood people, which implies sharing power with them. Pepinski's proposal [64] (the procedural outline for a neighbourhood policing program, summarized in chapter 4) illustrates how a form of authority sharing might take place.

SUMMARY – THE SENIOR CRAFT IN THE ECHELONS OF GOVERNMENT

This chapter has argued that supervision by government has sheltered policing from development rather than promoted its occupational growth. This has been achieved through the fragmentation of policing into many municipal departments, its dependent status as the regulated agency of a senior government, and its quasi-professional status, that is, as an unorganized occupation without stature in the larger array of the professions. Policing was part of the first reform movement in government, the occasion of its early depoliticization and emphasis on the law-enforcement function. Its standing as a craft made it peripheral to the professionalization and compartmentalization of government – police do not figure in the offices, boards, and commissions of government. Yet, the law-enforcement function gave it a protected place under the dominant influence of the provincial government. The perspective on policing tends to be administrative rather than geographical and political, a feature that has unquestionably impoverished thinking about police services.

The police occupation centred on managerial competence and bureaucratized departments then settled on the vital and esoteric practices of law enforcement. During the early nineteenth century, health care was accepted as a vital public service; it received largely local funding and was entrusted to a professional but local medical community, which, then as now, had impressive policy as well as administrative responsibilities and a considerable depth of occupational resources. The postwar decades brought the province and senior professionals into the dominant policy and management roles that we are now accustomed to. However, the medical profession itself – autonomous and perhaps not unbiased – staffs the relevant offices of government and does much to contribute to public dialogue on health-care policies and priorities (the debate about funding, which is subject to provincial largesse, is an example).

The authority for setting priorities among policing programs and of allocating resources accordingly carries considerable weight, for it implies a profound knowledge of, for example, the degree to which the security of citizens and the order of various neighbourhoods is threatened, the nature of the threats, and the costs of not attending to them. That authority may be rooted in legislation, but if it is not also rooted in knowledge and competence, given the nature of the consequences, it can and arguably should be at least accessible and accountable to the concerned clientele. These requisites of knowledge and competence are not met by board members or government officials, and they are inadequately met by the police occupation itself.

Postindustrial society is characterized by the shift from a man machine mode of production to knowledge-based services; the common form of wealth is no longer property but knowledge. This society is marked, not by goods, but by quality of life. Beyond security, as Bell has said, the chief determinants of quality are health and education, followed by such prominent desirables as recreation, information, and communication.[65] Failure to meet the need for decent living environments leads to growth in government, particularly local government, the level at which such needs have to be met. The appropriate size of the social unit organized to provide and manage the provision of some service may well vary according to the nature of the service. Municipal governments may no longer have the capacity to provide the major services of formerly local jurisdiction that today's transformed, expanding urban concentrations require. Provincial authorities that respond to an intractable problem with a diagnosis of municipal inadequacy is handling the matter often overlook the more basic, shifting complexity of scale. As a result, it has been suggested that "regions" could be redefined or accepted as geographically variable according to the nature of the service, each perhaps having a different overlay on the political map and, one presumes, a more variable governmental arrangement of the sort exemplified by regional and planning areas of the recent past. Thus, one may examine the regional fit of a service along existing political/demographic lines; according to the optimum size of the administering bureaucracy (as determined, for example by its sensitivity to relevant interests); or along public and private lines (in terms of ownership, funding, and purpose, of which profit might be one). These are by no means the only useful distinctions to be made between organized social units. In this way the level of government at which a police department is organized can be tailored to the nature and scope of its programs and the size and diversity of its clientele. This kind of thinking is not radical: hospitals, after all, tend to be arranged along these lines.

Bell suggests that the processes of innovation are as much political as technical because of their effects on the structure of society in a time of rapid change. In speed and scope, this is the greatest political revolution of our times. This brings me to technical decision making, which calls for people with the skills to forecast the constraints ahead and to formulate alternative responses in detail. The rigours of technical complexity will shift power from legislative to executive bodies as planning takes central stage. The outcome of the impending conflict between technocratic and political approaches cannot be predicted with certainty. Society, however, is becoming more communal; groups seek to establish rights where rights were once the domain of the individual. Occasions for conflict among competing interests will increase. The bases for settlement will not be technical but political. Bell predicted a societywide uprising against bureaucracy (including professionalization and technical decision making) and a widespread desire for participation. It is becoming axiomatic, even with policing, that people ought to be able to influence the decisions that affect their lives.

In the postindustrial society, the nonprofit sector (largely based on public funding) will grow. Government, universities, hospitals, research laboratories, and welfare organizations will be major employers, but few of their functions will be suited to the current system of planning and management and are evolving even now. Governmental approaches and policing itself are surely being challenged by these changing political/bureaucratic arrangements.

CHAPTER SEVEN

Competent, Accountable, and Autonomous – Professionals in Urban Society

THE MATTER OF PROFESSIONALISM

Leonard O. Gertler and Ronald W. Crowley characterized professionalism as the joining of competence and advanced technology to the ideals of social service and social justice.[1] The professionalization of occupations is a widely accepted, common method by which to ensure their continued competence, and accountability, in serving the vital interests of clients. In the modern context, a nonprofessionalized police occupation is an anomaly. The issue of police professionalism bears directly on their occupational competence, responsiveness to social needs, accountability, and capacity to evolve.

Terrence J. Johnson suggested a more economical definition of professionalism as an occcupation's statutory authority to manage itself[2] (in Canada, professions are chartered by provincial legislation). The characteristics of existing professions are so variable there is little hope of drawing out a more informative definition.

Typically, an occupation moving towards self-management displays the following characteristics.

- The service it provides is devoted to a common, vital interest of society.
- It lays exclusive claim to a substantial body of systematic knowledge and exercises a capacity to maintain that knowledge; members are required to be competent in its use and to contribute to it.
- Valid methods, common within the profession, are used to test and add to the knowledge base so that it is continually being refined and expanded.

- Qualifying for entry requires a substantial commitment of time and effort.
- The occupation is self-regulating; it has strong ethics, the authority to preserve these ethics, and a capacity to promote excellence and commitment to service.
- The occupational code of ethics is internalized so that there is a high level of self-control.
- Members are committed to the interests of clients, which stand before all other interests.
- The occupation is autonomous and bears overall responsibility for maintaining standards in serving clients.
- It has the right to declare incompetent an external evaluation of its performance.
- In part at least, it can assert that communication with clients is privileged.
- It has a monopoly of practice; that is, it exercises control over the characteristics of those admitted to the occupations over the method of entry, and over those attempting to practice or claim professional status.

These characteristics are also relevant: the occupation must be involved in some way with public policy;

- commitment, the salience of a set of beliefs, a way of life; and
- concern for the well-being of others.

James Q. Wilson includes in his definition of a profession the authority to certify that, through education and apprenticeship, the arts and skills necessary for competence have been achieved. Members must willingly embrace the professional code of ethics and have a sense of duty to colleagues; they are subject to the regulation and discipline of professional sanctions, including decertification. The occupation is self-governing through a collegial body. The authority of nominal superiors is restricted. Their reputation among their fellow professionals is taken seriously, and some of them devote themselves to enhancing the professional knowledge base through writing and research.[3]

Johnson holds that many of the characteristics used to define a profession are merely part of a variable set of qualities that predispose an occupation to professional eligibility. His expansion on the above list is equally informative:[4]

- Professional occupations draw on a heterogeneous source of clientele – the public at large – that has generally unrestricted access to the profession's services. (There is an implied dependency here, for the sick must seek the physician, who can potentially acquire authority over them; the sick thus risk exploitation. A numerous undifferentiated clientele is the basis for extended authority – contrast the influence and authority of architects, who have few clients, with the broader influence of lawyers. If differences among clients are expressed along systematic lines, then there will be pressures for differentiated services tailored to categories of clients: "client specialization" is common in law, architecture, psychology, and medicine, among others.)

- Specializations within an occupation are relatively few but not necessarily absent; an occupation must present itself as a coherent grouping without competing offerings of service. That is, members must not be allowed to offer themselves as specifically competent in a particular area and thereby breach the myth of equal competence the occupation necessarily presents to its clientele. (Later, specializations will develop but on a contained basis. Generalists, for example, will retain positions of authority and the professional may well be barred from publicly indicating a special area of work; however, where there is a scientific expansion into more differentiated areas to satisfy needs, new specializations in older occupations will tend to emerge, rather than new occupations.)
- Members display a common identity in a collegial community under their own, usually self-imposed control and accept the myth of equal competence.
- Professions emerged as part of, and in alliance with, the still-growing urban middle class in Victorian England, a politically influential social grouping of people that now, in postindustrial society, increasingly constitutes a distinct class.
- An occupation exists as a profession insofar as the public agrees, and then its voice will be accepted as socially authoritative, which is an extension of the authority of science or knowledge.
- Professionals have shared identity – "the myth of a community of people of equal competence" initially attained through a common means of assimilation (i.e., a single means of entry; inculcation of occupational norms during training, close supervision, and apprenticeship; effective control of vocational schools by practitioners; later, with growth and stability, the establishment of major institutions, such as medical schools and hospitals; a powerful association that includes within its membership virtually all practitioners; and a recognized credential-granting agency).
- Professions lay claim to cognitive exclusiveness, that is, substantial, systematic knowledge in the exclusive possession of practitioners by

which an area of service is monopolized. (Schön noted that, while major professions are grounded in systematic, fundamental knowledge, of which scientific knowledge is the prototype, minor professions have no exclusive claim to a defined body of knowledge and suffer, as juniors, from unstable institutional contexts of practice, especially at the hands of those in the major professions.[5] There are many examples; teaching, in transition to fuller professional status, once had a less specialized body of knowledge, a shorter training period before qualification, less-widely accepted status, less well established rights to privileged communication, and an autonomy greatly curtailed by a bureaucratic employment context with social and political interventions. A scientific-technological base has to exist and appear to exist; thus, for example, librarians become "information scientists," one of many such terms that tend to mask an occupation as minor rather than a fully fledged profession.

Johnson further asserts that professionalism arises where the tensions inherent in the practitioner-client relationship are controlled by means of an institutional framework based upon occupational authority; otherwise put, professionalism is the mechanism of managing that relationship.[6]

The notion of uncertainty in practitioner-client relations invites a comment on those aspects of professionalism that are related to occupational management and accountability. Historically there were four professions attending to the whole person: the religious ministry for the soul; professors for the mind; physicians for the body; and lawyers for one's relations with others. The four were distinguishable by distinctive garb, a monopoly of one sort of work, apparent poverty (for a higher calling was presumed), privileged communication, and jargon. In time, their capacity to abuse or seriously harm others was recognized as sufficient to warrant regulation to lessen uncertainty: a profession is an occupation that is potentially dangerous when its practitioners are irresponsible or incompetent.

Uncertainty is common in the producer-consumer relationship. "Goods satisfactory or your money back," like most product guarantees, is a form of a retailer's self-regulation designed to reduce and control uncertainty. Many largely single-occupation firms, such as travel agencies, may belong to an association that promotes service-wide standards and public confidence. The hugely expensive funding of professional schools and research programs are charges accepted by the public and reflect, in part, the desire to avoid uncertainties about competence.

Uncertainty is accentuated by the client's dependency on the practitioner, an apparent imbalance of power, as well as by an element of the unknown in the eventual outcome of the transaction; it may be a matter of whose definition of "goodness" will prevail, the client's, practitioner's, that of the public at large, or even that of the law. The practitioner's esoteric knowledge can baffle clients likewise professional reticence, the solemn rituals of many professions, and the routine use of jargon.

Taken together, high levels of uncertainty and exclusive, effective knowledge and skills permit an occupation to impose its definition of the practitioner/client relationship to a remarkable degree. Medicine comes to mind here. Further, if the profession has an extensive alliance with an influential group, for example lawyers with legislators, it may be able to expand its general definition of the relationship with clients to embrace more and more client interests, that is, to expand the bounds of its monopoly. Such strongly professionalized occupations can minimize intrusions into their relationship with clients by others such as government, preserve favourable working contexts, and set noncompetitive fee schedules.

The strength of a profession depends on its demonstrated ability to "manage" uncertainty; this ability forms the basis for exclusion of other practitioners, who may then be classified as charlatans or quacks. There are some major areas of professional practice that are not defined in legislation. Some may overlap; the line between architects and engineers, for example, is left unspecified. Urban planners are slow to claim legislated professional status in some provinces because they are unable to define their specific area of practice without overlapping onto other professions. The issue for an occupation may thus be the ability to command public recognition so as to defend a limited, often ill-defined area of service when only a part, even if the greater part, of it applied knowledge and skills is exclusive to the occupation. If knowledge and skills are not thought to be exclusive to a given occupation, professionalization will receive scant support.

In Victorian England, members of the professions came largely from the upper and uppermiddle classes, where political power lay.[7] Mutual trust within the influential classes, essential to the development of self-regulation, was a given. The path to self-regulation was eased by the politics of the days and particularly unpopular governmental limitations on commerce. In the United States, on the other hand, until about a century ago, no qualifications were required of lawyers.[8] Industrialization and urbanization were accompanied by the emergence of the suburban middle class whose prospering members were the primary clients of the professions, sharing their values and promoting their self-regulating monopolies.

Specialized divisions of labour have always been a characteristic of urbanizing societies. New occupations and professions and the specializations within them continue to come into existence. In Ontario, in the health-care field, seven occupations – midwifery, dietetics, audiology, occupational therapy, speech pathology, medical-laboratory technology, and respiratory therapy – were far along the path to self-regulation in the early 1990s. But even though professions are now of commoner coinage, they are still important social institutions of some status.

The vital nature of professional service necessarily dictates that client interests come before its own; under self-management, the integrity of the practitioner/client relationship rests on the primacy of the client's interest. Therefore, responsibility and accountability are fixed on the practitioner and, corporately, the profession. Where members of an occupation can inflict only minor damage on the public interest, as with the travel business or real estate, some form of external regulation suffices. Social workers constitute a "professional" workforce but the crucial specialist/client relationship is mediated by the employing government bureaucracy, often with the public purse rather than the client in mind.[9] (Social-welfare specialists have an association whose membership they control and professional departments in universities, so there are so-called professional processes involved; there is no "pure" example of professional responsibility wherein the specialist/client relationship is never modified or changed in one way or another.) The anomalous or quasi-professional status of social-welfare specialists is a result.

THE KNOWLEDGE OF
PROFESSIONALS AND SOCIETY

Knowledge is the stuff of professionalism. The validity of knowledge rests on scientific methods and implies an essential capacity to be expanded, as the professional schools at universities and the huge sums they spend on research affirm. Where the criteria of validity are not met, a modern occupation does not merit professional status because it cannot guarantee competence and diminish the uncertainties of clients. This raises the issues of specialist knowledge as public knowledge, integrity and the validity of knowledge, the instrumentality of knowledge in the service of the public, and professionalization in the management of change, all of which have significant social effects.

The notion of "expertise" and its role in public policy role was prominent during the pre-war years and on into the immediate postwar period. The term expert was often invoked during the professionalization of government, until experts were displaced by professionals. In terms of knowledge, the distinction between expert and professional qualifications was that of experience versus substantial educational. From this perspective, the still-current idea of police professionalism is characterized more by "expertise." Samuel Walker, reflecting on the history of police reform over the past century, noted that the dominant features of modern US police administration – bureaucratic, semimilitary, and hierarchical, with a tightly knit subculture – had taken shape by the end of the 1930s.[10]

Experts were sometimes said to have such intense experience with in their subject area that common sense was sacrificed to it and the ability to see around it lost. Experts and technocrats, wedded to the orthodoxies of their subject matter, resisted change. It was an inertia, in Dewey's terms, of tradition and habit, or, according to Mill, the despotism of custom. Such was the thinking when the concept of the expert police administrator-specialist was being promoted. When initiatives belonged to the expert, as they did to August Vollmer and O.W. Wilson, a bureaucracy developed along with its vices. Among them, in Harold Laski's words, the mistaking of technical results for social wisdom.[11] In contrast, the wisdom of the "plain man" lay in day-to-day experience, in common sense and a sense of the rightness of things, so that on election day, ordinary folk could express themselves collectively on matters of broad directions, if not on details. The hierarchy of social values lay outside the domain of expertise, so the place of social values in policy making was said to be the preserve of lay people. Laski suggested that an expert's conclusion is a second best until it has been examined in terms of a scheme of values unrelated to that person's area of specialization. He noted that expert leadership contrasts with democratic leadership in that political wisdom depends on an understanding of "common" life.[12]

Management by experts and the assessment of their products posed practical problems, though less so now, in the administration of government. The "statesman," that gifted amateur, was invented to stand between the expert and policy; this wise public servant, appointed or elected, was adept at reconciling the antagonistic views of experts. He could make decisions without giving reasons and saw things in a general way, simplifying and coordinating. Experts developed policy options from among which this Solon selected. But it seems that expert leadership and the wisdom derived from everyday life are rarely combined in the same person, including politicians. The "statesman," sufficiently wise and intuitive, proved elusive, so a conglomerate of virtue –

a board, for example, in its collective wisdom – was substituted. This reasoning may have been appropriate in its day. But the place of the professional in governmnet is quite different, and the place of the professional in the government of a postindustrial society different again, if not always clear.

With the current surge in accessible knowledge, urban living becomes more complex and professional occupations multiply. Where they are not swamped by the esoteric, lay people have the means to expand the common knowledge in technical and social areas that are relevant to urban life. This is a growing phenomenon, but not new. It was suggested as early as 1936 that the common understanding of many physical events and material things – even of historical events and peoples – had become a new social force: the product of scientific inquiry widely shared. This understanding gained in social authority; any conflict between, say, theology and science, faith and evidence, had to do, not with theories, but with alignments of authority. Productivity in education, science, and communication means that the "plain man" is becoming an even more informed person – in matters of nutrition, health, and the prevention of illness; increasingly so in matters of the environment; in the processes of education; and in the priorities of the market place. With better education and bountiful means of communication, we are more and more literate in technical matters. Moreover, since the issues we face – in cities, for example – are tough, the incentive to know about them is powerful.

From the pre-war period on, we have witnessed the spread of cities across a once-rural landscape and the spread of science-based knowledge across our intellectual landscape. Knowledge, I suggest, now mediates between specialist and policy maker, replacing experts and the search for statesmen.

Though specialized knowledge is the well-spring of innovation, society need never be wholly technocratic. The power to initiate, to direct public attention to particular needs or possibilities for action, lies in a coalescence of knowledge, interests, and attitudes within society, so that a new communal ethic – a widely shared, revised morality or structure of values aligned to the social authority of knowledge – may be coming into being.[13] This revised ethic, it seems to me, occasions anticipation in the way that an electorate, or some part of it, will expect that the political élite will communicate intentions and promote discussions on matters of significance. Society, then, is becoming more fractious and the implications for policing, police accountability, and politics are significant.

Does the specialist/professional offer advice or speak only when spoken to? Do specialists have political, strategic, or moral concerns that allow them to advise not just on narrow technical matters but on broad policy as well? In simpler days, as Bell suggested, technical matters could be left to the expert.[14] Now the technical dimension is no longer divorced from policy; the specialist has inevitably become an advocate for one policy or another but usually on rational rather than political grounds. The crux of the matter, of course, is the locus of policy making in the social/political area, for example, for the community-policing function. Must a public-service institution or profession be sheltered from political considerations so as to pursue, unfettered, activities on rational/legal grounds? Ordinarily, one heeds the advice of the competent: a doctor, an orchestra conductor, or a chemical engineer. However, people are increasingly knowledgable about political processes and choices (involving, for example, costs, effectiveness, and bias) so that heeding advice touching on public interests has new shades of meaning. However, according to Bell, "it is more likely ... that the post-industrial society will involve *more* politics than ever before, for the very reason that choice becomes conscious and the decision centers more visible ... Since politics is a compound of interests and values, and these are often diverse, an increased degree of conflict and tension is probably unavoidable in the post-industrial society."[15] The growing ranks of technical and professional people, especially in government bureaucracies, indicate the increasingly technical nature of political decisions, so the need to strike a balance between technocrats and those in a political system who respond to major interests becomes an issue. There will be a common core of problems centring on the relation of science to public policy, and these can be solved in different ways and for different purposes.[16]

To repeat, the newer actor on this stage is knowledge, widely shared in the form, often, of nontechnical generalities and integrated into public attitudes and purposes, so that the rational and political are blended all the more in the discussions of policy. The dilemma – the persistent matter of accountability in high-utility, high-technology professions that serve public purposes – is being redefined rather than lost in a surge of technical rationality.

The proposition is twofold. First, there is growing public awareness of the ineffectiveness of familiar policing programs and the unresolved problems of security. It is no surprise that a rethinking of the purposes of policing and a search for new approaches to ongoing problems is becoming common. Since we still have a long way to go, new knowledge of policing will pervade the urban consciousness and become authoritative. (Knowledge is now the authority that commands respect, while the trust and deference given public institutions has declined.) It is reasonable to conclude that public/political arrangements that foster timely discussion of policing purposes, programs, and outcomes will emerge. And, if professionalized, the police will become more practical.

As knowledge of urban life and of policing becomes disseminated and widely discussed, public attitudes may increase the pressure for a redeveloped policing occupation. As noted elsewhere, the public is commonly disposed to the law-and-order bent in urban policing, and the customary expert-based game plan of policing still holds sway. The attitudes behind these positions, set out in chapter 2, are strongly held in and out of policing. Advances in policing and the professionalization of the occupation may well be severely impeded, even unlikely, without a better informed citizenry.

In scientific or professional areas, the collective intelligence is disciplined by the rigours of learning. The method of learning is an open and accepted process through which advances (i.e., evidence for this or that proposition) are achieved. Contrasting ideas and divergent theories may surface, but the method itself is central and unchallenged. As evidence collects, knowledge makes its way against what John Dewey called inertia, entrenched traditions and habits surmounted by an emotional halo.

Integrity is rooted in the highly personal endeavour of acquiring both knowledge and the skills to apply it; it places an explicit value on the limits and uses of knowledge, thereby constituting an internal standard that is immediately recognized and professionally acceptable. A professional's reputation among colleagues hinges on this point. No professional association can successfully regulate its members in a climate of less internalized standards. An administrative structure of professional calibre, of collegiality, openness, and trust, is based on integrity thus defined. Maintenance policing – rather than legal force – engenders a high standard of similar values based on what James Q. Wilson called civility.

THE EXPERIENCE OF EDUCATION

Preparatory education or training can be said to occur on four levels: the level of crafts, where higher education is not involved and there is no reliance on theory or verbal abstractions; that of technicians, which involves postsecondary education; the professional, which demands advanced university education; and the managerial, which stands in weak relation to higher education and makes no claim to professionalism. Whether an educated police officer is more effective on the street is tangential: education is a principal means by which advanced knowledge can be brought to bear on urban problems, in policing education is an occupational or corporate endeavour, untried but eminently promising.

It has been suggested that the goals of education should be effective thinking and communication, the ability to discriminate between values, and the ability to make relevant judgments; these are the rather vague aims of a liberal-arts education. Professional schools, on the other hand, are sometimes faulted for concentrating exclusively on technical subject areas, thereby producing technocrats rather than educated professionals. A debate on the issue is beyond my scope here, so I postulate a twofold educational purpose: the advanced development of the faculties of the mind (critical thinking and the ability to handle ideas and values) and the exercise of these faculties in specialized and general subject areas.

A professional education is also directed at the development of internalized standards of behaviour based on well-understood goals of service and methods of the performance – in short, integrity. It is concerned with the various ways and means of achieving its goals in varied cases, not merely with the acquisition of some technical formula or recipe. It strives for a mastery of principles and, accordingly, a capacity to identify or discriminate among problems, relationships, and responses. In a similar vein, the select panel assembled in 1979 to advise the Canadian Police College on its senior officer training program noted the importance of intellectual skills that enable officers to identify problems, define them, and seek alternative solutions within the context of the basic role of the organization.[17]

It has been said that "keeping abreast" is possible only if one is educated in the first instance to think and study independently; education must leave an enduring habit of learning. One commonplace characteristic of the professional is a personal commitment, across a working life, to at least keeping abreast. The achievement of the rank of Ph.D. or executive is but a milestone in this process.

Learning is also an explicit process. Mere participation in events is without usefulness and such participation, though it is given the label experience, is a poor teacher of nuance and meaning in a world of cause and effect. Generally, it teaches understanding of none but the plainest matters. On the other hand, treating a specific segment of experience as a test of the usefulness of some particular knowledge reinforces or modifies what was learned and a true experience is gained. Thus, experience is no proxy for knowledge; experience alone is insufficient for the continued performance of a critical role in society.

Much of this discussion has been based on Schön's concept of "re-flection in action," (i.e., the use of specialized, scientific knowledge in problem solving through a particular approach to a task, an approach common in professional work).[18] Professions have known ends and their method of practice, "reflection in action," is instrumental in achieving those ends; method is the bridge between relevant knowledge and the problem at issue. Such knowledge has four qualities: it is highly specialized; firmly bounded (i.e., limited in scope and, with exceptions, exclusive to the specialists); scientific; and standardized (i.e., recognized for specific uses within the occupation). But it is neither fixed nor complete, but tentative. The evidence of its usefulness in different situations is variable and never absolutely convincing. Hence, to minimize uncertainty, such tentative knowledge must be fastidiously applied according to some simple prescriptive method. The methods of less technical occupations are inadequate.

A client's problem, according to Schön, is not a given but must be constructed from the materials of the client's problematic situation, which is often puzzling and uncertain. In order to formulate a problematic situation as a problem, a practitioner must do a certain kind of work. "Reflection in action" describes the process by which a problem is defined along with the desired ends and means of solving it within the scope of the technology and its accepted uses. Elements of a problematic situation are screened for the technical information they may convey as to the nature of a problem (much as pain and fever do in medicine). Problems differ one from another, so a practitioner requires a mechanism by which to classify and assess them. To make sense of a problem, however unique and unfamiliar, one must tentatively locate it in the relevant sector of specialist knowledge by identifying familiar elements. Next, the similarities to and differences from what is known and tried must be explicitly identified.[19] This is the start of the process of informed selection and rejection of information that indicates the technical constituents of a problem. Plainly, a client's problem – be it in medicine, law, architecture, or chemical engineering – must be redefined on the basis of its technical properties; the desired outcomes must be established on a similar basis, and the means to achieve them fashioned accordingly. No step is certain, each is a matter of reflection; problems in the human condition are infinite. There are few ready prescriptions and no bottom-line techniques of general applicability in the practices of a modern profession.

The outcomes or resolutions sought in any one situation, as well as the level of success, is variable. Once selected, the means of their achievement have to be invented (though the process is interactive, the selection from among possible outcomes being influenced by probabilities of success, or costs, of any one set of means). The presence of certainty or of a routine solution suggests a task that will probably be assigned to a professional junior. The reflection-in-action version of the professional method can be called a unique habit of a working mind.

There are other habits of the working mind, approaches characteristic of other occupations – the performing arts, administration, politics, flying high-performance jet aircraft – each differing from the next. We tend to be unaware that the habits familiar in one's occupation, though rational and results oriented, may be dissimilar to others and so misunderstood as being, perhaps too pragmatic or too "academic," hopelessly impractical and intellectual. The community-policing approach, if well developed, is a potential example of reflection-in-action.

In spite of the contributions of science to society, most people doubt that social ills can all be cured. If the purpose of professional knowledge is to meet the needs and problems of society, one might question whether it is adequate to the task.[20] Still, contributions are being made. As crime and disorder persist in our imperfect and complex communities – the unstable context of police practice – society will surely come to expect that police equip themselves with the discipline and competence that professional education and habits bring.

There are no Canadian university programs offering an education in the practice of policing – no "professional" schools of urban policing. In the absence of suitable options, officers engaged in part-time studies typically choose subjects in the social and behavioural sciences, such as psychology or the psychology of abnormal behaviour, in an often questionable belief that these fields have something to do with policing. A commentary on the possible content of police education is out of place at this point, and little would be served by reviewing the many studies of the successes or failures of higher education for the police, which tended to measure success and failure in terms of the immediate improvement in performance, or lack thereof, of recruit and experienced officer alike. Few studies, if any, addressed the contribution of appropriately educated people to the resources and competence of the occupation itself.[21]

Goldstein, in speaking of the ends of police education, suggested that higher education has come to be "synonymous with a commitment to challenge, questioning, criticizing and analyzing" and a way of instilling new values and broader perspectives."[22] Knowledge relevant to urban policing, is substantial, valid, and increasingly available, more so now than when the Law Enforcement Education Program ran its ill-fated course in the United States. When immense sums were given over to police education under that defunct program, commensurate improvement on the part of the individual or the occupation overall was not found. One analysis pointed convincingly to the low quality of the educational programs, which were intellectually shallow, conceptually narrow and provided by a faculty that is far from scholarly, and noted that undemanding programs, part-time, piecemeal routes to graduation credentials, were not capable of instilling the desired intellectual discipline.[23] The failure was attributable in part to police input or advice, for they seek training oriented to technique and operations but will concede that a program is legitimate to the extent that it is staffed by experienced, if retired, officers. A program of police education, then, was not the boon it promised to be. This recent experience provides lessons, few of which are positive, but no patterns for the next time around. The targets of learning (the discipline of the intellect in handling matters of principle and discrimination among ideas and values) and the habits of learning were both missing from these educational exercises. On a more modest scale, the Canadian experience with two-year "law enforcement and security" community-college programs was similarly disappointing vis-à-vis novice or prospective police officers.[24] (However, should there develop more that one category of police officer, each differing according to the tasks to be performed, then as in many other areas, community-college programs may well be an essential resource.)

It was mentioned earlier that of the vast public resources devoted to occupational education and training in Canada, a minuscule part goes to policing, a major public institution; there has been scant pressure, from public and political forums or from the occupation itself, to remedy this situation.

THE FOCUS AND ELEMENTS OF SELF-MANAGEMENT

T. Culyer Young, Jr. observes that "There is a basic tension – even conflict between modern democracy and professionals. Modern democracy is a complicated social equation built on the axiom that any person's view on any matter must be considered to be as valid and worthy of serious consideration as another's ... Professionalism is, or can be, the antithesis of this position: only those who are truly well informed on a subject and who are therefore professionals can have a valid and worthwhile opinion on that subject."[25]

Young, a museum curator and member of an occupation that is in the process of becoming professionalized, is understandably sensitive to the possibility, indeed the reality, of the intrusion of external influences into professional practice. His conclusion, though, may be given an unwarranted, sweeping interpretation, that all external assessments will be invalid in the esoteric realm of the occupation. It was noted earlier that a profession is a practical social invention whereby knowledge becomes an instrument in the resolution, however imperfect, of its problems. The institutions we have put in place to attend to matters of order, law, and crime, especially the police, have this fundamental quality: they are society's instruments for the resolution of some of its ills.

Young's comment – that the esoteric nature of occupational knowledge provides a bulwark against external assessments or other interventions into a professional matter – may be valid if the matter under discussion falls within the narrow limits of purely technical know-how or within a practitioner/client relationship. Occupational knowledge depends on the rigorous application of scientific knowledge and methods and thus on the quality of evidence on which they are based; the assessment of that evidence and the resulting codification of that knowledge are appropriately restricted to the professional.

A police executive enjoys considerable autonomy in setting priorities, in allocating and deploying resources, and, unquestionably, in selecting programs through which major functions are carried out. The executive and the department remain largely free of the processes of oversight for a board, committee of council, or mayor tend to act as intervening baffles. In this context, the issue will be who contributes to the definition of a problem of order and who selects the particular outcomes to be achieved and deems costs and means acceptable. Public/political participation is missing. In a more fractious society, the meanings and measures of policing success will be of obvious, open concern.[26]

When public interests are involved, valid, substantial, even unique knowledge – advice – if not always forthcoming, is expected to be provided from within a science or profession whose objectivity is unruffled by the pressures of the day. A community at large is being served. However, when a profession claims to serve an undifferentiated clientele, "the public at large," it must be understood that the public at large constitutes a "pool" of potential clients from which those who are actually served are drawn – in the case of the police, those with acute problems of security. The claim of serving the public at large obscures the place of a specific public interest and diffuses the place of accountability. (The "agency" model of professional practice, discussed below, helps to sort out client and practitioner roles. It dictates that both a recognized element of the public and the esoteric knowledge of the specialist have central roles.) Maureen Cain, a British scholar, disputed the notion that police operational matters are professional, so highly technical in all respects as to be nonpolitical; she suggested that this position was no more than an organized ideological force pre-empting the field of debate. (The autonomy of police in the pursuit of individual criminal cases is not in dispute here.) She suggested that the implied ability of police to speak for the public is demagoguery, even if it is a part of a rhetoric that shapes public attitudes. She noted that it is not the place of the police to question or challenge social changes but to understand or know them and to facilitate them, involving, as they do, diversity and conflict.[27] But, in the practices of local authorities or boards in Britain as in Canada, the items for accountability still amount to matters of housekeeping and administrative efficiency.

A claim to the authority of exclusive knowledge beyond the understanding of informed lay people and untranslatable into common parlance is crudely simplistic. Canadians are said to defer to ideas and relevant knowledge rather than to institutions and politicians. But where the public interest is involved, one might expect that a claim to authority based solely on such arcane knowledge would arouse suspicion and a sense of risk. This is an élitist stance. A claim to unfettered discretion is a signal for caution. There are narrow occupational matters which only the "truly well informed" have a valid opinion of, for example, technical practices recognized within the occupation as acceptable. On broader matters, those involving public interests, or when an occupation enjoys no knowledge, the claim to an exclusive opinion in a technical area is clearly deficient. An insistence that knowledge and understanding of policing are the exclusive preserve of those who have joined the brotherhood, as it were, is a deficient claim.

Self-regulation is concerned with three things: the assurance of competence; the independence of the professional and thus the protection of the practitioner/client relationship; and integrity, or the ethical quality of performance. Without reference to the "infrastructure" of a profession, such as professional schools, the research programs through which professional knowledge and technological support are expanded, professional associations, and self-administered codes, these three attributes include, among other things:

- specification of the qualifying process (typically by way of substantial, specialist education followed by practical training such as internships and articling) and a mechanism for certifying the practitioner-to-be, for example, examinations;
- a monopoly of practice, control of the rights to titles (e.g., the right to offer oneself to the public as a psychologist), specification of who may enter into practice, and, usually, what activities constitute practice;

- development and application of codes of ethics aimed at the protection of the client, and the capacity to discipline offenders including decertification;
- regulation of advertising and fees (in some professions, it is felt that marketplace competition is ineffective in ensuring competence, so fee schedules or guidelines are permitted), offering or advertising oneself as a specialist within a profession, including law (banned in the past, professional advertising is now more permissible, regardless of its effect on the notion that all members of a given profession are of equal competence);
- a prohibition, in some jurisdictions,[28] on partnerships with nonprofessionals; the legal profession, for example, prevents nonlawyers from practising law or influencing law partners in their practice, and prohibits fee splitting and employment in the practice of law where an employer, if a nonlawyer, could intervene in a lawyer/client relationship; and
- regulation of situations leading to potential conflicts of interests.

So, professional associations manage the nature of the practitioner/client relationship; differences between professions in the handling of this relationship are dictated by the nature of the occupation and its clientele and by the nature of the employment situation.

This brings me to the agency model of professional practice, the one most apt for policing. According to John Quinn, this model describes an individual practitioner with the ability to relate a general body of knowledge and the discipline of applying it to a specific problem or task on behalf of a client.[29] It is eminently consistent with Schön's reflection-in-action process, discussed above.

The model fixes responsibility and ensures accountability through the service relationship between practitioner and client, producer and consumer. What makes this a professional model is the agency function defined by client dependency in which the client, who is without specialist knowledge, must trust the professional, who acts as the client's agent. Second-order decisions flow from this: about what information is to be collected from the client and from specialist sources in the first instance so as to define the problem; what the possible solutions are; and which solution to choose and how to implement it. In this formulation of the professional approach, the place of the client is central, for the client, though acting on advice, makes the decisions; there is no special need for the client to share the knowledge and skills of the specialist provided the competence of the specialist is assured and the client's interest paramount.

The model also has agency and service components. The agency tasks include:

- determining what information is relevant and collecting it from the client, with client cooperation, and from professional and other sources;
- making tentative diagnoses of the problem or issue after scanning a complex array of professional knowledge for congruence with the information gained from the client, so as to reach approximate definitions of the problem (except in the most routine matters, such as spots with measles or a simple actionable breach of contract, conclusions have a tentative quality);
- again using a complex array of knowledge and experience, determining the options to which the problem may be amenable – an invention of means; and
- providing advice, which often includes an estimate of the degree of success, the resources required, and nature of client involvement, by which the client may select the option to be undertaken (one common option, to do nothing, is usually available).

The service tasks include:

- implementing the selected strategy with client cooperation; and
- assessing the results.

The basic obligation that client interests be dominant is assured by the specialist in the following ways:

- Any condition or influence that threatens client interests (such as serving the conflicting interests of a second client, or being in a subordinate position to another person – say, an employer out for profit – or organization with conflicting interests) is barred from the process.
- At a minimum, the specialist complies with recognized standards of competence, which include acquiring any new occupational knowledge and skills as they are advanced and codified;
- Given the near infinity of human situations, the specialist realizes that a client's problem will have unique aspects beyond the reach of ready prescription; the tentative quality of various strategies that may be used and the equally tentative promise of success suggest the humbling position of a practitioner in serving a client.
- The specialist respects confidentiality.

A manager, perhaps one who claims professional status through possession of a MBA, has no client but the employing firm and need not recognize ethics other than those shared within the firm. Managers are qualified for a variety of employments in government, industry, and commerce, a sphere of human endeavour for which no rigorous discipline or body of exclusive knowledge exists.

Though the revitalization of urban policing is at an early stage, some few police programs do approach the agency model, if loosely. The following steps, which involve joint community-group/police activity, were suggested for the establishment of a foot-patrol program. There is an implicit assumption in the neighbourhood foot-patrol manual[30] that the community has recognized a need for police intervention and that the initiative is taken by some person or group, either police or citizen-clients, concerned about community conditions.

1 Specification of the problem – information collection:
   – information gathering, in particular about reported and unreported crimes and crime rates and the remedies that may already have been instituted;
   – analysis of the community, its economic base, cultural make-up, social organizations, official systems and agencies, history of crisis management.
2 Resources – community participation and contributions:
   – identification of relevant systems, those units of social organization that may contribute support and resources to a patrol program;
   – identification of community leaders.
3 Identification and selection of options:
   – bringing leaders together to work out strategies;
   – citywide and neighbourhood meetings;
   – setting goals, determining resources, matters of implementation and evaluation;
   – implementation, including selection of officers, their training, management, and control.

Here, the "agency model" step of identifying a possible strategy is incomplete because of the prior commitment to a single means only, the foot-patrol program, though such programs have flexibility and perhaps are assured of success for that reason. The other main components of the model seem commonsensical, though certain features include a reliance on fairly technical information gathered to support a carefully achieved definition of the problem; a previously researched, evaluated and documented, adaptable program (neighbourhood foot patrol); a reliance on particular knowledge and skills (that is, on the leadership of line-level officers) for successful implementation. And while neighbourhood groups have no role in supervising or managing the program, there is an accountability to them for protecting neighbourhood interests. Adaptability and other less immediate benefits derive, as Trojanowicz noted, from the central concept of foot patrol, which has wide applications, including that of having the officer involved with the community.[31] For police officers to become advocates of the particular neighbourhoods in which they work is often undesirable. The risk of being subjected to local influences may be controlled, as in the agency model, if the program is designed along narrow lines with neighbourhood interests limited to goals set out through a prior understanding. The vested interest of elected politicians in public-agency programs within their wards is undeniable.

A foot-patrol program (like community policing, this sometimes seems to be a multiprogram label), with its built-in adaptability, is offered as a rather singular approach to addressing community ills, like some general, all-purpose therapy. But it is still an advance: it is experimental (the authors note that not all problems have been foreseen or adequately resolved); it is well researched; and it adds considerable substance to the meaning of community policing. Another relevant observation is that the program is based on scientifically valid evidence, a growing amount of esoteric knowledge to be found largely at Michigan State University.

Two aspects of the agency model of professional practice stand out. First, competence is reflected in the innovation involved in determining remedial strategies based on a complex array of knowledge and, again, inventing the means of their application. Second, the client is active, with definable responsibilities that include the initial determination of some issue or problem, the provision of information, the vital decision to accept the specialist's definition of the issue, and the further decision to accept the proposed solution and its costs and to participate in its application.

Bearing immediate responsibility for the interests of a client has a disciplining quality, if corporately recognized; without it, external supervision or regulation of an occupation becomes necessary, if not imperative. As noted earlier, it is from within an undifferentiated public that clienteles are found (groupings of people variously differentiated by need). Consider, for example, the occurrence of a disease, especially an epidemic. The way it is distributed among distinctly different categories of people in the community is germane to any response. Health-service resources will respond not only to the fact of the disease but also to the nature of its transmission and other relevant particulars. So, with the growing complexity and volume of specialist knowledge and its capacity for tailored response, specialists rather than generalist, tend to be seen as the most useful in the occupations and institutions that attend to social problems.

Political practices distinguish among constituents by shaping and allocating resources according to their diverse needs. In contrast, any so-called equitable (i.e., uniform) distribution of services is neutral with respect to clients and politics; it was a characteristic of the foot-patrol program in Flint, Michigan, for example, that uniform distribution of resources was needed to blunt the edge of criticism by politicians. The belief that the appearance of bias can be avoided by such uniformity of practice with the people as a whole as clients brings the inertia of comfort and is essentially misleading. That the biasing quality of politics may not mesh with the differing needs of different sets of clients is a reality and the basis for an argument that political authority be limited, for example, to a determination of a public agency's goals. The conventional position – that influence over policing, including political influence with its greater potential for bias, can only serve narrow interests – reflects the fact that the interests of sets of clients were not historically factored into the practices of policing.[32] Client-free functions characterize the depoliticization of policing in the context of the modernization of government administration discussed in the previous two chapters. In Ontario, ninety-one regulatory agencies and 580 agencies of all kinds deliver public services. When there is intervention in the practitioner/client relationship, the interests of the intervenor are also served. Such interests, usually those of government, are powerful, if not dominant.

The power shared with the people of a neighbourhood in community policing can be compared with that shared in a practitioner/client relationship. It does not imply the compelling authority of one over the other – quite the opposite. But it takes a tough reorientation in thinking and practices, by police and community alike, – to work out the type of transactions and accountability implied by the agency model; the dominant interest of the client may not be of an "added-on" superficiality typical of crime prevention or similar projects. I noticed, for example, that the Canadian Police College offers a course in "Community Problem Analysis and Program Management" for a person "tasked with researching, planning, implementing and evaluating new and innovative approaches to community problems," with topics including community policing, community studies, media arts, and others – the course, at the time, was two weeks long.

These comments highlight the point that we are not used to thinking about the clients of urban policing. Factoring them into a discussion of the maintenance of order, even if implicitly, carries what I called the disciplining quality of immediate responsibility and thus has a bearing on police accountability and the nature of the job. A client group is, inescapably, one half of the community-policing equation. In amongst the various interests, social, legal, and political, involved, the identification of the client group, including the ready example of neighbourhood people, has not been recognized as the crucial point it is. Instead, we have the *New York Times* expressing concern that the move to community policing is again putting temptation in the officer's way, this time in the form of lucrative drug-trade profits.[33] The legacy of O.W. Wilson continues to set the agenda.

TWO EMPLOYMENT CONTEXTS
FOR SPECIALISTS

We have seen that the police occupation does not fully recognize the significance of research and related intellectual endeavours; that it does not value high entry qualifications; that police officers are action-oriented and value prescriptions with immediate effect but little value, and possibly diminishing effects, in the longer term; that departments are hierarchically organized with policing/managerial competence tied to rank; that no widely accepted occupational organization exists; that senior officers are occupationally distant from line officers; and that people with relatively junior qualifications tend to employed in useful specializations.

A discussion of professional employment contexts and their effects on occupational status and practice does much to explain these issues as they relate to policing.

In a profession, the integrity of the practitioner/client relationship is of primary importance since otherwise the relationship is open to intervention. Methods of supervision and accountability imposed by the employer/intervenor may be so intrusive that services are modified accordingly. It will be shown that intervention by government can and often does shape the occupation itself, impeding growth in occupational competence.

Specialists are increasingly employed by large organizations, which complicates the nature of the client relationship. The employing organization itself may be the client, as with banks that employ their own accountants or school boards that hire public-health nurses. Some organizations are staffed solely by professionals and generally take the form of partnerships. The variations among nontraditional employment situations are numerous, and when these situations allow some form of intrusion into the specialist/client relationship, the term "near professions" comes into play. Two near-professional employment situations merit discussion, the first being what Terence Johnson called "patronage."[34]

Many organizations are increasingly sophisticated consumers of specialist services. Consider a physician employed by an insurance company to medically examine applicants: the client relationship is absent and there is no professional tie beyond basic ethical considerations. When the employer leaves only technique to the specialist's discretion, a pseudoprofessional relationship results (though it is common for technical roles to be alluded to as professional). This is a patronage situation. In contrast, the same physician under contract to a mining company will readily identify injured workers as patients; interference in the client relationship will not be tolerated.

In a patronage situation, technical skills that serve the immediate needs of the employer will be favoured (by specialist and employer alike) at the expense of wider or deeper knowledge directed to longer-term but less-certain results. So the patronage setting cannot be expected to advance occupational competence, let alone its knowledge-generating research capacity.

When the employing organization is bureaucratic and thus hierarchical (to distinguish from the more collegial context of physicians in a hospital or partners in a law firm), differing levels of competence are recognized rather than the single level of professional qualification: the higher the organizational status, the higher the competence ascribed – the administrative authority of a senior depicts the junior as a specialist of lesser ability. The bureaucratic context leads to overt fragmentation of the integrity of the occupation as junior technologies emerge to relieve the higher-status specialist of the more routine work.

A second major working context for professionals is the government as patron, a special case because of the broad sociopolitical purposes and power involved. Mediation or intervention in the relations with a client is virtually inevitable; defining client needs as well as determining the appropriate procedures to respond to those needs are not the exclusive domain of the practitioner. Occupational self-management is eroded. Government intervention, in a social-worker/client relationship, for example, stresses broader social consequences of a particular service. Here also, an occupation may be described as a nearprofession, and a professional employed in this context faces an intractable issue of divided commitment or loyalty. Government purposes may be, and usually are, imprecise, so the means of providing a service may be taken as proxies or substitutes for goals. In the case of policing, so-called deterrent patrols and reduced-response time, the diffusely stated goals nesling in the rhetoric of "servants of the law" or of serving the "people as a whole" are bolstered. The patron-government guarantees a clientele (and usually resources) to practitioners and thereby enhances the primacy of its own interest; and the service is shaped by the attention necessarily paid to the employer/government interest.[35] Even when an administrative-bureaucratic matter arises, intervention is likely, and patron interest is usually favoured over that of a client.

Obviously, a bureaucratic method of providing some vital service is not the only or better option. For example, hospitals are nonhierarchical; they foster professional collegiality and standards with no confusion about who the client may be. No government array of goals or unwanted administrative practices intrude into the relationship except perhaps for budgetary pressures.

About two-thirds of salaried physicians in the US work in private health-care institutions. The trend continues and mediation plays an increasing role as insurance organizations vigorously attempt to control costs. Salaried medical specialists are not a new phenomenon, of course; those in the armed forces are a case in point. But a new dimension is emerging. When the employing organization emphasizes low cost medicine, curtailed services, and paper-based procedures for approval of more expensive treatment, such interventions weaken the dominant interest of a patient and deform the thrust of practitioner competence.

Specialists of managerial rank, who are required to attend to administrative and regulatory matters, succumb to the potent influence of the rewards offered in administrative/management work, including promotion and high status, none of which are intrinsic to their professional worth. Immediate, visible achievements – those readily recognized and rewarded in bureaucracies – set the specialist's focus. Short-term efficiencies that benefit the bureaucracy take precedence over wider considerations. The political pressures of the day are rarely out of mind. (The collegiality of the specialist occupation is diminished in this bureaucratic context; occupational loyalty is weakened, along with ties to a professional association.)

With occupational standards in the hands of a bureaucratic agency, occupational associations tend to become simply self-interested pressure groups. Teaching associations come to mind and, I suggest, police associations. As the collegial or professional function of an association diminishes, membership becomes devalued, fragmented or restricted. Job security, pay, and promotion are cast as the occupation's ultimate objectives.

The relationship between specialist and government employer, then, has a tremendous capacity to erode an occupation's self-concept and thus generate confusion. Social work, for example, has self-governing status throughout Canada except in Ontario. The Ontario association's 1989 consideration of the desirability of legislation to enable the society to set entry standards and supervise professional conduct met internal opposition. There was fear that this professionalization would result in a more extensive dependency on government, an apparent collusion with it, with the association becoming a part of established interests that would detract from its focus on the interests of clients.

The ideology and attitudes of practitioners in close contact with clients are likely to differ markedly from those in central and higher places of authority. In policing, the differences, even distrust, that arise between line officers and management officers are now well known throughout Canada and the US.[36] Rank requires standing and credibility in policing (of having earned one's credentials on the street) and thereby maintains the illusion, if not the reality, of specialist competence. But higher rank carries administrative and related duties that actively deflect from that competence, which soon fades. Many specialists have refused promotion so as to continue their practice at the client level, or, when this was not possible, quit. Echoes of this are found in policing as I indicated earlier.

The price that the specialist pays for government/patron employment is the narrowing of vision and perspective. The professional outlook deteriorates when the larger organization's needs take precedence over those of the clients for whom the specialization ultimately exists. Occupationwide values and activities come to seem of negligible significance.

THE VAGARIES OF POLICE PROFESSIONALISM

Urban police provide a vital service and thus have a professional aspect, but they fulfil this service in familiar, once-effective, but nonprofessional ways that are imbued with all the pale attributes of discretion hampered by bureaucratization, which substantially limits, even distorts, the discretion of line officers.

Klockars described the police-executive approach to professionalism, thus: "To them [police administrators] it meant tighter administrative control, a more heavily centralized administrative structure, and more extensive regulation of officer discretion. What is peculiar about this sense of "professional" is that it is almost exactly the opposite of what "professional" means when it is applied to all other occupations ... that a broad range of discretion will be accorded to the professional, who will be entrusted with handling situations in an atmosphere marked by a lack of supervision."[37] He argued that a genuine professionalism was required because the police officer is entrusted with a substantial and highly consequential right: the right to use and to threaten to use coercive force in an almost infinite variety of situations.[38] It is this sense of "professional," rather than the one long promoted by police administrators, that order-maintenance policing requires. "Choices about exercising that right will regularly be made out of sight of supervisors and other reliable evaluaters. Moreover, while there is no doubt that 'the law' bears some relationship to what the police officer does, it is better understood as a tool he may see fit to use when he believes a situation calls for it than a guide or set of instructions for how he ought to behave ... Policing has long been a real profession whose identification and acceptance as a profession have been prevented by a series of historical accidents."[39] These accidents include the effects of the reform movement, especially, in the United States, the emphasis on managerial competence, the distancing of patrol officers from the public they serve and a hierarchical structure marked by a disciplinary climate and the mutual distrust of line and administrative officers, which is also marked in Canada.

What is meant by professionalism in much of policing, then, is the vital quality of service, "progressive" management, central control, and neutral, competent, generalist officers.[40]

There is another claim to professionalism within policing, a modern meaning of the word that hinges on technical expertise and the fairly extensive applications of technology to a variety of tasks (communications, identification, forensic laboratories, and so on). The lead is taken by national departments, which have the resources but, significantly, not the functions of truly urban departments. FBI Special Agent Deakin has written a rather thin and predictably orthodox account of the move in US policing towards a more technically based enterprise with better-educated and trained people. Using the jargon of the day, he suggests that the realization, beginning in the 1960s, of the failure of policing to deter crime marked the beginning of the current renaissance in police professionalism, which is reflected in a willingness to experiment, a "rebirth of the spirit of service to the community," and particularly in a return to the concept of order maintenance and the conviction that the whole community bears a responsibility for the collective quality of life. However, the evidence of progress offered in Deakin's book is indicated by its section titles: the International Association of Chiefs of Police; Forensic Science and Laboratories; Identification Systems; Hoover's FBI; Uniform Crime Reporting; The FBI Law Enforcement Bulletin, etc.[41] – in all, a complacent, superficial view based in large part on innovation in technological applications.

James Q. Wilson observed that professionalism in policing involves not only a reassessment of how police should function but the identifi-

cation of problems as they arise in the community. The ability to perform these tasks depends on whether policing has an assured place as
a profession in society. Occupations with tenuous claims to professionalism, as I noted in the previous chapter, make their case by identifying
themselves in the public and political mind with some visible, vital
role. The language, the rhetoric of legitimacy – "the war on crime," "to
serve and protect," "the people as a whole," "the community at large,"
or "servants of the law" – has shaped public attitudes about crime and
sustained public support. Similarly, Barbara Price suggested that "professionalism" in policing rests more on rhetoric – she added such slogans as "working for the good of society," "closer contact with the
public," and "specialization through training" – than reality. Any substance behind the words is found in bureaucratic initiatives such as the
add-on units for public and community relations and crime prevention.[42]

COMMENTARY ON THE HINDER-ANCES TO A PROFESSIONALIZED POLICE OCCUPATION

According to Louis A. Mayo, "The concept of professionalism which
embodies an established philosophy of policing derived from formal-
ized ethical standards, is almost the opposite of what is frequently
meant by professional policing in the police literature. The absence of
a well-articulated philosophy of policing leaves chiefs without substantive guidance in policy formation, policy setting and program implementation."[43]

A 1980 Task Force on Policing in Ontario concluded that police
professionalism entailed police sharing in the values and attitudes
common in society as well as evincing a capacity to exercise discretion
in the light of these shared values. The dissonance between public expectations and what the police believed the job of policing to be was
considered resolvable by education. [44]

Among the barriers to police professionalization are: lack of professional knowledge; bureaucratic organizations; and the leadership
structure. With regard to the first, which echoes the task force and
Mayo, the generation of new theoretical knowledge that could lead to
innovations in strategies and organization has been singularly absent
from policing. There are two reasons for this, the first being employment in a bureaucratic organization. The second is that the practices
of police work are akin to those in a craft setting with only a department and not an occupation-wide agency providing the locus in which
standards and roles are shared. A change in leadership may be wel-

comed, but an innovative officer who has moved up the ladder faces several problems, most notably that some of the officer's innovations are bound to fail. In a traditional organization any such failure will reflect back on the officer; there will be a subsequent erosion of personal authority within the department, where such authority may already have been diminished through delegation in a collegial way. Naturally enough, those in the upper echelons foresee a shrinking of their own policy-making and managerial roles, and the prospect might seem, if not threatening, then unnecessary.

The rhetoric of professionalism is used to request or defend a budget, and to defend a department against public or political criticism. It is used sparingly.[45] A police executive is not always aware of its effectiveness, and uncertainty about its full implications induces some caution. There is a sense that the credibility of "professional" rhetoric is dependent on some corresponding action. More importantly, it carries the threat that it will lead to more autonomous line officers and to participatory management, which it does in fact do. The development of professional competence is not only a long-term task but one that must anticipate errors and embrace experimentation. For a police executive, errors spell public complaints and experiments often fail.

In another vein, W. Clinton Terry maintains that police actively foster in the public mind the notion that policing is highly stressful. This is aimed at gaining occupational legitimacy and prestige as well as securing coherence within the police subculture, "By dovetailing the idea of dangerousness with the ideal of personal dedication and service to others, the notion of police stress gives to the police occupation the ideological coherence needed for professional status and recognition."[46] The police seek to create in the public mind an association between the moral order exemplified by law, that higher ideal under which they serve, and their service, thereby achieving legitimacy with it all its enabling authority. It is an integrating ideology, embracing public, police subculture, and law. It portrays to the world a responsibility for the lives of others and justifies the autonomy of their occupational activities under the authority of "some higher ideal."

Order maintenance consumes the largest part of police time and resources; by its nature, as Terry noted, it better parallels the services of older professions,[47] though it is the law-enforcement ethic of commitment and dangerousness that is sought. Job stress, danger, and trauma offer a greater sense of unity, "an integrating ideology" that guides members and permits the representation of the occupation as a unified one with a doctrine of vital public service.[48] Thus, however real the stress, this version of the police image is but a proxy for professionalism and an obstacle to it.

Knowledge of policing is not exclusive to police officers – there is no systematic body of knowledge that is occupationally recognized, least of all one that is effective in reducing crime and victimization. Professionalism conveys the idea of great skill or proficiency, but as David Perrier has noted, police training in Canada is deficient and the contribution of technology to the apparent professionalism of police lies in law enforcement, while the deficiency is in peace keeping, which highlights the dearth of internally held knowledge.[49] Further, the occupation does not systematically add to its fund of knowledge and makes no attempt to put in place institutions for doing so. I quoted Swanton earlier to similar effect, that most institutions dealing with matters relevant to police development generally are not integral to the (police) science. These external institutions, especially universities, reflect a concern about the nature and quality of the police occupation. He was writing of Australia, the United States, Britain, New Zealand, and Canada.

Endemic occupational uncertainty about the range of its activities and concerns is inconsistent with the responsibilities of a profession. In policing, there is no monopoly of practice within a well-defined area; the many other police and quasi-police agencies of government and ubiquitous private agencies have overlapping functions. The maintenance of order, however, generally remains exclusive to the police.[50] Chief Raymond C. Davis indicated that the basic direction of a more advanced police occupation "must emerge from within the community and be grounded on a recognition that the mission of police is public service. There are hazards in the police role of community organizer, but there are also tremendous benefits. The spectrum of areas needing police attention differs from locale to locale, but the only limiting principle I would advocate is that police efforts must be aimed at improving quality of life within the community."[51]

B.W.H. Bingham examined the professional status (indicated by education) of executives in American municipal governments through an extensive survey of cities and professional associations, including police, and found that, among civilians at executive level, 65 percent had advanced degrees (about 15 percent held no degree) but among police chiefs, only 31.5 percent had advanced degrees (41.4 percent held no degree). The survey was conducted within the International Association of Chiefs of Police, which has 11,250 members from sixty-four countries. Bingham found that government directives, grants of money, and formal (chiefs') association endorsements determine what type of innovation is adopted, which explains, in part, why some projects are so common among departments. The value of professional associations to municipal officials lies in the horizontal transmission of knowledge of innovations, but in policing this effect is diminished by the highly restricted membership of chiefs' associations, national and state.[52]

Carl Klockars has argued that "police officers already have a genuinely professional role and the obligations and responsibilities that go along with it; what they lack is the education, status and organizational environment that recognize that fact ... If policing is indeed an unacknowledged professional task it may be asked why it should not be allowed to continue in the unrecognized role it currently occupies."[53]

The ethics of a professional practitioner are internalized, for the most part, rather than imposed, and one can argue that a disciplinary, regulatory approach to supervision in the tradition of O.W. Wilson is anachronistic in an occupation with highly discretionary activities. The commitment of operations officers to the mores of street work, reflected in their often beleaguered and embattled sense of brotherhood, suggests that subcultural values dominate, in part, in the absence of an occupation-based consensus about roles and standards.

The autonomy of a professional in private practice contrasts with the often lapsed supervisory practices in policing, even though much discretionary activity is involved. Some explanations may be found in the cohesiveness and influence of line officers (for example, the tendency to co-opt supervising sergeants), which has been mentioned elsewhere, and the often truculent stance of the union. Officers expect tolerance in their performance on the street from their fellows and the turning of "blind eyes," except when their conduct exceeds group bounds. Certainly, general loyalty to department and peers blurs a wider sense of accountability, so misconduct can be seen simply as an offence against a code for which no one need share the onus. Damage to a department is contained. The salience of deeply rooted subcultural standards, particularly those bearing on conduct, is illustrated by vigorous police opposition to external regulation and complaints boards. Such regulation cannot be forced effectively on a hostile group. Their persistent opposition to external review reflects, it seems, a basic disagreement about what standards are to be applied, even though the argument is often set out in terms of the inability of outsiders to understand the nature and essentials of street work.

Having developed along bureaucratic lines, especially of tight regulation, the police working context came to be deeply inconsistent with the line officers' exercise of discretion and the working habits suited to demanding tasks. (In James Q. Wilson's words, an operations officer's view is that "the power of the administrator is to be checked because the administrator, if he is a strong man is 'out to get us' and, if he is a weak one, is 'giving way to outside pressure.'"[54] Given management's neglect of these issues, it would seem likely that employment associations may become involved in professional matters by default.

In the context of the postindustrial society, the continuing professionalization of the workplace poses long-term questions about the union movement, whose membership has declined over the years except, significantly, in public-sector unions. The entry of young, educated workers may well challenge both the common organization of work and its character, and the structures of trade unionism and professional organizations. Most technology-based groups organize into associations, or do so before long. However, the eventual character of their organizations – whether professional organizations in a guild form, or militant unions – remains to be seen. Young entrants, Bell speculated, may be more militant and with increasing employment by government under fiscal restraints, they may lean towards militant rather than professional organization, as the history of teachers' associations indicate.[55]

In the emerging postindustrial society, while employment in services is flourishing and will continue to do so, employment in government has become the growth area, particularly in local government, and the central occupational categories are the professional and technical (in the United States the largest growth has been in teaching, followed by professional health care, then science and engineering).[56]

Functions that displace property as the foundation of esteem and status imply, according to Bell, activity that seeks to realize the ideal of social purpose, a professional one.

In terms of the professional class – the newer, larger status group – the appropriate notion is one of vertical "layerings" based on levels of intellectual endeavour in the acquisition and application of knowledge; access is gained through education and co-optation. The ethos is different; power includes political authority for these new élites that are based on knowledge and planning – "the basic requisites for all organized action in a modern society." The technical élites are essential to the formulation and analysis of decisions on which political judgments have to be made. They are the new constituency, the technical and professional intelligentsia.

Order, the City, and the Occupation

The two major functions of urban police, law enforcement and the maintenance of order, have distinctive purposes and means, though they are often inseparable on the ground. The goals of law enforcement align it with the criminal-justice system. Its rules and procedures circumscribe police activity. The maintenance of order, in contrast, is concerned with an ill-defined range of human activity that is covered by the somewhat loose term disorder. It has social and political purposes and practices, all malleable and mutable. Not law but the particulars of persons, places, and events are its determinants and discretion, therefore, is its watchword.

Crime animates our attention. It vicariously touches our primary concern with survival, especially when it hits close to home. Detection and punishment are fundamental to our sense of the rule of law; competent law enforcement, we believe, indicates that society is functioning well. The criminal-justice system enacts a morality play featuring obedience and respectability and retribution for transgressions.

Disorder, in contrast, seems banal, errant – not necessarily unlawful – behaviour. The restoration of order, if done well, escapes public attention.

Crime also attracts police resources. Publicity about crime rates prompts targeted patrols, intensive investigative work, and placebos like the 911 systems. Yet, as we have seen, a fear-of-crime attitude is more closely tied to disorder and the quality of neighbourhood life than to the reality of crime rates. The consequence remains: police attention is drawn away from order-maintenance programs.

As our understanding of urban life deepens, however, the central role of order maintenance is revealed. The customary authority of ide-

202 Urban Policing in Canada

ology may well yield to a rational, science-based realignment to issues of social well-being, disorder, and victimization.

Common sense suggests that the policing environment, the city, should determine policing priorities and programs. The familiar law-enforcement strategies of police patrols, on-call and nonintrusive, combined with managerial competence and a fortuitous technology, defined a "new" police professionalism. Suburbs were well served and few occasions to question police functions and status provided.

As exurbia evolves, however, novel challenges – some already apparent – to the police-on-call tradition emerge. In any case, these familiar programs obviously have not served inner-city neighbourhoods by any measure, be it crime rates, fear of crime, or the prevalence of disorder. Police, depoliticized and insulated from local issues as they are, tend to persist in a law-enforcement-oriented approach that resists transformation according to the particulars of problems and pressures.

It is not that police cultivate a blind insensitivity to the problems of their city. Being apolitical, though, they remain aloof from the pressures other civic agencies face in trying to ameliorate them. Much policing activity is political by nature and the chief is a leading civic politician, but there is scant involvement in relevant processes centring on the concerns of the neighbourhoods served. The dominant police attitude, that the public should have no say in policing matters, is as pervasive as it is defensive.

Policing remains craftlike in its methods of transmitting knowledge and skills within its ranks; it is locked into minimal standards of entry and certification (brief training and apprenticeship). Few, if any, extrinsic rewards for educational achievement are offered. One can hardly avoid the conclusion that, as the general level of education rises, young people who see no place for themselves in advanced education may be attracted to policing.

As an experience-based occupation, policing lacks the means and habits of verifying program effectiveness and then generalizing from it to ensure its availability as knowledge, and it lacks the inclination to do so. It has no occupational memory in the modern sense. Corporately, it does not display an interest in the knowledge of policing generated by academic and research communities. Many departments are undertaking innovative or experimental projects; some are realigning themselves using a variant of community policing. But this kind of effort is atypical.

Modern administrative practices were once needed, but the structure they inhabit is now inflexible and resistant, for example, to the decentralization demanded by community policing. Departments remain hobbled by personnel practices based on antiquated in-at-the-bottom minimal-qualification recruitment. Tenacious internal attitudes favour the *status quo* in functions and accountability.

I have explained the prevailing approach to police supervision and accountability. One common Canadian practice has been to assign of supervision to local boards of police commissioners, or committees of council, all under the influence of provincial-government offices. These provincially ordained practices have produced anaemic supervision, leaving the relationship between police functions and community issues in department hands, the better to ensure a nonpolitical climate. In consequence, this practice also depoliticizes local concerns about policing. However, in a democratic system police can be given direction and their accountability made explicit without risk of any influence, including that of local politics, subverting the processes of justice.

That security and order are public-policy issues would seem to be self-evident, but continuing police absence from the policy-making arena reflects an inadequate appreciation of community problems of security on the part of the supervising bodies. To tell a police chief what his priorities should be requires a sound knowledge of the threats to the security and order afflicting various neighbourhoods and of the human costs of not attending to them. This is a grave responsibility in the current context. Exhortations to a department to implement the "add-ons" of community policing, such as more foot patrols, do little more than illustrate the inherent deficiency of government supervision. Neither the run of policing programs, it seems, nor the *modus operandi* of supervisory offices reflects a sufficient understanding of urban order and how to sustain it.

Government bureaucracies are voices of authority, often of technical competence and certainly of power, in their own right. Widely based professions can and do have balancing voices of authority in the politics of public-policy matters. Professionals themselves, it was noted, may occupy pertinent offices of local and senior government; the professional context is one of stature and, if well established, of significant consequence. The police occupation has a marginal or insubstantial position in the workings of government. Martin Laffin's analysis of the "politics" of occupations and professions in government revealed that government professionals, while able to intervene in public policy making, also seek to attain their own goals and do so by claims of exclusive competence in their functional area.[1] They are involved in maintaining, and enlarging on, the acceptance of those claims in areas of public concern. This is a political process. Laffin identified four factors or "resources" relevant to this process. The first is the possession of a distinct and systematized body of knowledge and skills that is scientifically valid and resistant both to acquisition by others and to fragmentation into discrete subspecialties. If a core body of knowledge is not in evidence, as in policing, then acceptance as an occupation with a valid claim to some area of competence is resisted. The occupation, then, will variously attempt to control the transmission of its knowledge to ensure exclusiveness, guard its legislated area of authority and practice, emphasize the vital nature of its services, or, raise standards by promoting both research and the diffusion of knowledge among its members. Obviously, an occupation bound to the practices and resources of a craft will neither value nor use all its options.

The second professional resource, the provision of an important, vital service to the public and the premise that the occupation is thoroughly oriented to that service, remains potent in preserving and enlarging on its command of public support, its stature.

The third resource consists in members occupying strategic positions and the not-uncommon achievement of professional concentration in a local-government department headed by one from their own ranks, as with a police department, though some may perform administrative or nontechnical functions. Where local or provincial elements of government, including commissions, are not headed or staffed by specialists, then it seems the claim to exclusive knowledge has not been accepted. If truly professional, specialists may occupy positions between local and senior governments (e.g., provincial commissions and boards of directors, mainstays of the legal profession). These positions may constitute a major channel of communication, if not the main channel, between those governments. Few police officers gain senior positions in government, so there are only weak-voltage channels of communication between governments, their departments, the occupation, and its associations.

The fourth resource of an occupation consolidating its position in government is support from segments of the public organized around a particular sociopolitical interest that is congruent with the occupation's area of competence, such as environment-related technologies, and the helping professions. Professionals may well ally themselves so as to be on the "right side" of public opinion providing the apolitical image of public service is not put at risk. It is this resource that buttresses the police claim to strong public support for the "war-on-crime" orientation and the emergency-call style of policing.

If the police occupation is assessed along these lines, its marginal position seems undeniable. Its primary resource weakness is the failure to pursue the attainment of exclusive but valid knowledge, but its strength lies in its justifiable claim of serving a vital public interest. The ready public support of police is general; police shun specific support for specific reasons. Further, their antipathy to catering to public opinion and influence, especially political influence, has been well demonstrated.

An occupation on the path to becoming a profession will have acquired, among other qualities and resources, the means to ensure the competence of members, both on entry and throughout a career; an association of which most practitioners are members; concern for certifying competence and for ethics; and the resources and habits of generating specialized and accessible knowledge and skills. Thus, occupational resources are needed to provide advanced, specialized qualifications as a prerequisite to certification. There should be a professional association that would eventually be empowered to certify competence and develop performance standards and professional ethics. And there must be a capacity to experiment on a department-by-department and cross-department basis.

I and others have recommended that the police be professionalized. Better education and a revised occupational structure, while just a beginning, would be considerable developments. Optimism is rare among students policing; some are convinced of the apparent futility of attempting improvement or major surgery, such splitting off from the occupation functions that could be readily carried out by other, more technically qualified people.

Certain intangible resources in policing programs are cause for optimism. Rather than contemplate radical remedies, it is useful to reflect on the Flint foot-patrol program and similar experiences. The discretion and initiatives allowed to patrol officers were a significant factor in the Flint program's success. Projects cited in fear-of-crime research report similar findings. An evaluation of a foot-patrol project in Canada indicated the motivating influence of the ability to use discretion and initiative. These results contrast with the core thinking that continues to shape the way policing is organized. It is not unreasonable to imagine a flow of thinking, exemplified by community policing, that might redefine officers' tasks so as to tap and exploit those factors of motivation and innovation. The strong police subculture is another potentially influential resource. In Canada, with its less-complex, less-fragmented policing structure, some further impetus to this sort of change may be found – from outside policing, in the context of a professionalizing society, and perhaps from within policing, under the stimulation of a potential threat to the monopoly of police practice.

There are no surprises in the conclusion that the professionalization of policing should follow a client-centred, self-managing direction; the former dictates the assurance of competence and the latter an occupationwide support of standards and common ethics. Obviously, there are many steps that must be taken to achieve this redirection. Each step is tied to its own daunting problems – the in-at-the-bottom personnel structure being but one – the answers to which are not available by prescription. It seems to me that the prudent course would be to set this general direction towards professionalism and then, taking a step-by-step approach, work out the resolution of problems as they arise and, with patience and time, gain experience and discover options. There is no bureaucratic fix; any "promising" ones have undoubtedly been tried or, wisely, rejected.

That entrenched public institutions have the capacity to undergo revolutionary change in a crisis-free climate is implausible, but persistent, incremental change exploiting the trends in a complex social environment can be achieved, with patience. Herman Goldstein, in speaking of the implementation of problem-oriented policing, noted that in large bureaucracies, change grows out of varied developments so that it is often more a matter of taking advantage of opportunities than of some systematic approach or plan.[2] Though change comes about in often messy ways, each change will be in the right direction (if only in some minor way) as long as some notion of an adequate, if not ideal, police service has been articulated.

The police occupation exists formally only in the hundreds of largely autonomous, discrete departments, most of which are small, with limited resources. Members are without an effective corporate affiliation; their allegiance is without focus and their occupational interests unrepresented. An essential step, then, is providing a focus for the occupation; an institution devoted to the competence of urban police is suggested – one or more centres for studies, scholarship, and research in urban policing. Such centres, the establishment of which is a provincial matter, are needed to develop and employ a critical number of urban-policing specialists and provide the opportunity for officers to qualify for advanced roles, including those in government. They may also meet a critical need for an information resource – libraries, publications programs, and storage and retrieval systems. Surely the advanced education of at least some police is a goal to be nurtured.

One major purpose of a professional education is to instil a life-long habit of learning; as John F. Kennedy said of his military officers, that their careers must not consist of four years education and thirty years of experience; rather, they must study and grow mentally if they are to acquire a basis for making balanced decisions.[3] Advanced education has come to be viewed as synonymous with a long-term commitment to challenging, questioning, criticizing, and analyzing existing institutions, and as a way of instilling new values and broader perspectives. An exceptional part of this process is that the scientific method of obtaining knowledge – through experimentation – is well learned; it is a crucial skill. There is also a wide public platform on which the police specialist should have a part. Daniel Bell quoted Zbigniew Brzezinski to the effect that social problems are less the consequence of deliberate evil than the unintended by-products of complexity and ignorance; solutions cannot be sought in emotional simplifications but in the use of accumulated social experience and scientific knowledge. At present, the measurement of social ills – crime, property loss, sickness, unemployment, and family disruption – is extensive but lacks refinement; importantly, there have been few attempts to link these problems to underlying conditions and no proper assessment of costs or progress.[4] The crudity of crime statistics is an example: on what else is the enhanced stature of the occupation to be based?

James Q. Wilson was quoted earlier to the effect that the considerable discretion exercised by line officers, far removed from the police chief in larger departments, is still not fully recognized and accepted but that controlling such discretion to the satisfaction of the community is most difficult.[5] Two paths to control are the command-oriented bureaucracy and the more internalized collegial arrangement. These represent conflicting values and any organization will have great difficulty harbouring both. The latter, it seems to me, is becoming a characteristic of postindustrial society and the former, increasingly anachronistic.

From a divergent viewpoint, Robert Reiner has argued that "the hope for policing that respects the rights of minorities lies not in democratic control through elected authorities, but a re-assertion of the traditional legal and professional ideals of the police embodying a universal and impartial authority, albeit one sensitive to the need for public acceptance."[6] This is a conservative attitude but it still draws attention to the undesirable nature of further pursuit of "control through elected authorities." The Canadian experience with both elected authorities and boards suggests that their supervision has not been entirely effective. Reiner's alternative, a recourse to a legal ideal, will be as deficient as it has been in the past.

One troublesome factor is the nature of public attitudes to order, security, and the functions of urban policing. Advances in the nature and quality of services are unlikely unless they are stimulated and supported by the reshaped attitudes of a newly informed public.

Vital occupations continually face crises as society and the human condition change: the emergence of AIDS is a clear example. The notable crises are ones of competence. Our officers are dedicated and cities comparatively well policed, but acclaim does not long endure as cities change; it is in this context that my assessment of the Canadian police occupation is to be understood. For greater relevance, then, any assessment of policing should be weighted towards deficiencies of competence and function, not cost, corruption, abuse of authority, or crude inefficiencies. Canadian police have retained their legitimacy. The nub of the matter is what is to be done, and how, in modern urban communities.

One can only hope that this book has delivered on its promise to provide an anatomy of an aging craft. It seems to me wise, in this case, to end at the beginning, by alluding to a first step in the occupational renewal of policing. The entrenched attitudes and programs discussed here present an obstacle to change precisely because adaptability was never assumed to be essential to a police force oriented to the enforcement of criminal law. The contemporary emphasis on the reform of government may distinguish this period as one during which the salience of order maintenance and the place of a versatile and inventive policing occupation were recognized.

Notes

PREFACE

1 Braiden, *Bank Robberies*, 3.
2 Reiner, *Politics*, 212.

CHAPTER ONE

1 Thompson, in *Respectable Society*, dwells quite extensively on the establishment's attitude that the underclasses should be encouraged to behave in a virtuous way and hence given the incentives to achieve respectability as an outward social goal. See in particular 141–75. Reiner, in a different approach, suggested that in a situation of widespread instability, what was required was to enable the working classes to participate in the political processes of the country. He writes, "[The] working class, the main source of intial hostility to the new police, came to be incorporated into the political and economic institutions of British society. Police acceptance was mutually interdependent with a wider process of pacification of social relations" (*Politics*, 51). I also found Bentley's *Politics without Democracy* most informative.
2 Bentley, *Politics without Democracy*, 91.
3 Crime rate had little to do with starting up police forces. Monkonnen (*Police in Urban America*, 57) points out that in the US, during the years in which urban police forces were established, crime rates were not a significant factor. What was happening at the time was the modernizing of munic ipal governments, which included the establishment of functional departments, the police being one. Reiner makes a similar case for Britain (*Politics*, 39ff.).

4 Moore and Kelling, " 'To Serve and Protect,' " 54.
5 See, for example, Thompson, *Respectable Society*, 203.
6 Ibid., 330.
7 Reiner, *Politics*, 52–61.
8 Ibid., 47.
9 Thompson, *Respectable Society*, 330.
10 Alderson, "Police and the Social Order," 25–6.
11 See, for example, Reiner, *Politics*, 45.
12 Ibid., 116.
13 Moore and Kelling, " 'To Serve and Protect,' "54.
14 Ibid., 57.
15 James Q. Wilson, *Varieties*, 25.
16 Ibid., 27.
17 Ibid., 26.
18 Ibid., 11.
19 Ibid., 6.
20 Alderson, 31.
21 Sewell, *Police – Urban Policing*, 139.
22 Klockars, "Order Maintenance," 317.
23 Emsley, *Policing and Its Context*, 135–8.
24 Moore and Kelling, " 'To Serve and Protect,' " 55.
25 James Q. Wilson, *Varieties*, 30.
26 Patrick V. Murphy, "Ethical Issues," 95.
27 Ibid., 95.
28 Ibid.
29 Bopp, *O.W. Wilson*, 5–6.
30 Klockars, "Order Maintenance," 312.
31 Moore and Kelling, " 'To Serve and Protect,' " 57.
32 Ibid.
33 Klockars, "Order Maintenance," 312.
34 Samuel Walker, " 'Broken Windows,' " 76.
35 Bell, *Post-Industrial Society*, xvi.
36 Ibid., 364ff.
37 Ibid., 129ff.
38 See Moore and Kelling, " 'To Serve and Protect,' " 55 and Braiden, "Bank Robberies," 9.

CHAPTER TWO

1 Bell, *Post-Industrial Society*, 479.
2 Reiner, *Politics*, 132.
3 I have relied on Berki, *Security and Society*, for much of what follows in this part. See in particular 48ff. and 203ff.

4 Lea and Young, *What Is to Be Done,* 59.
5 Thompson, *Respectable Society,* 320.
6 Berki, *Security and Society,* 203.
7 Klockars, "Order Maintenance," 314.
8 Reiner, *Politics,* 111ff.
9 Berki, *Security and Society,* 51.
10 Trojanowicz, *An Evaluation,* 5.
11 Berki, *Security and Society,* 8.
12 Cited in Berki, ibid., 56.
13 See, for example, Wilson and Boland, *Effect of Police,* on Kelling et al., *A Summary Report.*
14 Berki, *Security and Society,* 206.
15 Reiner, *Politics,* 103.
16 Berki, *Security and Society,* 11.
17 Ibid., 64.
18 Ibid., 30ff.
19 James Q. Wilson, *Varieties,* 16ff.
20 Berki, *Security and Society,* 94.
21 Lea and Young, *What is to Be Done,* 55.
22 Thompson, *Respectable Society,* 193ff.
23 Timothy Appleby, "more Police, Prisons, Prosecutors Called key to Winning Drug War," *Globe and Mail,* 18 October 1989.
24 Kelly and Kelly, *Policing in Canada,* 626.
25 Ibid., 599.
26 Ibid., 611.
27 See, for example, James Q. Wilson's comments on the maintenance of order, in *Varieties,* 17ff.
28 Bell, *Post-Industrial Society,* 477.
29 Ibid., 112ff.
30 Ibid., 213ff.
31 Ibid., 364ff.
32 Ibid., 447ff.
33 Ibid., 482.

CHAPTER THREE

1 Lachman and Downs, "Neighborhoods," 214–24.
2 Blumenfeld, "Continuity and Change," 50.
3 Higgins, *Local and Urban Politics,* 2.
4 Wilson and Herrnstein, *Crime,* 299–300.
5 Russell, "Individual Liberty," 112.
6 Klockars, "Order Maintenance," 311.
7 Emsley, *Policing and Its Context,* 129.

8 Kelling et al., *A Summary Report*, 3–4.

9 Gertler and Crowley, *Changing Canadian Cities*. Pages 308–23, which include exerpts from literature, is interesting and informative.

10 For population statistics I have relied on: Dominion Bureau of Statistics, *Canada 1958*; Dumas, *Current Demographic Analysis*; George and Perrault, *Population Projections for Canada*; and Foot, *Canada's Population Outlook*.

11 Fishman, *Bourgeois Utopias*, 10–12.

12 Ibid., 9.

13 See Adams, "Residential Structure," 176–9; and Pool, "Communications," 453.

14 Adams, "Residential Structure," 178–9.

15 John Sewell, *Globe and Mail*, 8 February 1988.

16 Samuel Walker, " 'Broken Windows,' " 82.

17 Kelling, "Urban Police," 21.

18 Wilson and Herrnstein, *Crime*, 411–12.

19 Ibid., 425–6.

20 Monkonnen, *Police in Urban America*, 83–5.

21 A study of one Canadian city illustrates this point. See McGahan, "Criminogenesis," 218–20.

22 Herbert, "Deprivation," 462.

23 Wilson and Herrnstein, *Crime*, 306, 445–6.

24 Herbert, 462.

25 James Q. Wilson, *Varieties*, 140ff., 172ff., and 200ff.

26 Ibid., 203–6.

27 Wilson and Boland, *Effect of Police*, 12.

28 Lea and Young, *What is to Be Done*, 172–5.

29 Wilson and Boland, *Effect of Police*, 4.

30 Ibid., 13.

31 Wellman and Leighton, "Networks," 245–6.

32 Cohen, *Symbolic Construction*, 12ff.

33 McGahan, *Police Images*, 43.

34 See, for example, McGahan, "Criminogenesis," 210; and Wellman and Leighton, "Networks," 185.

35 James Q. Wilson, *Thinking about Crime*, 30ff.

36 Higgins, *Local and Urban Politics*, 245ff.

37 James Q. Wilson, *Thinking about Crime*, 30ff.

38 Bourne, ed., *Internal Structure*, 4.

39 Wellman and Leighton, "Networks," 247–50.

40 Ibid., 249.

41 Ibid., 250–2.

42 Ibid., 251.

43 Wilson and Herrnstein, *Crime*, 306, 311, 410–11.

44 McGahan, "Criminogenesis," 219.

45 Gertler and Crowley, *Changing Canadian Cities*, 327ff.

46 Wilson and Herrnstein, *Crime*, 301.

47 Ibid., 302–3.

48 Rose and Deskins, "Felony Murder," 521.

49 Hylton, "Public Attitudes," 253–6.

50 Merry, *Urban Danger*, 153–62.

51 Manning, "Modern Police Administration," 63.

52 Trojanowicz, *An Evaluation*, 2.

53 Brian Dexter, "Let Us Help Fight Jane-Finch Drugs Citizens Suggest," *Toronto Star*, 27 April 1988.

54 Wilson and Herrnstein, *Crime*, 308.

55 Wellman and Leighton, "Networks," 252ff.

56 Ibid., 251–2.

57 Fishman, *Bourgeois Utopias*, 155–72.

58 Hayes, *The Dispersed City*.

59 Fishman, *Bourgeois Utopias*, 184.

60 Ibid.

61 Cox and Nartowicz, "American Metropolis," 384.

62 Higgins, *Local and Urban Politics*, 17.

63 Castells, "The Wild City," 580.

64 Cox and Nartowicz, "American Metropolis" 386–7.

65 Fishman, *Bourgeois Utopias*, 201–2.

66 *Toronto Star*, 22 August 1989.

67 Richard Mackie, "Toronto Region Forecast to Lead Population Growth," *Globe and Mail*, 10 August 1989.

68 Bell, *Post-Industrial Society*. See, for example, 171.

69 Blumenfeld, "Continuity and Change," 51.

70 Hiss, *The Experience of Place*, 141, 178–86.

71 Ibid., 181–2.

72 Alonso, "The Population Factor," 546.

73 Kelling, "Urban Police," 18.

CHAPTER FOUR

1 Lindsey et al., "The Oasis Technique," 322.

2 James Q. Wilson, *Varieties*, 278ff.

3 Ibid., 214.

4 Ibid., 290.

5 Ibid., 287.

6 Trojanowicz and Harden, *Community Policing Programs*, 5.

7 Feldman and Graham, *Bargaining for Cities*, 105.

8 Bob Hepburn, *Toronto Star*, 28 April 1986.

9 McGahan, "Criminogenesis," 219, 221–3. His conclusions are tentative given the unavoidable problem of aggregating data.

10 Trojanowicz, "Neighborhood Patrol Strategies," 96, 100–1.

11 Wilson and Kelling, "Making Neighborhoods Safe," 48.

12 Pate et al., *Reducing Fear of Crime*, 26–33.

13 Murphy and Verteuil, *Community Policing Survey*, 2.

14 For more general background, see Cain, "Toward a Political Sociology," 27–51; Reiner, *Politics*, 200; and Lea and Young, *What is to Be Done*, 199, 217–18.

15 Scarman, *The Scarman Report*, cited in Reiner, *Politics*, 200.

16 Sacco, "Perceptions of Crime," 96–9.

17 Lindsey et al., "The Oasis Technique," 326.

18 Ibid., 327.

19 Goldstein, *Problem-Oriented Policing*, 3.

20 Sherman, "Effective Policing," 136.

21 See Kelling, "Urban Police," 17, and Scott, "The Current Climate," 42ff. Goldstein describes this as a new "common wisdom" on the police. See *Problem-Oriented Policing*, 11, 168–72.

22 Canada, House of Commons, *Debates*, of 23 January 1986, vol. 90/92, col. 253/254.

23 Reiss, "Serving the Community," 63.

24 A symposium on community policing was conducted in March 1986. See Loree and Murphy, eds., *Community Policing in the 1980s*.

25 Scott, "The Current Climate," 44.

26 Roach makes his point clearly in his discussion of the implementation of community-oriented policing in the Metropolitan London Police. See "Community Based Policing," 88.

27 Reiss, "Serving the Community," 63.

28 Sherman discusses this point generally in "The Police Executive as Statesman."

29 Scott, "Serving the Community," 44.

30 Roach, "Community Based Policing," 77.

31 Reiss, "Forecasting," 146.

32 Reiss discusses the need for experimentation, research, and planning within police departments. See "Forecasting," 140–3.

33 Trojanowicz and Banas, *Job Satisfaction*, 11–13, and Klockars, "Order Maintenance," 318–19.

34 Thomas G. Koby, quoted in Andrew H. Malcolm, "Cities Try Out New Approach in Police Work," *The New York Times*, 29 March 1989.

35 Pate et al., *Reducing Fear of Crime*, 35; and Trojanowicz, "Neighbourhood Patrol Strategies," 12.

36 Hunt, "Planning and Implementation," 65–7.

37 MacDonald's study illustrates this point as well as others with respect to the police ideology. See *A Study of Leadership*, 74–5.
38 Ontario, Ministry of the Solicitor General, *Community Policing*, 4–5.
39 Walker, Walker, and McDavid, *A Three Year Evaluation*, 2–8. For a wider discussion, see also Christopher Walker, "The Community Police Station."
40 Walker, Walker, and McDavid, *A Three-Year Evaluation*, 4.
41 Ibid., 65–70, 72–5.
42 Hornick et al., *An Evaluation*, 97–102.
43 Trojanowicz, *Neighbourhood Patrol Strategies*, 96–7, and Trojanowicz and Banas, *Uniform Crime Reporting*, 114.
44 Trojanowicz, "Neighborhood Patrol Strategies," 96–7.
45 Reiss, "Serving the Community," 63–4.
46 Lachman and Downs, "Neighborhoods," 219–24.
47 Kelling, "Order Maintenance," 297–8.
48 James Q. Wilson, *Varieties*, 278–9.
49 Kelling, "Order Maintenance," 297–8.
50 Reiner, *Politics*, 171–4.
51 Roach, "Community Based Policing," 85.
52 Epstein and Vanderhoef, *Paraprofessionalism*.
53 Pepinski, "Better Living," 254–5.
54 Ibid., 264.
55 Ibid., 261.
56 Goldstein, "Improving Policing," 236–58.
57 Goldstein. *Problem-Oriented Policing*, 1.
58 Ibid., 33.
59 Ibid., 29.
60 Ibid., 173.

CHAPTER FIVE

1 Reiner, *Politics*, 52–3.
2 Cooper, "Police Officers," 101–3.
3 Chief James Harding spoke of this contradiction in an informal statement at, the Workshop on Community Policing, Canadian Police College, 1986; Wilson's discussion of the order-maintenance duties of patrol officers is general but pertinent. See *Varieties*, 17–34. See also McGinnis, "Career Development in Canadian Policing: Part II," 258–9.
4 MacDonald and Martin, "Specialists," 189–91.
5 Terry discusses police stress as the ideology that served to bring coherence to job tasks among officers. This ideology implies "dovetailing the idea of dangerousness with the ideal of personal dedication and service to others." See "Police Stress as a Professional Self-Image," 502–503.
6 MacDonald, *A Study of Leadership*, 73–5, 157–8.

7 Goldstein, *Problem-Oriented Policing*, 163–4.

8 Gruber, "Promoting Police Officers," 387ff.

9 Kelling, "Urban Police," 20–1.

10 MacDonald and Martin, "Specialists," 211.

11 Ibid., 202.

12 Ibid., 217.

13 Stolovitch and MacDonald, "A Quasi-Policy Statement," 86–7.

14 Select Panel, "Police Manager Development Study," 256.

15 Swanton, *Police Institutions*, 336–9.

16 Ibid., 336ff.

17 Klockars, "Order Maintenance," 319.

18 Swanton, *Police Institutions*, 4–5.

19 Police Chief Executive Committee, *Report*.

20 Ontario, Ministry of The Solicitor General, Task Force, *Policing in Ontario*, 99–100.

21 President's Commission on Law Enforcement and the Administration of Justice, *The Challenge of Crime*, 274.

22 Martin, "Issues in Higher Education," 215.

23 Ibid., 215.

24 Sherman et al., *The Quality of Police Education*.

25 Bopp, *O.W. Wilson*, 80–2.

26 O'Reilly, "Programs of Study," 173–6.

27 Goldstein, *Policing a Free Society*, 291–304.

28 Patrick O'Flaherty, "Stupidity is Alive and Well (Thanks to TV)," *Globe and Mail*, 19 January 1988.

29 Select Panel, "Police Manager Development Study," 256.

30 Roosevelt, "Municipal Administration," 183.

31 See Kelling, "Changing Function," 12–13, and Klockars, "Order Maintenance," 310–17.

32 Wilson and MacLaren, *Police Administration*.

33 Bopp, *O.W. Wilson*, 7–8.

34 Ibid., 6.

35 Klockars, "Order Maintenance," 312.

36 The police often substitute means for ends and matters of organization and organizational capacity for goals, and they need to handle problems rather than incidents alone. Goldstein discusses this from several angles. See *Problem-Oriented Policing*, 1, 35–6, and 154–5.

37 See MacDonald, "Some Alternative Models," 171–3; and Neave et al., "Management Issues," 33–4.

38 See, for example, Price, *Police Professionalism*, 95.

38 Manning, "Police Administration," 59.

40 Kelling, "Order Maintenance," 296.

41 Moore and Kelling, "To Serve and Protect," 60.

42 Reiner, *Politics*, 64.

43 Klockars, "Order Maintenance," 319.

44 Bopp, *O.W. Wilson*, 58–9.

45 Carpenter, *Evaluation Systems*, 49.

46 Coutts, "Senior Police Administration," 27.

47 Goldstein, *Problem-Oriented Policing*, 27–9, 150.

48 For a discussion of some aspects of this matter, see Neave et al., "Management Issues," 36ff.

49 Goldstein, *Policing a Free Society*, 259.

50 MacDonald, *A Study of Leadership*, 129–35.

51 Kelly and Kelly, *Policing in Canada*, 199.

52 See James Q. Wilson, Varieties 279, 283, and MacDonald, *A Study of Leadership*, 129–135.

53 See MacDonald, *A Study of Leadership*, in particular the discussion beginning on p. 29.

54 Neave et al., "Management Issues," 44.

55 James Q. Wilson, *Varieties*, 29ff.

56 MacDonald, *A Study of Leadership*, 141–3.

57 Neave et al., "Management Issues," 33.

58 For a brief discussion of this point, see Murphy, *Assessing Police Performance*.

59 MacDonald, *A Study of Leadership*, 174–82.

60 Neave et al., "Management Issues," 53.

61 Cited in Goldstein, *Policing a Free Society*, 227.

62 Neave et al., "Management Issues," 33.

63 Reiss, "Forecasting," 136.

64 MacDonald and Martin, "Specialists," 217.

65 Reiss, "Forecasting," 139.

66 Ibid., 143–8.

67 Ibid., 132–3.

68 Ibid., 133.

69 Ibid., 140.

70 Ibid., 140–1.

71 Ibid., 148.

72 Reiner, *Politics*, 198.

73 MacDonald, *A Study of Leadership*, 74–5.

74 McDougall, "The Occupational Dimension," 6.

75 MacDonald, Martin and Richardson. "Physical and Verbal Excesses," 295–7.

76 Sallman, "The Police and the Criminal Justice System," 189.

77 Cooper, "Police Officers," 103.

78 MacDonald, *A Study of Leadership*, 74–5; MacDonald, Martin, and Richardson, "Physical and Verbal Excesses," 310.

79 Reiner, *Politics*, 85ff, 198–203.

80 Reuss-Ianni's *Two Cultures of Policing* refers to operations officers and their sergeant supervisors on one hand and police management on the other. Patrol officers and their sergeants share a commonality of attitudes and approach to work.

81 Forcese, "Police Unionism," 111–12.

82 Ibid., 87, 97, 111.

83 Ibid., 111.

84 Goldstein, *Problem-Oriented Policing*, 150, 164–5.

85 Reiss, "Forecasting the Role," 150.

CHAPTER SIX

1 Andrews, "Political Independence," 11.

2 James Q. Wilson, *Varieties*, 11, 64ff.

3 MacDonald, *A Study of Leadership*, 84ff.

4 Patrick V. Murphy, "The Prospective Chief's Negotiation," 32.

5 Sewell, *Police – Urban Policing in Canada*, 201–7.

6 James Q. Wilson, *Varieties*, 231.

7 Bell, *Post-Industrial Society*, 159–60.

8 Andrews, "Political Independence," 12.

9 Rousseau, *The Social Contract*, 403.

10 Higgins, *Local and Urban Politics*, 26.

11 Sewell, *Up against City Hall*, 164ff.

12 Simmonds, "An Address," 181.

13 Swanton, *Police Institutions*, 329–31.

14 Higgins, *Local and Urban Politics*, 10–11.

15 Rhodes, "'Power Dependence,'" 13ff.

16 Higgins, *Local and Urban Politics*, 18.

17 Ibid.

18 Ibid.

19 Ibid., 72–4.

20 Monkonnen, *Police in Urban America*, 52ff.

21 Higgins, *Local and Urban Politics*, 239–40.

22 Ibid., 244–5.

23 Reiner, *Politics*, 37–9.

24 Higgins, *Local and Urban Politics*, 124–5.

25 Rhodes, "'Power Dependence,'" 18ff.

26 Ibid., 18–19.

27 McDougall, "A Case Study," 10ff; see also Laffin, "Professionalism," 18–25.

28 McDougall, "A Case Study," 15.

29 Ibid., 22.

30 Feldman and Graham, *Bargaining for Cities*, 5.

31 McDougall, "A Case Study," 21.

32 Laffin, "Professionalism," 24–5.
33 Jane Coutts, "Direct Election Is Panned," *Globe and Mail*, 14 November 1990.
34 Higgins, *Local and Urban Politics*, 126.
35 Ibid., 234.
36 Ibid., 251.
37 Ibid., 247
38 Ibid., 248–9.
39 Feldman and Graham, *Bargaining for Cities*, 111–22.
40 Reiner, *Politics*, 17.
41 Higgins, *Local and Urban Politics*, 124–5.
42 Ibid., 126–7.
43 Ibid., 254.
44 Reiner, *Politics*, 3.
45 Waterloo Region Review Commission, *Police Governance*, 83–102.
46 Sallman, "The Police and the Criminal Justice System," 188–96.
47 Stenning, "Community Policing," 88.
48 Hann et al., "Municipal Police Governance," 28–9.
49 Baldwin and Kinsey, *Police Powers and Politics*, 107–8.
50 McDougall, "A Case Study," 26.
51 Hann et al., "Municipal Police Governance."
52 McDougall, "A Case Study," 13.
53 Hann et al., "Municipal Police Governance," 16–20.
54 Ibid., 5ff.
55 Ibid., 32–8.
56 R. v. Metropolitan Police Commissioner, ex parte Blackburn, *All E.R.* 763 at 769, 1968.
57 Hann et al., "Municipal Police Governance," 43–7.
58 Ibid., 37.
59 Ibid., 26–8.
60 Ibid., 16–18, 50–1.
61 Ibid., 13–14.
62 Susan Eng, "Police Costs: Time to Gore Sacred Cows?" *Toronto Star*, 4 October 1990.
63 Hann et al., "Municipal Police Governance," 13–14.
64 Pepinski, "Better Living," 261–4.
65 Bell, *Post-Industrial Society*, 127.

CHAPTER SEVEN

1 Gertler and Crowley, *Changing Canadian Cities*, 309.
2 Johnson, *Professions and Power*, 45.
3 James Q. Wilson, *Varieties*, 30.

4 Johnson, *Professions and Power,* 19ff.

5 Schön, *The Reflective Practitioner,* 23.

6 Johnson, *Professions and Power,* 43–4.

7 Thompson, *Respectable Society,* 64–5.

8 Speiser, *Lawsuit,* 139. Speiser gives a brief account of the continuing development of the law profession and its numerous specializations.

9 Scott, "Professional Employees," 131–4.

10 Samuel Walker, " 'Broken Windows,' " 77.

11 Laski, "The Limitations of the Expert," 164.

12 Ibid., 162ff.

13 Bell, *Post-Industrial Society,* 112–19.

14 Ibid., 401.

15 Ibid., 263.

16 Ibid., 119.

17 Select Panel, "Police Manager Development Study," 255.

18 Schön, *The Reflective Practitioner,* 49ff.

19 Chapter 5of Shön's *Reflective Practitioner,* "The Structure of Reflection-in-Action," beginning on p. 128, is particularly useful to the points I am raising here.

20 Ibid., 8ff.

21 See analysis of police eduction in Martin, "Issues in Higher Education."

22 Goldstein, *Policing a Free Society,* 254.

23 Sherman et al., *The Quality of Police Education,* 1–12.

24 O'Reilly, "Programs of Study," 174–5.

25 Young, "Democracy vs Professionalism," 5.

26 Andrews, "Political Independence," 12.

27 Cain, "Toward a Political Sociology," 37–8.

28 Quinn, *Multidisciplinary Services,* 24–7.

29 Ibid., 3–6. He summarizes the agency model of professional practice as it was first described by Tuohy and Wolfson.

30 Trojanowicz and Smyth, *A Manual,* 4.

31 Trojanowicz, *An Evaluation,* 4–6.

32 Kelling, "Urban Police," 12–18.

33 Andrew H. Malcolm, "Going beyond Jails in Drive to Make U.S. a Safer Place," *The New York Times,* 10 October 1990.

34 Johnson, *Professions and Power,* 63ff.

35 Ibid., 77–80.

36 MacDonald, *A Study of Leadership,* 84. See also James Q. Wilson, *Varieties,* 71ff.

37 Klockars, "Order Maintenance," 318.

38 Ibid.

39 Ibid., 318–19.

40 Moore and Kelling, "To Serve and Protect,'" 50.

41 Deakin, *Police Professionalism.* See Table of Contents.
42 Price, *Police Professionalism, Rhetoric and Action,* 94–8.
43 Mayo, "Leading Blindly," 410.
44 Ontario, Ministry of the Solicitor General, Task Force, *Policing in Ontario,* 94ff.
45 Terry, "Police Stress as a Professional Self-Image," 502.
46 Ibid.
47 Ibid., 507–8.
48 Ibid., 504–6.
49 Perrier, "Police Professionalism," 209–11.
50 This point is illustrated by Swanton on the tables in *Police Institutions,* 336–9.
51 Davis, "Organizing the Community," 95.
52 Bingham et al., *Professional Associations,* 69–70, 89.
53 Klockars, "Order Maintenance," 318.
54 James Q. Wilson, *Varieties,* 73.
55 Bell, *Post-Industrial Society,* 144–5.
56 Ibid., 221ff.

EPILOGUE

1 Laffin, "Professionalism," 20.
2 Goldstein, *Problem-Oriented Policing,* 31. The book's final chapter is also insightful on implementation.
3 Claflin, *JFK Wants to Know,* 281.
4 Bell, *Post-Industrial Society,* 77, 333–6.
5 James Q. Wilson, *Varieties,* 8–11.
6 Reiner, *Politics,* xii.

Bibliography

Adams, John S. "Residential Structure for Midwestern Cities." In *Internal Structure of the City*, 2d ed., edited by Larry S. Bourne. New York: Oxford University Press, 1982.

Alderson, John C. "Police and the Social Order." In *Police and Public Order in Europe*, edited by John Roach and Jurgen Thomaneck. London, UK: Croom Helm, 1985.

Alonso, William. "The Population Factor and Urban Structure." In *Internal Structure of the City*, 2d ed., edited by Larry S. Bourne. New York: Oxford University Press, 1982.

Andrews, Allen H., Jr. "Structuring the Political Independence of the Police Chief." In *Police Leadership in America: Crisis and Opportunity*, edited by William A. Geller. New York: Praeger, 1985; Chicago: American Bar Foundation, 1985.

Baldwin, Robert, and Richard Kinsey. *Police Powers and Politics*. London, UK: Quartet Books, 1982.

Bell, Daniel. *The Coming of Post-Industrial Society*. New York: Basic Books, 1976.

Bentley, Michael. *Politics Without Democracy 1815–1914*. London, UK: Fontana Paperbacks, 1984.

Berki, R.N. *Security and Society: Reflections on Law, Order and Politics*. London, UK: J.M. Dent & Sons, 1986.

Bingham, B.W.H., B.W. Hawkins, J.P. Frendreis, and M.P. LeBlanc. *Professional Associations and Municipal Innovation*. Madison: The University of Wisconsin Press, 1981.

Blumenfeld, Hans. "Continuity and Change in Urban Form." In *Internal Structure of the City*, 2d ed., edited by Larry S. Bourne. New York: Oxford University Press, 1982.

Bopp, William J. *O.W. Wilson and the Search for a Police Profession*. Port Washington, NY: Kennikat Press, 1977.

Bourne, Larry S., ed. *Internal Structure of the City.* 2d ed. New York: Oxford University Press, 1982.

Braiden, Inspector Chris. "Bank Robberies and Stolen Bikes." *Canadian Police College Journal* 10, no. 1 (1986): 1–30.

Cain, Maureen. "Toward a Political Sociology of the British Police: A Review of 1979 and 1980." In *The Maintenance of Order In Society,* edited by Rita Donelan. Ottawa, Canadian Police College, 1982.

Canada. House of Commons. *Debates,* 23 January 1986. Vol. 90/92, col. 253/254.

– Statistics Canada. *Education in Canada, 1973.* Ottawa: Information Canada, 1973.

Castells, Manuel. "The Wild City." In *Internal Structure of the City,* 2d ed., edited by Larry S. Bourne. New York: Oxford University Press, 1982.

Carpenter, G.J. *Police Officer Performance Evaluation Systems.* Ottawa: Canadian Police College, 1989.

Claflin, Edward B. *JFK Wants to Know: Memos From the President's Office, 1961–1963.* New York: William Morrow, 1991.

Cohen, A.P. *The Symbolic Construction of Community.* London, UK: Tavistock, 1985.

Cooper, William H. "Police Officers Over Career Stages." *Canadian Police College Journal* 6, no. 2 (1982): 93–112.

Coutts, Larry M. "Senior Police Administration: The Identification of Training Needs." *Canadian Police College Journal* 13, no. 1 (1989): 18–28.

Cox, Kevin R., and Frank Z. Nartowicz. "Jurisdictional Fragmentation in the American Metropolis: Alternative Perspectives." In *Internal Structure of the City,* 2d ed., edited by Larry S. Bourne. New York: Oxford University Press, 1982.

Davis, Raymond C. "Organizing the Community for Improved Policing". In *Police Leadership in America: Crisis and Opportunity.* edited by William A. Geller. New York: Praeger, 1985; Chicago: American Bar Foundation, 1985.

Deakin, Thomas J. *Police Professionalism, The Renaissance of American Law Enforcement.* Springfield, IL: Charles C. Thomas, 1988.

Desaulniers, Louise, ed. *Selections from 119 Years of the Atlantic.* N.p.: Atlantic Monthly Co., 1977.

Dominion Bureau of Statistics. *Canada 1958.* Ottawa: Queen's Printer, 1958.

Downie, Bryan M., and Richard L. Jackson, eds. *Conflict and Cooperation in Police Labour Relations.* Ottawa: Supply and Services Canada, 1980.

Dumas, J. (Statistics Canada). *Current Demographic Analysis.* Ottawa: Supply and Services Canada, 1984.

Elcock, Howard. *Local Government: Politics, Professionals and the Public in Local Authorities,* 2d ed. London, UK: Methuen, 1986.

Emsley, Clive. *Policing and Its Context 1750–1870.* London, UK: Macmillan, 1983.

Epstein, Joyce, and Sheila Vanderhoef. *Paraprofessionalism – A Study for the Winnipeg Police Commission.* Winnipeg: Institute of Urban Studies, University of Winnipeg, 1977.

Ericson, Richard. *Reproducing Order – A Study of Police Patrol Work.* Toronto: University of Toronto Press, 1982.

Etzioni, A. *The Semi-Professions and Their Organization: Teachers, Nurses, Social Workers.* New York: The Free Press, 1969.

Feldman, Lionel D., and Katherine A. Graham. *Bargaining for Cities: Municipalities and Intergovernmental Relations – An Assessment.* Toronto: Institute for Research on Public Policy Butterworth, 1979.

Fishman, Robert. *Bourgeois Utopias: The Rise and Fall of Suburbias.* New York: Basic Books, 1987.

Foot, David K. *Canada's Population Outlook.* Toronto: James Lorimer, 1982.

Forcese, Dennis. "Police Unionism: Employee-Management Relations in Canadian Police Forces." *Canadian Police College Journal* 4, no. 2 (1980): 79–129.

George, M., and J. Perrault. (Statistics Canada). *Population Projections for Canada, Provinces and Territories, 1984–2006.* Ottawa: Supply and Services Canada, 1985.

Gertler, Leonard O., and Ronald W. Crowley. *Changing Canadian Cities: The Next 25 Years.* Toronto: McClelland and Stewart, 1976.

Goldstein, Herman. *Policing a Free Society.* Cambridge, MA: Ballinger, 1977.

– "Improving Policing: A Problem-Oriented Approach." *Crime and Delinquency* 25 (1979): 236–58.

– *Problem-Oriented Policing.* Philadelphia: Temple University Press, 1990.

Gruber, Gerald P. "Promoting Police Officers: A Job Analysis Approach." *Canadian Police College Journal* 8, no. 4 (1984): 386–94.

Hann, Robert G., James H. McGinnis, Philip C. Stenning, and Stuart Farson. "Municipal Police Governance and Accountability in Canada: An Empirical Study." *Canadian Police College Journal* 9, no. 1 (1985): 1–85.

Haskell, T.L., ed. *The Authority of Experts.* Bloomington: Indiana University Press, 1984.

Hayes, Charles R. *The Dispersed City: The Case of Piedmont, South Carolina.* Research Paper no. 173. Chicago: University of Chicago Press, 1973.

Herbert, David T. "Deprivation: Definition, Measurement, and Spacial Qualities." In *Internal Structure of the City,* 2d ed., edited by Larry S. Bourne. New York: Oxford University Press, 1982.

Higgins, Donald, J.H. *Local and Urban Politics in Canada.* Toronto: Gage, 1986.

Hiss, Tony. *The Experience of Place.* Toronto: Random House, 1990.

Hornick, Joseph P., Barbara A. Burrows, Ida Tjosvold, and Donna M. Phillips. *An Evaluation of the Neighbourhood Foot Patrol Program of the Edmonton Police Service.* Canadian Research Institute for Law and the Family. Ottawa: Solicitor General of Canada, 1989.

Hunt, Deputy Assistant Commissioner R.A. "The Planning and Implementation of Change in a Police Department: The London Experience." In *Community Policing in the 1980s,* edited by D. Loree and Chris Murphy. Ottawa: Solicitor General of Canada, 1987.

Hylton, John H. "Public Attitudes towards Crime and the Police in a Prairie City." *Canadian Police College Journal* 4, no. 4 (1980): 243–76.

Jackson, Richard L. "Police Management under Fiscal Restraint." *Canadian Police College Journal* 7, no. 3 (1983): 230–42.

Johnson, Terence J. *Professions and Power.* Toronto: Macmillan, 1972.

Kelling, George L. "Order Maintenance, the Quality of Urban Life, and Police: A Line of Argument." In *Police Leadership in America: Crisis and Opportunity,* edited by William A. Geller. New York: Praeger, 1985; Chicago: American Bar Foundation, 1985.

– "The Changing Function of Urban Police: The Historical and Political Context of Community Policing". In *Community Policing in the 1980s,* edited by Donald J. Loree and Chris Murphy. Ottawa: Solicitor General of Canada, 1987.

– "Acquiring a Taste For Order: The Community and the Police." *Crime and Delinquency* 33 (1987).

Kelling, George L., Tony Pate, Duane Dieckman, and Charles E. Brown. *The Kansas City Patrol Experiment: A Summary Report.* Washington: Police Foundation, 1974.

Kelly, William, and Nora Kelly. *Policing in Canada.* Toronto: Macmillan, 1976.

Klockars, Carl B. "Order Maintenance, the Quality of Urban Life and Police: A Different Line of Argument." In *Police Leadership in America: Crisis and Opportunity,* edited by William A. Geller. New York: Praeger, 1985; Chicago: American Bar Foundation,1985.

Lachman, M. Leanne, and Anthony Downs. "The Role of Neighborhoods in the Mature Metropolis." In *The Mature Metropolis,* edited by Charles L. Leven. Lexington, MA: Charles C. Thomas, 1978.

Laffin, Martin. "Professionalism in Central-Local Relations." In *New Approaches to the Study of Central-Local Government Relations,* edited by G.W. Jones. London, UK: Gower, 1980.

Larson, M.S. *The Rise of Professionalism: A Sociological Analysis.* Berkeley: University of California Press, 1977.

Laski, Harold J. "The Limitations of the Expert." In *Man and the State,* edited by William Ebenstein. New York: Rinehart, 1947.

Lea, John, and Jack Young. *What Is to Be Done about Law and Order?* Harmondsworth, UK, and Markham, ONT: Penguin Books, 1984.

Leven, Charles L. "Growth and Nongrowth in Metropolitan Areas and the Emergence of Polycentric Metropolitan Form." In *The Mature Metropolis,* edited by Charles L. Leven. Lexington, MA: Charles C. Thomas, 1978.

Lewis, Roy. *A Force for the Future.* London, UK: Temple Smith, 1976.

Lindsey, William H., Ronald Cochran, Bruce Quint, and Mario Rivera. "The Oasis Technique: A Method of Controlling Crime and Improving Quality of Life". In *Police Leadership in America: Crisis and Opportunity,* edited by William A. Geller. New York: Praeger, 1985; Chicago: American Bar Foundation, 1985.

Loree, Donald J., and Chris Murphy, eds. *Community Policing in the 1980s.* Ottawa: Solicitor General of Canada, 1987.

MacDonald, Victor N. *A Study of Leadership and Supervision in Policing.* Ottawa: Canadian Police College, 1986.

– "Some Alternative Models of Police Operation." *Canadian Police College Journal* 4, no. 3 (1980): 171–83.

MacDonald, Victor N., and M.A. Martin. "Specialists and the Personnel Structures of Canadian Police Forces." *Canadian Police College Journal* 10, no. 3 (1986): 189–226.

MacDonald, Victor N., M.A. Martin, and A.J. Richardson. "Physical and Verbal Excesses in Policing." *Canadian Police College Journal* 9, no. 3 (1985): 295–341.

Manning, Peter C. "Modern Police Administration, The Rise of Crime-Focused Policing, and Critical Incident Analysis." In *The Maintenance of Order In Society,* edited by Rita Donclan. Ottawa, Canadian Police College, 1982.

Marin, Judge Rene J. *Professionalization of the Canadian Police Officer through Education and Training – Myth or Reality.* An Address to the Fifth Annual Police Trainers Conference, Toronto, May 1978.

Martin, M.A. "Issues in Higher Education for Canadian Police." *Canadian Police College Journal* 3, no. 3 (1979): 214–36.

Mayo, Louis A. "Leading Blindly: An Assessment of Chief's Information about Police Operations." In *Police Leadership in America: Crisis and Opportunity,* edited by William A. Geller. New York: Praeger, 1985; Chicago: American Bar Foundation,1985.

McDougall, Allan K. "Policing in Ontario: A Case Study in Administrative Balkanization." Unpublished paper, 1969.

– "Policing in Ontario: The Occupational Dimension to Provincial-Municipal Relations." Ph.D. dissertation. Department of Political Economy, University of Toronto, 1971.

McGahan, Peter. "Criminogenesis and the Urban Environment: A Case Study." *Canadian Police College Journal* 6, no. 4 (1982): 209–24.

McGinnis, James H. "Career Development in Canadian Policing: Part II." *Canadian Police College Journal* 9, no. 3 (1985): 254–94.

Merry, Sally Engle. *Urban Danger: Life in a Neighborhood of Strangers.* Philadelphia: Temple University Press, 1981.

Monkonnen, E.H. *Police in Urban America 1860–1920.* New Rochelle, NY: Cambridge University Press, 1981.

Moore, Mark H. and George L. Kelling, " 'To Serve and Protect': Learning From Police History." *The Public Interest* 70, (Winter 1983): 49–65.

Murphy, Christopher. *Assessing Police Performance: Issues, Problems and Alternatives.* Programs Branch User Report No. 1985–19. Ottawa: Solicitor General of Canada, 1985.

Murphy, Chris, and Jacques de Verteuil. *Metropolitan Toronto Community Policing Survey (Working Paper No. 1, 1986–47).* Ottawa: Solicitor General of Canada, 1986.

Murphy, Patrick V. "The Prospective Chief's Negotiation With the Mayor." In *Police Leadership in America: Crisis and Opportunity*, edited by William A. Geller. New York: Praeger, 1985; Chicago: American Bar Foundation, 1985.

– "Ethical Issues in Policing." *Criminal Justice Ethics* 4 (1985).

Murphy, Patrick V., and Thomas Plate. *Commissioner*. New York: Simon and Schuster, 1977.

Murphy, Thomas P., and John Rehfuss. *Urban Politics in the Suburban Era*. Homewood, IL: The Dorsey Press, 1976.

National Advisory Commission on Criminal Justice Standards and Goals. *Police*. Washington: US Government Printing Office, 1973.

Neave, E.H., W.H. Cooper, V.N. MacDonald, and E.R. Peterson. "Management Issues in Canadian Municipal Policing." *Canadian Police College Journal* 4, no. 1 (1980): 32–66.

Ontario, Ministry of the Solicitor General. *Community Policing: Shaping the Future*. Toronto: Queen's Printer for Ontario, 1990.

– Task Force on the Racial and Ethnic Implications of Police, Hiring, Training and Promotion and Career Development. Report of the Task Force. *Policing in Ontario for the Eighties, Perceptions and Reflections*. Toronto: Ministry of the Solicitor General, 1980.

O'Reilly, Robert R. "Programs of Study for Law Enforcement Personnel in Canadian Community Colleges." *Canadian Police College Journal* 2, no. 1 (1978): 162–76.

Pate, Anthony M., May Ann Wycoff, Wesley G. Skogan, and Lawrence W. Sherman. *Reducing Fear of Crime in Houston and Newark: A Summary Report*. Washington: Police Foundation, 1986.

Pepinski, Harold E. "Better Living through Police Discretion." *Law and Contemporary Problems* 47 (1984).

Perrier, David. "Police Professionalism." *Canadian Police College Journal* 2, no. 2 (1978): 209–14.

Police Chief Executive Committee. International Association of Chiefs of Police. *The Police Chief Executive Report*. Washington: Law Enforcement Assistance Administration, 1976.

Pool, Ithiel De Sola. "Communications, Technology and Land Use." In *Internal Structure of the City*, 2d ed., edited by Larry S. Bourne. New York: Oxford University Press, 1982.

Porteous, J. Douglas. *Environment and Behaviour*. Toronto: Addison-Wesley, 1977.

President's Commission on Law Enforcement and the Administration of Justice. *The Challenge of Crime in a Free Society*. New York: Avon, 1968.

Price, Barbara Raffel. *Police Professionalism, Rhetoric and Action*. Lexington, MA: Lexington Books, 1977.

Quinn, John. *Multidisciplinary Services: Organizational Innovation in Professional Service Markets*. Toronto: Ministry of the Attorney General, Professional Organizations Committee, 1978.

R. v. Metropolitan Police Commissioner, ex parte Blackburn. *All E.R.* 763 at 769, 1968.

Reiner, Robert. *The Politics of Police.* New York: St Martin's Press, 1985.

Reiss, Albert J., Jr. *The Police and the Public.* New Haven: Yale University Press, 1971.

– "Forecasting the Role of the Police and the Role of Police in Social Forecasting." In *The Maintenance of Order In Society*, edited by Rita Donelan. Ottawa: Canadian Police College, 1982.

– "Shaping and Serving the Community: The Role of the Police Chief Executive." In *Police Leadership in America: Crisis and Opportunity*, edited by William A. Geller. New York: Praeger, 1985; Chicago: American Bar Foundation, 1985.

Reiter, B.J. *Discipline as a Means of Asssuring Continuing Competence in the Professions and Tables of Discipline Activities by Profession.* Toronto: The Professional Organizations Committee, Ministry of the Solicitor General, 1979.

Reuss-Ianni, Elizabeth. *Two Cultures of Policing: Street Cops and Management Cops.* New Brunswick, NJ: Transaction, 1983.

Rhodes, R.A.W. " 'Power Dependence' – Theories of Central-Local Relations." In *New Research in Central-Local Relations*, edited by Michael Goldsmith. Aldershot, UK: Gower, 1986.

Roach, Commander Lawrence T. "Implementing Community Based Policing in the London Metropolitan Police." In *Community Policing in the 1980s,* edited by D. Loree and Chris Murphy. Ottawa: Solicitor General of Canada, 1987.

Roosevelt, Theodore. "Municipal Administration; The New York City Police Force." In *Selections from 119 Years of the Atlantic*, edited by Louise Desaulniers. N.p: Atlantic Monthy Co., 1977.

Rose, Harold M., and Donald R. Deskins, Jr. "Felony Murder: The Case for Detroit." In *Internal Structure of the City*, 2d ed., edited by Larry S. Bourne. New York: Oxford University Press, 1982.

Rousseau, Jean Jacques. *The Social Contract.* [1762]. Vol. 38 of *Great Books of the Western World*, edited by Robert M. Hutchins. Chicago: Encyclopaedia Britannica, 1952.

Sacco, Vincent F. "Perceptions of Crime and Anomic Adaptations." *Crimcare Journal* 1, no. 2 (1985): 86–108.

Sallman, Peter A. "The Police and the Criminal Justice System." *Canadian Police College Journal* 5, no. 4 (1981): 187–210.

Scarman, Lord. *The Scarman Report.* London, UK: Penguin Books, 1982.

Schön, D.A. *The Reflective Practitioner: How Professionals Think in Action.* New York: Basic Books, 1983.

Scott, Deputy Chief Peter. "The Current Climate of Canadian Policing: Prospects for Change." In *Community Policing in the 1980s*, edited by D. Loree and Chris Murphy. Ottawa: Solicitor General of Canada, 1987.

Scott, W. Richard. "Professional Employees in a Bureaucratic Structure." In *The Semi-Professions and Their Organization Teachers, Nurses, Social Workers*, edited by Amitai Etzioni. New York: The Free Press, 1969.

Select Panel. "Police Manager Development Study" *Canadian Police College Journal* 3, no. 3 (1979): 254–60.

Sewell, John. *Up against City Hall.* Toronto: James Lewis and Samuel, 1972.

– *Police – Urban Policing in Canada.* Toronto: James Lorimer, 1985.

Sherman, Lawrence W. "The Police Executive as Statesman." In *Police Leadership in America: Crisis and Opportunity*, edited by William A. Geller. New York: Praeger, 1985; Chicago: American Bar Foundation, 1985.

– "Effective Policing: Recent Contributions." In *Community Policing in the 1980s*, edited by Donald J. Loree and Chris Murphy. Ottawa: Solicitor General of Canada, 1987.

Sherman, Lawrence W., and The National Advisory Commission Higher Education for Police officers. *The Quality of Police Education.* San Francisco, CA: Josey Bass, 1978.

Simmonds, Commissioner R.H. "An Address to the International Conference on Police Accountability." *Canadian Police College Journal* 6, no. 3 (1982): 179–87.

Skolnick, J.H. *Justice without Trial: Law Enforcement in a Democratic Society.* New York: John Wiley, 1967.

Speiser, Stuart M. *Lawsuit.* New York: Horizon Press, 1980.

Stenning, Phillip C. "Community Policing: Who's in Control?" In *Community Policing: Proceedings, 2–3 August 1984* (AIC Seminar Proceedings, no. 4), edited by Superintendent James Morgan. Canberra, AUS: Australian Institute of Criminolgy, 1984.

Stewart, James K. "Research and the Police Administrator: Working Smarter, Not Harder." In *Police Leadership in America: Crisis and Opportunity*, edited by William A. Geller. New York: Praeger, 1985; Chicago: American Bar Foundation, 1985.

Stolovitch, Harold D., and Victor N. MacDonald. "A Quasi-Policy Statement on the Role of Formal Management Training and Education in Police Management Development." *Canadian Police College Journal* 5, no. 2 (1981): 81–97.

Swanton, Barry. *Police Institutions and Issues.* Canberra, AUS: Australian Institute of Criminology, 1979.

Terry, W. Clinton III. "Police Stress as a Professional Self-Image." *Journal of Criminal Justice* 13 (1985): 501–12.

Thompson, F.M.L. *The Rise of Respectable Society, A Social History of Victorian Britain, 1830–1900.* London, UK: Fontana Press, 1988.

Trojanowicz, Robert. *An Evaluation of the Neighborhood Foot Patrol Program in Flint, Michigan.* East Lansing, MI: School of Criminal Justice, Michigan State University, 1982.

– *Uniform Crime Reporting and Community Policing: An Historical Perspective.* East Lansing, MI: National Neighborhood Foot Patrol Center, Michigan State University, 1985.

– "Neighborhood Patrol Strategies: The Flint Michigan Experience." In *Community Policing in the 1980s*, edited by Donald J. Loree and Chris Murphy. Ottawa: Solicitor General of Canada, 1987.

Trojanowicz, Robert C., and Dennis W. Banas. *Job Satisfaction: A Comparison of Foot Patrol Versus Motor Patrol Officers*. East Lansing, MI: The National Neighborhood Foot Patrol Center, Michigan State University, 1985.

Trojanowicz, Robert, and Hazel A. Harden. *The Status of Contemporary Community Policing Programs*. East Lansing, MI: The National Neighborhood Foot Patrol Center, Michigan State University, 1985.

Trojanowicz, Robert C., and Paul R. Smyth. *A Manual for the Establishment and Operation of a Foot Patrol Program*. East Lansing, MI: The National Neighborhood Foot Patrol Center, Michigan State University, 1984.

United Kingdom. Royal Commission on Police. *Final Report*. London, UK: Her Majesty's Stationery Office, 1962.

Van Maanen, J. *The Boss: First Line Supervision in an American Police Agency*. Cambridge: Alfred P. Sloan School of Management, 1983.

Walker, Christopher R., "The Community Police Station: Developing a Model." *Canadian Police College Journal* 11, no. 4 (1987): 273–318.

Walker, S. Gail, Christopher R. Walker, and James C. McDavid. *The Victoria Community Police Stations: A Three-Year Evaluation*. Ottawa: Canadian Police College, 1992.

Walker, Samuel. *A Critical History of Police Reform: The Emergence of Professionalism*. Toronto: D.C. Heath, 1977.

– "Broken Windows' and Fractured History: The Use and Misuse of History in Recent Police Patrol Analysis." *Justice Quarterly* 1, no. 1 (1984): 75–89.

Waterloo Region Review Commission. *Police Governance in Waterloo Region*. Toronto: Queen's Printer, 1978.

Wellman, Barry, and Barry Leighton. "Networks, Neighborhoods, and Communities: Approaches to the Study of the Community." In *Internal Structure of the City*, 2d ed., edited by Larry S. Bourne. New York: Oxford University Press, 1982.

Wilson, James Q. "Dilemmas of Police Administration." *Public Administration Review* 28 (1968).

– *Varieties of Police Behavior*. Cambridge: Harvard University Press, 1970.

– *Thinking About Crime*. New York: Basic Books, 1975.

Wilson, James Q., and Barbara Boland. *The Effect of Police on Crime*. Washington: US Government Printing Office, 1979.

Wilson, James Q., and Richard J. Herrnstein. *Crime and Human Nature*. New York: Simon and Schuster, 1985.

Wilson, James Q., and George L. Kelling. "Police and Neighborhood Safety: Broken Windows." *The Atlantic Monthly* (March 1982).

– "Making Neighborhoods Safe." *The Atlantic Monthly* (February 1989): 46–52.

Wilson, Orlando W., and Roy C. MacLaren. *Police Administration*. 4th ed. New York: McGraw-Hill, 1977.

Young, T. Culyer, Jr. "Democracy vs Professionalism." *Rotunda* 20, no. 1 (1987): 5–7.

Index

Academies, police; *See* Police colleges and academies

Accountability, of police, 16, 17–18, 141; to government, 146; and law enforcement, 144; to neighbourhoods, 87; to police boards, 164; political nature, 143; and problem-oriented policing, 95; professional, 17–18; to public, 161

Agency model of professional practice, 186, 188–9

Alberta, 65–7

Alderson, John, 7, 13

Alonso, William, 67

Apprenticeship system, 19, 23, 99, 100, 101, 114. *See also* Police Training and education

Arrest rates, 12–13, 71, 72

Associations, police, 136, 137, 153, 199; Canadian Association of Chiefs of Police, 137; International Association of Chiefs of Police, 35, 136, 198

Authority, of police to act, 68, 89, 90

Autonomy: in government, 156–7; meaning, 142; police, 50, 142–3, 153, 166, 184–5; professional, 18

Baldwin, Robert, 163

Bell, Daniel, 19–20, 144, 168, 178, 200; *The Coming of Post-Industrial Society*, 65

Bennett, William, 35

Berki, R.N., 27, 30, 32

Boland, Barbara, 49

Bopp, William J., 117

Bourgeois Utopias (Robert Fishman), 43

Braiden, Chris, 85

Bramshill police staff college (Britain), 121

Brandon, Manitoba, 163

Britain: 19th century police, 5; Home Office Inspectorate of the Constabulary, 162; local control of police, 162–3; Metropolitan Police Act, 5; police structure in, 33; professional class, 174; public acceptance of policing in, 3, 5–6, 33, 99; race-related riots, 77–8; Reform Act

(1832), 4; Royal Commission on police (1962), 111; Unit Beat System, 119

British Columbia, 164

British common law, 165

Brzezinski, Zbigniew, 207

Cain, Maureen, 184–5

Calgary, 44

Calgary Police Service, 103

Canada: community college police education, 183; exurban forms in, 62; municipal government reform, 148–50; municipal police boards, 163–4; police departments, 135; public acceptance of policing in, 99; suburban development, 42; urbanization, 42–3, 44, 150

Canadian Association of Chiefs of Police, 137

Canadian Police College, 108, 114; management courses, 118, 120, 180, 190; report on performance evaluation (1989), 120

Cars, 21, 48, 87

Castells, Manuel, 63

Chicago police department, 115

Children's Environments Research Group (City University, New York), 66

Cities, 41–5; characteristics, 40; dispersed, 62; focus of police mission, 67; garden, 62; government functions in, 147; lost city thesis, 53, 54; population, 42; satellite, 62; saved community thesis, 54; social diversity, 147

Civilians: action against drug trafficking, 75; employment in police departments, 104, 105; volunteers in police projects, 84

Class distinction, 43–4; and morality, 27; and policing, 7, 11, 33; professional, 174–5; in us policing, 91–2

Client/practitioner relationship, 181–2, 186; in professional working context, 191–3

Cohen, A.P., 50–1

Colleges, police; See Police colleges and academies

Coming of Post-Industrial Society, The (Daniel Bell), 65

Command orientation, 122–4, 125, 128

Communal model, 73

Communication, 60

Communities: access to government, 169; characteristics, 54–5; definition, 50–1; human connections in, 53–4; of interests, 51; liberated, 60; order in, 32; and policing, 131, 166–7, 188–9; political relationship with police, 68; and service-style policing, 71–3; and technology, 60; types, 60–1; and watchman-style policing, 70

Community policing, 69, 79–82; acceptance, 82; community influence in, 90–2; and discretion, 82, 90; distribution of services, 80; effect on working conditions, 140; example of reflection in action, 182; foot-patrol programs, 85–7; and municipal government reform, 159, 160, 162; new roles for personnel, 129; Ontario Community Policing Manual, The, 82; political nature, 80–1, 87–8; power sharing in, 190; projects, 83–7; research on, 74, 95–6

Competence, 120

Computers, 124

Connections, personal, 53–4, 60

Consensus, political, 6, 7, 34–5

Conventional ideology, 25–6, 29, 35

Corruption, of police, 4, 16, 114

Cox, Kevin, 63

Craft: educational level, 179; orientation of policing, 70, 167

Crime: neighbourhood patterns, 75–8; organized, 153; and police resources, 201; serious, 10, 12, 16. See also Fear of crime; War on crime

Crime control, 161–2

Crime deterrence, 28, 30; evolution of patrol program, 118; field interrogation, 49; rational-deterrence approach, 35; value, 29–30, 36

Crime prevention, 6; civilian volunteers for, 84; and law enforcement, 35–6; policing orientation, 83; in reactive administration, 127

Crime rates: in Toronto, 83; in Vancouver, 83; in Victoria, 83–4; in us cities, 46; age group, 67; Canadian statistics, 83–4; in high density areas, 55; in inner city, 46; neighbourhood patterns, 75–8; and policing styles, 49; public perception, 58, 59; statistics, 207; in suburbs, 47; and urbanization, 46; and war, 3; of young males, 46, 47

Criminal-justice system: and crime control, 161–2; and law enforcement, 201

Crisis management, 127

Crowley, Ronald W., 42, 55, 170

Danger, perception of, 58–9

Davis, Raymond C., 198

Deakin, Thomas J., 195

Declaration of the Rights of Man and of the Citizen (France, 1789), 26

Demand management, 129

Denmark, 103

Detectives, 6

Devon and Cornwall Constabulary, 13

Dewey, John, 176, 179

Discretion: and bias, 31; and community policing, 82, 90; control, 118, 119, 120, 122, 141, 207; and law enforcement, 11; and order maintenance, 9, 14–15, 74, 99; in political policing, 31; in problem-oriented policing, 95; problems, 142; and professionalism, 134, 194; training in, 123, 124

Disorder, 12, 201; application of laws against, 90; arrest solution for, 72; in neighbourhoods, 73, 89; police control, 90–1; political nature, 31–2; privatization, 70; in suburban areas, 72. *See also* Order; Order maintenance

Distrust: officers and management, 118, 120, 121, 122, 142, 194

Downs, Anthony, 88

Drug trafficking and abuse, 26, 35, 75, 115

Economic restraint, 21–2

Edmonton Neighbourhood Foot Patrol Program, 85–6

Education, 114, 179, 180. *See also* Police training and education

Emsley, Clive, 14

Enlightenment, 25

Epstein, Joyce, 91

Experience, educational value of, 180

Expertise: judgement of, 176–7; and knowledge, 176

Exurbia, 57, 61–5; characteristics, 61–2; inner city, 64; physical layout, 63; policing in, 64; political jurisdiction, 62–3; postexurban city, 65

Families, 51, 57, 67

Fear of crime, 30, 56, 57–9; definition, 59; and disorder, 201; fear-reduction studies, 76–7, 122; neighbourhood reactions, 59–60; police response, 59

Feldman, Lionel D., 159

Fishman, Robert, 62, 63; *Bourgeois Utopias*, 43

Flint, Michigan: Foot Patrol Program, 9, 75, 86–7, 190

Foot-patrol programs: and agency model of professional practice, 188–9; basis on research, 189; comparison with car patrol, 87; distribution of resources, 190; in Edmonton, 85–6; in Flint, Michigan, 9, 75, 86–7, 190; projects, 59, 75, 85–6, 122; and public security, 59; value, 73–4. *See also* Patrol strategy

Forcese, Dennis, 137, 139

Fragmentation, of police occupation, 105, 135–6, 206

France, 5, 26

Freedom, individual, 7, 26, 30–1

Germany, 103

Gertler, Leonard O., 42, 55, 170

Goldstein, Herman, 78, 114, 120–1, 182; problem-oriented policing, 92, 96, 206

Government: appointment of police commissioners, 161; and origins of policing, 4, 33; police support of government interest, 129–30; provision of services, 150–1, 168–9; responsiveness, 145–6; role of professionals, 150–2, 167–8, 177, 192–3; supervision of police, 143, 162, 167, 203
– municipal: autonomous bodies in, 156–7; citizens access to, 158; and community policing, 159, 160, 162; depoliticization, 149; focus and role, 147, 148, 152, 169; political nature, 157–8, 159; private-corporation model, 149; reform, 148–50, 157–9, 159; regionalization, 155–6, 157; relationship to central government, 148; relationship to provincial government, 150–5, 152, 153, 155; role of professionals, 153–5; supervision of police, 146, 152–3
– provincial: policing policy areas, 152–3; relationship to municipal government, 150–5

Graham, Katherine A., 159

Hann, Robert, 163, 165–6, 166

Harden, Hazel A., 73

Hart, Roger, 66

Herbert, David T., 47, 51

Herrnstein, Richard, 46, 47, 55–6

Higgins, Donald, 40, 63, 145, 156–7

Hiss, Tony, 66

Hobbes, Thomas, 25

Home Office Inspectorate of the Constabulary (Britain), 162

Hoover, J. Edgar, 117

Houston, Texas, 76–7, 81, 122

Ideology: conventional, 25–6, 29, 35; police, 134

Incidents, grouping of, 92

Industrialization, 3–4, 36–8

Inner city areas: characteristics, 51–2; crime and disorder rates, 46; and exurbia, 64; and lost city thesis, 54; population growth, 52; separation from suburbs, 43; social problems, 52; stability, 55; and watchman-style policing, 55

International Association of Chiefs of Police, 35, 136, 198

Interrogation, field, 49

Johnson, Terrence J., 170, 171–3, 191–3

Kansas City patrol experiment, 42
Kelling, George, 45, 67, 89, 115, 119
King's Peace, 90
Kinsey, Richard, 163
Klockars, Carl B., 17, 27–8, 41, 109, 194, 199
Knowledge: accessibility, 177; and expertise, 176; occupational, 184; in postindustrial society, 19–20, 37, 168; professional, 18–9, 175–9; specialized, 177. *See also* Policing knowledge
Koby, Thomas (Assistant Chief of Houston), 81

Lachman, Leanne, 88
Laffin, Martin, 203
Landscape, 65–6
Laski, Harold, 145
Law: class bias, 33–4; discriminatory impact, 9; equality under, 14; and individual freedom, 26; intent and impact, 160–1; and morality, 27, 34; and order maintenance, 14; police adherence to, 6; police as representatives, 36; universal nature, 28–9, 161
Law and order, 25–6, 41. *See also* Order
Law enforcement, 12–13, 29, 201; alignment with criminal-justice system, 201; command orientation, 122–3; and crime prevention, 30, 35–6; emphasis on procedure, 11, 74, 123–4; and legalistic-style policing, 70–1; and order maintenance, 9, 13, 32; and police autonomy, 144; and police work, 27–8, 98, 109–10; political aspect, 28–9; and security, 27; and service-

style policing, 71; training orientation, 108
Law Enforcement Code of Ethics, 115
Law Enforcement Education Program (LEEP), 111, 113, 182–3
Lea, John, 26
Leadership, 107, 117, 120, 126
Learning, 180
LEEP; *See* Law Enforcement Education Program
Leighton, Barry, 54, 55, 60–1
Liberated community, 60–1
Locke, John, 25
London Metropolitan Police, 13, 45, 91; in 19th century, 6, 8–9; and community policing, 82; establishment, 3; public acceptance, 3, 5–6, 33, 99
Long-range planing, 131–2
Los Angeles, 61
Lost city thesis, 53, 54
Lost community, 60–1
Low-income areas: crime in, 56; potential for violence, 11

MacDonald, Victor, 125, 133, 141
McDougall, Allan, 133, 134, 151, 152, 153
McGahan, Peter, 55
Maintenance of order; *See* order maintenance
Males, crime potential, 46, 47
Managed landscape, 65, 66
Management, 117–18, 120–1; demand, 129; education for, 118, 120–1, 179; intermediate operation, 125; and line officers, 118, 120, 121,

138; long-range planning, 128–32; meaning, 143; proactive operation, 124, 125, 126, 128; reactive operation, 124–7, 128; structural changes, 127–8
Manitoba, 163
Manning, Peter, 59
Marin, Judge, 111
Mayo, Louis A., 196
Merry, Sally Engle, 58, 59
Metropolitanism, 62
Metropolitan Police Act (Britain), 5
Metropolitan Toronto Police, 77
Michigan State University, 189
Military: comparison with police, 105; influence on policing, 122; police use of paramilitary force, 8; retired officers in policing, 99; style of policing, 49
Mill, John Stuart, 145
Monkonnen, E.H.: *Police in Urban America*, 46
Montreal, 44
Moore, Mark H., 119
Moral authority, 68
Morality: 19th century, 3–4, 42–4; and class system, 27; and individual worth, 26; and law, 27; and religion, 27; shifts in values, 23, 64
Multinucleated cities, 62
Murphy, Patrick V., 15, 142

Nartowicz, Frank, 63
Natural landscape, 65
Neighbourhoods: categorization, 51; characteristics, 40, 54–5, 56; crime patterns, 75–8; declining, 55–6, 57, 76; definition, 50–1; evolution, 67; exclusive, 45; fear of crime, 57–9; inner city, 51–2; integrity, 45; new-

form, 66; order and disorder in, 32, 73, 89; police accountability to, 87; scattered, 65; security, 58; and technology, 60; varying values, 56
Netherlands, 103
Newark, New York, 76–7, 122
New Brunswick, 163
Newfoundland, 163; Royal Newfoundland Constabulary, 163
Newman, Sir Kenneth, 13
New York Police Department, 15, 114

Occupations: knowledge, 184; political resources, 203–4
O'Flaherty, Patrick, 114
Ontario: 19th century policing, 163; municipal police boards, 163, 164; Police Services Act, 152, 153; Task Force on Policing (1980), 196
Ontario Community Policing Manual, The, 82
Ontario Police College, 108
Ontario Police Commission, 153
Order: in communities and neighbourhoods, 32; concept, 31–2; local deterioration, 32. *See also* Disorder; Law and order
Order maintenance, 13–15; ambiguity of goals, 89; basis for police professionalism, 197; and crime reduction, 89; and discretion, 9, 14, 74, 99; and law enforcement, 9, 13; legal basis, 14; and legalistic-style policing, 89; and local order, 32; need for specialized knowledge, 109–10; police function, 13–15, 109, 201; political

nature, 9, 31–2, 87; and redefinition of policing, 162; and service-style policing, 71; and watchman-style policing, 48, 69–70. *See also* Disorder
Organization: categories, 129

Patrol strategy, 10, 50; central control, 126–8; as deterrent, 41, 118; and legalistic-style policing, 71; obsolescence, 41; position in department, 100; preventive, 49, 117, 126; rapid response, 21, 23, 74; reactive nature, 126; in suburban areas, 48; Unit Beat System, 119; zone-assigned personnel, 127. *See also* Footpatrol programs
Patronage, context of professional employment, 191–3
Peel, Sir Robert, 3, 99
Pepinsky, Harold, 91, 167
Performance evaluation, 120
Perrier, David, 198
Phoenix, Arizona, 61
Planning, long range, 128–32
Police and policing: adherence to law, 6; administration, 202–3; agents of social change, 129–30, 132; appraisal, 21–2; autonomy, 50, 142–3, 153, 166, 184–5; basis in experience, 202; civilian basis, 122; and class differences, 7, 11, 33; corruption, 4, 16, 73, 114; craft orientation, 70, 101, 167, 202; functions, 22–3, 109, 198, 201; future, 24; government supervision, 143, 146, 152–3, 162, 167, 203; history, 3–4; ideol-

ogy, 134; in industrial society, 36–8; organizational model, 79; orientation to fixed territory, 51; political nature, 10, 34–5, 202; political neutrality, 6, 9, 33, 130; public acceptance, 3, 4, 5–6, 33, 99; public control, 207; reform, 132; relationship with community, 68; research on, 15; as service providers, 6; task and mission, 11–12, 131, 198; unions, 137–9, 200; urban orientation, 45; use of minimal force, 6, 8; use of professional rhetoric, 197; use of research, 131–2; use of technology, 21, 124
Police boards, 156–7, 159, 163–7; control of administration, 164; government appointment of commissioners, 161; history, 163; mandate, 164; relationship with police chief, 166; responsibility for policing policy, 165–7
Police chiefs: educational level, 198; political role, 202; relationship with police board, 166; responsibility for policy, 165–6
Police colleges and academies, 101; Bramshill (Britain), 121; Canadian Police College, 108, 118, 120, 180, 190; Ontario Police College, 108; University of California (School of Criminology), 116; in Canada, 108; community colleges, 183; independence from police administration, 114; lack of professional schools, 182. *See*

also Police training and education

Police departments: bureaucratic organization, 6, 115, 118, 119, 122, 196; governance, 163; management, 117–18; and municipal government reform, 149; need of specialized skills, 104–5; ranks in, 103, 194; resistance to change, 96; size, 136; titles, 22; use of civilian specialists, 104, 105

Police Foundation, 15

Police in Urban America (E.H. Monkonnen), 46

Police occupation, 99–105, 203; assessment, 203–4; bottom entry policy, 99, 107, 140; corporate structure, 98; development, 136–7, 139; fragmentation, 105, 135–6, 206; generalist character, 104; leadership structure, 196–7; level of education, 99, 105, 198; military organization, 122; professionalization, 15–20, 50, 117, 134, 170, 194–9, 205–7; professionalization of, 176; regulation, 199; structure, 23–4

Police officers (line, patrol), 197; attitudes and beliefs, 132–5; benefits from unionization, 138; control of, 117; detectives, 6; discretionary powers, 10, 11, 74; fraternity and solidarity, 100, 101, 102, 133, 199; knowledge of social ills, 94, 95; motivation, 134; myth of "fatherly" type, 17; need for specialized knowledge, 105; preoccupation with danger, 13; relationship with

management, 118, 120, 121, 122, 138, 142, 194; relationship with public, 10–11, 134, 144–5; representatives of order and stability, 8; representatives of the law, 36; resistance to change, 134, 135; role in order maintenance, 13–15

Police Services Act (Ontario), 152, 153

Police training and education, 19, 23, 101–3, 108; in Canada, 103, 108; in US, 111, 113; comparison to military, 103; law enforcement orientation, 108; post-entry, 101, 103, 107, 108, 121, 206–7; and post-secondary education, 110–11, 182–3; practical orientation, 111, 113–14; problems with, 102, 108–9; public support for, 110, 183; role of O.W. Wilson, 115–16. *See also* Apprenticeship system; Police colleges and academies

Policing knowledge, 111–12, 184; community policing, 79; deficiencies, 198; development, 111; officers need for, 105; in order maintenance, 109–10; and policy, 168; professional, 19, 196. *See also* Knowledge

Policing styles, 48–9; legalistic, 49, 50, 70–1, 89; military, 49; political, 31; preventive, 6; problem-oriented, 92–7; service, 49, 71–3; team, 127; watchman, 48, 55, 69–70. *See also* Community policing

Politics: concept in government reform, 160; police role in, 144–5; in postin-

dustrial society, 178; process, 87

Population: urban percentages of, 42

Postexurban city, 65

Postindustrial society, 65, 144; in Canada, 19; characteristics, 37–8; politics, 178; professionalization in, 200; role of knowledge, 19–20, 168

President's Commission on Law Enforcement and the Administration of Justice (1967), 111

Price, Barbara, 196

Prince Edward Island, 163

Prisons, 35

Private security agencies, 110

Probation, 100

Problem, 92–3

Professionals and specialists: agency model of practice, 186–90; characteristics, 17–18, 170–1, 204; class orientation, 174–5; definitions, 170–3; education, 179, 180; employment contexts, 191–4; ethics, 185, 188, 199; growth and development, 18–19; and modern democracy, 183–4; and politics, 178, 203–4; in post-industrial society, 179; practitioner/client relationship, 172, 173–4, 175, 181–2, 186, 191–3; public service, 154; role in government, 150–2, 167–8, 177, 192–4; Specialization, 103–8

Program-effectiveness studies, 21–2

Promotion opportunities, 100, 101, 102–3; basis on experience, 120–1; in Canada, 120; qualifications for, 120–1

Proposition 13 (California), 21
Provincial police commissions, 108, 152, 162
Public: awareness of policing knowledge, 178–9; client role, 185–7, 189–90; relationship with police, 10–11, 134, 144–5
Public service professionals, 154
Punishment, 26

Quebec, 163, 164
Questioning tactic, 49
Quinn, John, 186–90

Racial problems, 10
Radios, 21, 48
Rank, 100, 103, 194
Rapid response strategy, 21, 23, 99; patrol program, 74; use in suburbs, 48
Rationalism, 25
RCMP; See Royal Canadian Mounted Police
Reflection in action, 181–2, 186
Reform, of municipal government, 148–50, 157–9
Reform Act (1832, Britain), 4
Reform movement (in US policing), 16, 17, 50, 115, 119, 155
Regina, 58
Reiner, Robert, 7, 9, 159, 207; approach to police reform, 132; policies for acceptance of policing, 6
Reiss, Albert J., Jr., 79, 80, 90, 128, 129, 140
Research: basis for foot-patrol programs, 189; on community policing, 95–6; for long range planning, 131–2; police use of, 131–2; on policing, 15; on urban crime rates, 46, 47, 55–6
Response time, 125

Rhodes, R.A.W., 147
Roach, Lawrence T., 81, 91
Robarts Commission report, 166, 167
Roosevelt, Theodore, 114
Rousseau, Jean Jacques, 25, 145
Royal Canadian Mounted Police (RCMP), 105, 108; employment of civilian specialists, 105; local role, 146, 163
Royal Newfoundland Constabulary, 163
Rural areas: and urban development, 65–6
Russell, Bertrand, 41

Sallman, Peter, 134
Satellite cities, 62
Saved community thesis, 54, 60–1
Scarman, Lord, 13
Schön, D.A., 173, 181–2, 186
Security: as absence of crime, 22–3; and individual freedom, 30–1; and law, 27, 28; personal, 29, 30; public sense of, 59; sources, 31; Western idea, 25
Self-regulation, 185–6
Selznick, Philip, 126
Service sector, 37
Sewell, John, 13, 145
Sherman, Lawrence, 113
Snowdon, W.J., 83–5
Social change, police role in, 129–30
Social control, 147
Social engineering, 87, 88
Social problems, 207
Social stability, 7
Social support, 147
Society: role in crime prevention, 36
Specialists; See Professionals and specialists
Statesman, 176
Status quo, 41, 129–30
Stop-and-search tactic, 49

Street life, 19th century, 5
Suburban areas: connection with nature, 56, 65; crimes rates in, 47; order in, 45–6, 47; policing, 20–1, 48; protection from decline, 53; and saved community thesis, 54; services and regulation, 44–5; and service-style policing, 49, 72; as social experiment, 45–6; social segregation, 47
Suburban development, 39, 42, 56–7; effect on municipal government, 155; and transportation, 44
Supervision, 143
Swanton, Barry, 109, 146, 198

Task Force on Policing (1980, Ontario), 196
Technician, educational level, 179
Technoburbs, 62
Technocities, 62
Technology, 20, 21, 124, 195
Telephones, 21, 48
Terry, W. Clinton, 197
Thompson, F.M.L., 7
Tocqueville, Alexis de, 145
Toronto: crime rates, 83; exurban development, 64; Metropolitan councillors, 156; problem areas, 77; suburban development, 44
Toronto Centered Region Concept, 65
Transportation, 44, 60
Trojanowicz, Robert, 28–9, 59, 73, 76, 86, 189

Uniforms, 41, 100
Unions, police, 137–9, 200
Unit Beat System (Britain), 119
United States: class bias in policing, 91–2; crime

rates in cities, 46; municipal government reform, 148; police history, 4, 115; police training and education, 111, 113; policing, 16, 17, 176; policing reform movement, 16, 17, 50, 115, 119; political control of policing, 4, 9; professional class, 174–5; public acceptance of policing, 4; urbanization, 150
United States Office of National Drug Policy, 35
University of California: School of Criminology, 116
Urban development, 65–7; and landscape, 65–6; postwar, 20–1; and rural areas, 65–6
Urban forms, 40
Urbanite: personal connections, 53–4, 60
Urbanization, 3–4; affect on policing, 39; in Canada, 44; and changes in policing, 67–8; and

crime rates, 46; demands on government, 150–1; trend toward, 42
Urban planning, 65–7, 158
Urban studies of policing, 39–40

Vancouver, 83
Vanderhoef, Sheila, 91
Victims, 29, 31
Victoria Community Police Station Project, 83–5
Violence: police, 6; potential in low-income areas, 11; against women, 51
Vollmer, August, 16, 118–19, 155

Walker, Samuel, 17, 45, 176
War on crime, 16, 17, 115
War on drugs, 26, 115
War on poverty, 40
Washington, D.C., 75–6
Waterloo Region Review Commission, 161, 166
Wellman, Barry, 54, 55, 60–1
Wilson, James Q., 10, 11, 123, 179, 207; defini-

tion of policing styles, 48, 69; definition of profession, 171; models of policing, 73; police behavioural change, 141–2; police resistance to change, 143; professionalism in policing, 195; research on urban crime rates, 46, 47, 55–6; variations of police strategy, 89
Wilson, O.W., 16, 115–18, 176; career, 115–16; focus on administrative efficiency, 125–6; ideas and influence, 116; ideas and influence, 41, 87, 115–16, 149; and police education, 113, 115; and US police reform, 97, 119, 155
Winnipeg, 158, 163
Working landscape, 65, 66

Young, Jack, 26
Young, T. Culyer, Jr., 183–4

Zone policing, 127–8